The Great Equalizer

The Great Equalizer

How Main Street Capitalism Can Create an Economy for Everyone

David M. Smick

PublicAffairs
New York

Published in the United States by PublicAffairs™, an imprint of
Perseus Books, LLC, a subsidiary of Hachette Book Group, Inc.

Printed in the United States of America.

PublicAffairs books are available at special discounts for bulk purchases in the U.S. by
corporations, institutions, and other organizations. For more information, please con-
tact the Special Markets Department at Perseus Books, 2300 Chestnut Street,
Suite 200, Philadelphia, PA 19103; call (800) 810-4145, ext. 5000;
or e-mail special.markets@perseusbooks.com.

Book Design by Amy Quinn

Library of Congress Cataloging-in-Publication Data
Names: Smick, David M., author.
Title: The great equalizer : how main street capitalism can create an economy
  for everyone / David M. Smick.
Description: First Edition. | New York : PublicAffairs, 2017.
Identifiers: LCCN 2016037061 (print) | LCCN 2016049687 (ebook) | ISBN
  9781610397841 (hardback) | ISBN 9781610397858 (ebook)
Subjects: LCSH: United States—Economic policy—21st century. | Creative
  ability in business—United States. | Small business—United States. |
  Economic development—United States. | BISAC: BUSINESS & ECONOMICS /
  Economic Conditions. | POLITICAL SCIENCE / Economic Conditions. | BUSINESS
  & ECONOMICS / Development / Economic Development.
Classification: LCC HC106.84 S65 2017 (print) | LCC HC106.84 (ebook) | DDC
  338.973—dc23
LC record available at https://lccn.loc.gov/2016037061

First Edition

10 9 8 7 6 5 4 3 2 1

Contents

Preface

This is a unique moment in American history. Our president can shift people's expectations about the future to positive goals and actions. The choice is between being an ideological placeholder or becoming a truly transformational president. In a counterintuitive way, today's public anger and disillusionment over lack of economic opportunity have produced a rare chance to achieve positive change. The public's message to their Washington policymakers: We are tired of economic mediocrity at home and terrified of a dangerous world. We crave a healthier, more robust economy. We want constructive change. We don't care how you get there. Be creative. Be pragmatic. Try different things. Cut bipartisan deals. Just get there! We want an economic environment of bottom-up dynamism. When all is said and done, economic growth is everything.

The Great Equalizer describes the new mindset that can achieve a better economy for everyone. It is a call for a set of new paradigms that inspire and empower average Americans to reboot their economy. It is a manifesto that argues with a new kind of economic policy of Main Street Capitalism, America's best days are still to come.

To be sure, many experts have concluded that America's best days are behind us, that mediocre long-term economic growth is baked in the cake, and that politically, socially, and racially, the United States will continue to tear itself apart. These experts are wrong.

True, the economy faces stiff headwinds. The policy tools of macro-economics have failed to achieve historic levels of economic performance. The central bankers have slashed interest rates and flooded the economy with liquidity. The economy has underperformed anyway. As a result, working- and middle-class families can feel the American Dream slipping away. For nearly two decades, their incomes have flatlined. Average folk are desperate. They yearn for a dynamic jobs-producing economy that works for everyone. They know in their gut America needs a new economic approach.

Americans feel besieged precisely because in recent decades, a Corporate Capitalism of top-down mismanagement and backroom deal-making has smothered their innovative spirit. Government and central bank policy now favors the big, the corporate, and the status quo at the expense of the small, the young, the new, the inventive, and the entrepreneurial. It favors Wall Street over Main Street. Because the economic system is compromised, people can feel it in their bones that their children's future is being frittered away.

In response, I envision a vibrant Main Street Capitalism of mass small business startups and bottom-up innovation, all unfolding on a level playing field. Main Street Capitalism is the Great Equalizer. It offers a climate of dynamism where every man or woman is a potential founder of a business startup. Women already start firms at twice the rate of men (based on 2014 data). Dramatic advancement by female entrepreneurs could become America's economic secret weapon. Just as important, Main Street Capitalism especially empowers those at the bottom rungs of the economic ladder.

As I'll show, the problem with today's economy is not a lack of monetary liquidity but a lack of the liquidity of confidence. People are terrified of the future. Investors are holding back. Innovators are starting firms at less than half the rate they did two decades ago.

There are reasons why America's economic dreamers and discoverers have become risk averse. The economic system is rigged. In the fight between David and Goliath, Goliath always wins. And in Washington, D.C., a stifling partisanship has meant nothing ever gets done to fix things. Meanwhile, our infrastructure is crumbling. I argue that the political and legislative tactics of two past presidents, Republican Ronald

Reagan and Democrat Bill Clinton, can offer a useful guide to better policymaking.

Today, the world is a terrifying place of massive debt, currency wars, dubious asset prices, and excess supply capacity, while ISIS rears its ugly head all too often. The new information economy is replacing the old, familiar, brick-and-mortar one of manufacturing. Technological change is coming at people so fast they are overwhelmed. Can technological innovation be made to benefit everyone, and not just a select few in Silicon Valley and their investors on Wall Street?

I contend that despite such daunting challenges, people are not going to give up on the American Dream without a fight. Thankfully, innovative dreaming and discovering have always been in America's DNA. The United States has been a land of innovative daring. That is why the American economy has traditionally been a massive, high-growth, jobs-producing machine, a hothouse of commercially attractive creativity. The United States still has many advantages. The building blocks are still in place to achieve higher levels of economic success. Today technology is sometimes feared, but actually innovative advancements in information and other technologies can produce a powerful bottom-up growth phenomenon. Because people are more connected, great ideas are more easily found and shared. All human knowledge is at everyone's fingertips, and essentially is free. The cost of reaching customers has never been cheaper. So *The Great Equalizer* is ultimately an optimistic book about rebuilding an awesome economic growth engine that is beyond the economists' ability to model. To show the way, I offer Main Street Capitalism's 14-Point Plan of bipartisan reforms that can help unleash America's creativity and confidence.

Ultimately, economies are more than statistical measurements of supply and demand, economic output, balance-of-payments deficits, and rates of return on capital. As I'll show, economies are people— their hopes, fears, dreams, and expectations. Economies entail what the English economist John Maynard Keynes in 1936 called the ebb and flow of "animal spirits." Economies are flesh and blood. And that's the good news.

Our economic future is not baked in the cake. Nor is our economic destiny a matter of luck. Human creativity and initiative are not irrelevant in determining economic success or failure. The level of the people's innovative daring is not preset. Americans have a history of rising to the challenge.

The Great Equalizer shows that with a new, bottom-up economic approach, a more robust economy is within our grasp. Americans want their leaders to write a new economic narrative. They want to rediscover the thing that has always made them exceptional: their can-do attitude and audacious spirit—their willingness to dream big and to dare big. Average working families are desperate for higher rates of economic growth. But the time to write that new story of American economic dynamism is now. The clock is ticking.

—*David M. Smick*

Introduction

When I was thinking about writing a book about today's global tsunami of working- and middle-class economic anger, it dawned on me that I may be both the worst and the best person to take on such a task. On the one hand, after a decade working as a staffer on Capitol Hill (and briefly in the U.S. auto industry), I have spent the last 30 years as a macroeconomic policy adviser to a number of world-class investors. I help my highly affluent clients war-game the threats and opportunities to the global economy. I am an investor myself.

On the other hand, I have also experienced life at a different level. I grew up in a working-class neighborhood in the city of Baltimore. My next-door neighbor drove a cement truck. A close friend's father was a plumber. While I was living at home into the late 1960s before leaving for college, my father never earned more than $8,750 a year. Economic thinking for most families in our neighborhood related not to global stock, bond, and real estate prices, but to how weekly paychecks could be stretched to cover food and housing expenses. This was a life of frequent economic anxiety.

A public school kid, I attended, though I didn't know it at the time, a junior high school later ranked as one of the ten most violent in the United States. To attend one of the city's two best public high schools, I took three transit buses, transferring my way across town and back for a total of two and a half hours a day. I was familiar with the neighborhoods at the center of the 2015 Freddie Gray riots. Nothing that happened there surprised me.

I worked my way through college as a janitor, house painter, member of a catering crew, hard-hat construction laborer, and country club dining room waiter. Working at the country club, I dealt with a lot of highly affluent club members. I grew to dislike those folks for their sense of superiority toward the wait staff, which adds a sense of irony to my current employment dealing with the global financial elite.

As my college years ended, no commencement speakers were telling my generation to follow our passions and believe in our destiny. It was the anxiety-ridden 1970s. We were just trying to figure out what to do about Vietnam and to find work in the worst job market since the 1930s. If you had told me back then that I would spend the bulk of my career working with some of the world's most successful money managers, I would have said you were crazy.

But here's the thing. Having come of age in Baltimore, I saw firsthand the combined ugly results of hyper-partisanship and the slow death of economic confidence, imagination, and hope. Baltimore is one of the most Democratic cities in the nation. Almost everyone in my neighborhood voted Democratic. In 1948, my father voted for Democrat Harry Truman for president. After turning 18, it seemed natural for me to register as a Democrat, which I did. Republicans seemed to be those rich people who lived in the horse country to the northwest of the city, the local pastures that support the Preakness racehorse activities. Their world seemed unapproachable.

But I was conflicted. I distrusted the rich but craved their financial security and was concerned about the Soviet Union's territorial ambitions. Fairly quickly, my political views began to develop. In presidential politics, I ended up working for the campaigns of Republican Ronald Reagan in 1980 and Democrat Bill Bradley in 2000. I admired Bradley precisely because of his lack of partisan narrow-mindedness and for his willingness to reach across party lines on tax reform and international economic policy issues. It was clear that Reagan's approach to the economy, although not perfect, was appropriately targeted at the small business, innovative sector—the frustrated economic risk-takers in waiting who could revive the American economy.

Looking back, particularly in the wake of the ugly race riots of 2015, I can see how much my hometown's working-class families suffered living in a city captured by a status quo mentality. With its beautiful harbor, Camden Yards baseball stadium, and downtown luxury hotels, the center of Baltimore was allowed to become a glamorous donut hole surrounded by the rotting dough of inner-city poverty, local political and police corruption, and hopelessness. The middle class moved to the suburbs seeking better schools and greater safety. The rate of small business startups collapsed. While a few large corporations propped up the municipal tax base and some tech hot spots appeared, any type of an empowering economy for average folk for the most part shriveled up and died.

Yet nobody rang the alarm. For decades, a complacent Baltimore leadership lived an illusion, convinced that the status quo of sub-par economic achievement was tolerable. Baltimore got by until one thing happened: The U.S. economy itself entered its current era of mediocre long-term economic growth. Then the wheels of the city came flying off. Racial tensions exploded. Just as Baltimore needs a new economic narrative for success, America today must also write a new economic and political narrative that raises the level of prosperity for all.

The American people are angry—and with good reason. Their country has fallen into a slime pit of mean-spirited partisanship that will be difficult to reverse. This new era of hatred has contributed to broad-based policy shutdown. Stalemate and division are two reasons for America's "new normal" of mediocre economic growth rates. So is Washington's blind devotion to bigness—that is, to large institutions. America's leaders have lost their way. The country has become risk averse. People are no longer starting new firms at the rate they once did. Existing businesses are not investing at a high enough rate to really expand the economy for everybody. Uncertainty toward the future reigns supreme. As former White House national security official Norman Bailey neatly summed up the ultimate reason for the public's deep anger and frustration: "Large segments of the population are nearly insolvent." More than half lack the liquid savings to cover even a month's worth of income if they lost their job, according to a survey by the Pew Charitable Trusts. No wonder people are terrified of the future.

Indeed, something important is underway in American society and throughout large parts of the world. A new economic nationalism and rejection of free-market capitalism is rising in popularity. A silent, and at times not-so-silent, public anger over slow growth and lack of opportunity has appeared. How our new president responds to this emerging public attitude could affect the country for decades.

Brexit, the decision on June 24, 2016, by the British people to leave the European Union despite the extraordinary economic risk of doing so, could for the rest of the world in coming years be remembered as the canary in the coal mine. For Washington, D.C., Brexit was a warning that Americans are desperate for a new politics and a more effective approach to economic prosperity. They want reforms that produce a dynamic economy that works not just for the privileged few in Silicon Valley and on Wall Street, but for all. They also want protection from a dangerous world.

The global economy has, indeed, become a horror show that could take us all down. Confidence worldwide has plummeted. Financial and geopolitical risk has soared. In some cases, global risk resembles the dangers that plagued the depression-ridden 1930s. As the world's central banks continue to pump out financial liquidity, something strange is going on: Total global liquidity continues to shrink.

Meanwhile, some of the world's biggest central banks have been forced to resort to negative interest rates. That's when the banks ask you to pay them to hold your money. In the 1930s, average folk just stuffed their cash in mattresses. Everyone talks about the problem of global liquidity. But the problem is not with liquidity itself; it again is with the liquidity of confidence.

The world looks terrifying. Since 2010, official global GDP and trade growth rates have dropped by more than half. Commodity prices have become highly unstable. Emerging markets led by China are bogged down with massive amounts of excess supply capacity. They blindly produce regardless of the demand for their products, spreading dangerous disinflationary pressure worldwide as price levels soften.

Meanwhile, emerging-market corporate debt has more than doubled. China's dangerous credit binge has been unprecedented in terms of the speed with which the debt has been accumulated. Europe is in long-term economic stagnation, with an ugly populist political threat lurking at the door. Japan is at risk of falling back into deflation. Its financial market, with the central bank the biggest net buyer of stocks and bonds, is no longer a real market. Brazil is in severe economic crisis that could risk a scenario of default. Collapsing Venezuela is on the verge of entering the Stone Age. And the world's total debt has skyrocketed to a level unimaginable even a decade ago—$180 trillion as of 2015 and now even higher.

Here's what is really scary. Throughout the world, the return on capital, the rate of income received from an investment, is often so low there are serious questions about how long borrowers will be able to service that massive debt, particularly when their debt is denominated in strengthening U.S. dollars. Worldwide there is now a dangerous shortage of dollars, which is why it has been difficult for the Federal Reserve to tighten credit as much as some policymakers there would like. One wrong move could be the tipping point unleashing a global tidal wave of defaults—and a worldwide banking crisis.

The global financial system, therefore, has become a dangerous paradox wrapped in a riddle. The matrix of inflation, deflation, slow income growth, excess productive capacity, dubious real estate and stock market asset prices, unprecedented public and private debt, and eye-popping geopolitical surprises is as confusing as ever. The vast majority of people worldwide believe their children's future is at risk. They can see that the global economic engine is sputtering in a world with no one in control. Around the world, things we thought could never happen are happening.

The American people are desperate to decouple from this global madness. It won't be easy, but doing so is not impossible. The experts argue that a long-term U.S. economic growth rate of only between 1 and 2 percent is all we can hope for. They call it the "new normal" of economic mediocrity. There's nothing we can do, even though slow growth makes us highly vulnerable to these nasty global risks.

The growth-is-limited theory is called "secular stagnation." It holds that lower population growth and a slowdown in the kind of transformative technological breakthroughs that lead to greater productivity performance (doing more with less) could hold the American economy back for decades. A dismal economic future for America, some experts say, is baked in the cake.

Because the rate of a nation's long-term growth has extraordinary implications, this book will outline the dangers that secular stagnation represents. The difference between the U.S. economy's historic average annual growth rate of 3.2 percent versus the disappointing 1.4 percent average annual GDP growth achieved during the period 2007–2016 is not more than a mere 100 percent jump in economic activity. It is more like a 500 percent spike in economic dynamism. It is the difference between a nation in deep economic anxiety, at war with itself, versus a nation where the American Dream is still a possibility for all. It is likely the difference between a successful two-term presidency or a one-term disappointment.

For America, however, all is not lost. Throughout history, the economic experts have almost always been too pessimistic. Their forecasting track record has been abysmal. With policy reforms and better leadership, there could be better times ahead. One extraordinary bright spot: Women in America are moving to the forefront of the process of starting new businesses. Economics has always entailed a high degree of unpredictability. The health of an economy depends on behavioral elements that don't always fit on an Excel spreadsheet or follow the confines of a predictable theory. A scenario of mediocre or no economic growth doesn't have to be baked in the cake. There could be more prosperous times ahead. Indeed, in a curious way the public's anger, as difficult as it is to imagine, may present our new president with a rare opportunity for bipartisan problem solving, particularly in the areas of debt reduction, infrastructure modernization, and the encouragement of more business startups. For a brief window with the election of a new president, the destructive partisan forces of stalemate may be held at bay.

The experts are pessimistic on growth precisely because the economics profession itself is in crisis. Since the 2008 financial collapse, economists have conducted a giant global monetary experiment. They have relied on massive supplies of central bank liquidity to try to spur higher economic growth. The experiment failed. What the experts found is that the role of central bank liquidity—of money—is a lot more complicated than they thought. Economies are a lot more than "money."

Economies involve a complex ecosystem and are linked to psychology, which cannot be understood via standard econometric models that try to reduce human behavior to mathematical equations.

Economies, again, are a mixture of the hopes, dreams, and fears of people. And that's the good news. Little about our economic future is necessarily preset. The success of an economy is heavily influenced by the behavior of people, by their level of confidence. And people are not just consumers; they are also investors, entrepreneurs, and, in some cases, dreamers of the kind of breathtaking innovation that can transform the lives and livelihoods of average working families.

Despite a dangerous, chaotic world, the ingredients are still there for Americans to achieve higher levels of economic success. The United States has many advantages. Unlike most parts of the world, it is for all practical purposes independent of the politically unstable Middle East for its supplies of energy. But what the United States desperately lacks is a new economic narrative told by a compelling leader.

In writing a new game plan, the first step is to examine recent history. What worked and what didn't? During the period from 1980 to the present, those presidents who, when they had no other choice, engaged in reasonable bipartisan compromise (and were wise to the growth-inhibiting effect of excessive regulation on the private sector) enjoyed economies twice as robust, with more than twice as many jobs created, as those presidents unwilling, or unable, to accept bipartisan compromise.

In other words, during the high growth, big jobs–producing presidencies of Ronald Reagan (1981–1989) and Bill Clinton (1993–2001), both political parties, when forced to, worked together for the benefit of the nation's economic welfare. Both benefited from the lagged effect of the previous deregulation of the trucking, airline, railroad, and other industries achieved under President Jimmy Carter (1977–1981). Both had economies helped by a period of stable prices while the global economy was enlarging and nationalism was at bay. But both sent the reassuring message to economic decision makers in the private economy that, if need be, Washington, D.C., could embrace the process of reaching bipartisan consensus. Policymaking represented a broad consensus of public opinion.

Since the turn of the century, however, America has undergone a disappointing transition. During the deeply partisan years of George W. Bush (2001–2009) and Barack Obama (2009–2017), policy stalemate reigned. Regulation of the private sector ratcheted up under Bush and zoomed to unprecedented highs under Obama, according to the American Enterprise Institute. The global economy kept shrinking, and nationalism returned in full force. The U.S. economy underperformed, and for most the American Dream began to slip away.

As a personal aside, I feel that in recent years Bill Clinton has gotten a bum rap. Although hardly flawless, his economic accomplishments have been smeared by unfair characterizations from both the right and the left. Facts are facts, and the Clinton economy was impressive. Bill Clinton's ability to achieve bipartisan compromise was not some flaw as many progressive commentators suggest. That willingness to compromise, along with a middle-of-the-road policy mix that encouraged an expansion in investment, were part of the secrets to the success of the 1990s. So, too, of course, were the end of the Cold War and the earlier elimination of hyperinflation.

During the 2016 Democratic primary, Bernie Sanders, the self-described Democratic socialist, argued that America's only choice was to travel down the road of overwhelming governmental control of the economy. He argued that capitalism itself was not only "rigged" but bankrupt. Such thinking has captured the ultra-progressive side of the Democratic Party. Bill Clinton's approach of working within the capitalist system is no longer popular with some Democrats, and others absolutely despise it. Yet the lesson here is that to be successful when it comes to the economy, a president would be wise to be a lot more like Bill than Bernie.

Capitalism comes in different varieties. In recent decades, a Corporate Capitalism of inside deal–making, elite special privilege, and dominance by large institutions has, indeed, exerted a stranglehold over the U.S. economy. The system *has* been "rigged." As a result, America's traditional can-do attitude and spirit of optimism have been shattered by a sense that there is no longer a level playing field. The corporate capitalists, of course, have always been around. But in the last decade their power has intensified to a mind-boggling level.

But is rejecting capitalism really the answer to insulating America from a dangerous world? Could we trust, say, the managers at the Department of Veterans Affairs to run something as complex as the U.S. economy? Or how about the experts who designed and implemented the

Obama Administration's healthcare website? Maybe the solution is not to abandon capitalism but to reboot capitalism. Instead of Corporate Capitalism, I call for a return to Main Street Capitalism.

Main Street Capitalism is the Great Equalizer in this time of inequality. It is the high-growth capitalism of bottom-up innovation, with a flood of business startups, all happening on a level playing field. The empowering force of Main Street Capitalism, where every man or woman is a potential entrepreneur, is what has historically made the U.S. economy the envy of the world.

I will never forget a conversation I had in the mid-1990s with Jean-Claude Trichet, then head of the French central bank, who later became president of the European Central Bank. Over lunch at the central bank in Paris, Trichet surprised me by uttering this: "The American economy is nothing short of a miracle. Your people's sense of daring, of a willingness to explore avenues of innovation, to take on risks is nothing short of breath-taking." He was applauding Main Street Capitalism, the Great Equalizer. He was congratulating America's global distinction as a land of dreamers and discoverers. At the time, unlike today, America's productivity rates were soaring. American innovators were on the move.

In economics, attitude matters. Washington policymakers continue to fiddle with the cyclical levers of monetary and fiscal policies. But, when all is said and done, a change in attitude and understanding is ultimately the thing that will raise the level of long-term potential economic growth. The secret to higher levels of prosperity comes down to these words: encouraging a groundswell of enthusiastic risk-takers to ignite an innovation revolution. Today's policy task is to change expectations—to fortify an intense optimism toward the future and to bolster people's courage to take on challenges.

The American people are conflicted. Gallup and other polls regularly show that Americans are intrinsically optimistic. Yet two out of three Americans now think that when their kids grow up, they will be worse off financially than their parents, according to polling by the Pew Research Center. They share this parental concern whether rich or poor, young or old, or male or female. Translation: Americans desperately want to be optimistic. Their policymakers simply need to give them sound reasons for being bullish on the future.

Greater innovation is the heart of the economic solution. Yet in recent years, the U.S. economy has been suffering from a kind of disease hampering its ability to perform at maximum output. That ailment is a decline in the rate of productivity and in the number of business startups resulting from a decline in innovative daring in many sectors of the economy.

America desperately needs a revolution in the public's spirit and attitude based on a new paradigm for vibrant growth. The stakes could not be higher. The U.S. government alone is nearly $20 trillion in debt, an amount that boggles the mind. As I'll show, innovation that raises the rate of productivity growth is America's only hope of protecting itself from a potentially ugly debt situation not very far down the road. There is a reason Steve Jobs worshiped the economy's innovators so much. He perceived their importance to the larger economy. He said they do nothing less than "move the human race forward." They are the secret to greater prosperity despite an economy loaded with debt.

The Great Equalizer in today's economy is policies that lead to higher achievement in education and greater innovation. As Northwestern University's John O. McGinnis argues, technological innovation, despite its disruptive nature, is a great tool to "help reduce inequality because it helps generate and harness ideas, and ideas are free. . . . Ideas can be shared equally in a way that material goods cannot, and the fact that technology increasingly makes ideas the drivers of our society and economy means that our circumstances are more equal than conventional income measures would suggest."

The high-tech venture capitalist Marc Andreessen stated the same concept in a different way: "The technology revolution has put the means of production within everyone's grasp."

Inspiring greater innovative success is not easy. And because innovation is an economic disrupter, innovative breakthroughs can produce paradoxical, sometimes troubling consequences. History shows that success in bringing about more transformational innovation that benefits average working families requires an aggressive style of entrepreneurial capitalism. It is the kind of capitalism in which every man or woman is a potential capital owner.

Greater innovation is essential for one other reason. For decades America's demographics (the rise of a huge baby-boom middle class to its productive years) served as a major economic tailwind, pushing the U.S. economy ever higher. But with the retirement of the baby boomers, demographics has become a headwind to growth. So returning to America's traditional growth rate above 3 percent will require a significant increase in the economy's performance—its productivity—from an innovation revolution. Thankfully, dreaming and discovering have always been a large part of America's DNA. That, again, is why this book is fundamentally optimistic about America's future.

Yet in today's new era of policy surrender, the experts remain convinced economic mediocrity is irreversible. Federal Reserve Chair Janet Yellen herself argues that today's slow growth is the "new normal." International Monetary Fund head Christine Lagarde calls it the "mediocre normal." Both phrases are euphemisms for copping out. Both policymakers are really saying, "I've done what I can. I'm out of ideas. Don't blame me." Yet how can anyone accurately measure the economic potential of nearly 325 million Americans if, backed by compelling leadership, they collectively become inspired to reinvent their economy? There are no facts about the future. To be sure, the U.S. economy faces challenges. The American people have gone into a hiatus of distraction and disillusionment. Many have lost faith in the future.

People may be the problem, but they are also the solution. People desperately yearn to take the initiative, but the compromised system is holding them back. The system has soured economic expectations. People have become risk-averse. Yet the United States still has in hand the means to construct a higher-growing economy. But the American people need first to reach down deep into their collective souls and find the thing that has always made them exceptional—their boundless joy and can-do optimism toward future possibilities.

This book is all about rebuilding an awesome economic growth engine the potential of which no economist can adequately model. This is a message about shifting the American people's expectations toward the future. This is a statement of optimism. Why am I so sure America's best days still lie ahead? My hunch is that people are not going to let the American Dream die without a fight. Americans are fighters at heart. They know the economic system has been rigged. Average folk collectively have more insight, are more hopeful, have better ideas, and are more courageous than their dysfunctional leaders.

We are, for sure, living in the ultimate age of discontinuity. Working families are desperate. They crave an end to the Washington partisan clown show of stalemate they know in their bones has helped sap the economy of its vitality. They want a revitalized economy for all. Our new president must, therefore, launch a national crusade based on a "grand bargain" of doable economic reforms. It is time to reject the political extremes—both right and left—and to make those reforms truly bipartisan. Our new president needs to shock the world by becoming the president of all Americans.

What I have outlined in this book is not an agenda either side, right or left, will find ideologically perfect. Instead, it is a set of reforms with which a majority of the American people already agrees. The United States has hit an inflection point. The world has become a dangerous place. America's only hope is to rediscover the roots of a dynamic, empowering Main Street Capitalism.

Ultimately, America's economic problem is our inability to come to an understanding of who we are as a people. As syndicated columnist Maureen Dowd colorfully asked, "Are we winners who have been through a rough patch? Or losers who have soured our sturdy and spiritual DNA with too much food, too much greed, too much narcissism, too many lies, too many pies, too many fat-cat bonuses, too many cat videos on the evening news . . . and too much mindless and malevolent online chatter?" In other words, is America still a purposeful country?

I believe we either move ahead with reform or risk suffocating stalemate, permanent national mediocrity, and ongoing vulnerability to the dangers of global economic and financial contagion. This is the moment of truth. This is the time we find out who we really are as Americans.

ONE

Growth Is (Almost) Everything

Nine months before the first stages of the 2008 financial crisis, I offered this observation to the other guests at a Washington dinner party: "Though it appears robust, the U.S. financial system is highly vulnerable. It could potentially wreck the entire world economy." All heads turned my way.

The big banks, I argued, had lost any understanding of the financial picture on their balance sheets, which were loaded with complicated paper instruments not tied closely to valuations of any credibility. Yet the prices of these "trust me" paper financial assets, including mortgage-backed securities, were considered so certain and safe that they, incredibly, had become the foundation of the entire financial system. "But how do we truly know these paper financial assets reflect the true value of America's housing market?" I asked. "Just because the experts say so? The experts are often wrong."

At the time, financial markets were booming. But it seemed the banks had done the equivalent of making a giant mixed salad of millions of securitized mortgages (financial paper) and were selling individual salad bowls throughout the world. The only problem? Some of those mortgage-backed securities were toxic. Consume a piece of lettuce with just one of those toxic bits, and you're dead. Yet in the global distribution of the giant mixed salad, no one could identify which bowls contained the toxic assets. Suddenly, the entire financial system was potentially contaminated. The crisis could come, I argued, if a fearful world stopped ordering salad.

My dinner party guests eyed me with a look of annoyance. I stopped talking. On the drive home, however, my wife, Vickie, remarked: "You should write a book about this financial risk." After some reflection, I wrote *The World Is Curved: Hidden Dangers to the Global Economy*, and it became a 2008 bestseller. The title was, of course, a response to *New York Times* columnist Tom Friedman's compelling 2005 book *The World Is Flat*. Another *New York Times* columnist, David Brooks, called *The World Is Curved* "astonishingly prescient." Bill Clinton's assessment? One of the three best books on the financial crisis.

My hunch that the global economy was at a tipping point proved correct. The world was hit with the most devastating financial collapse since the 1930s. The crisis was like an elephant stomping on the global financial market's chest. Forty percent of the world's wealth vanished in the night. The giant beast had stepped on the financial system's windpipe. The economy was suffocating. Yet what the people of the United States were experiencing was not just a financial calamity; they were facing the beginning of a monumental threat to the American Dream.

The financial crisis is now a familiar, and ugly, story. Through a combination of domestic and global factors, financial risk in the United States was allowed to become grossly underpriced. Combined with massive leverage by the big Wall Street banks and the politicization of mortgage lending by Washington politicians, low real interest rates caused stock, real estate, and other market valuations to rise to unrealistic highs. Then the bubble burst, the markets crashed, and the rest is history.

But that's all old news. The question now is—what's happened since the crash, and why are both the U.S. and global economies failing to perform at historic rates of growth?

To their credit, the world's policymakers responded boldly. The world's governments and central banks (including the U.S. government and the Federal Reserve) collectively committed in terms of both present and potentially future resources a mind-boggling $17 trillion—almost one-quarter of global gross domestic product at the time—for government bailouts, widespread financial guarantees, fiscal stimulus packages, and an ocean of new monetary stimuli (often in the form of massive excess reserves injected into the banking system). The size of the medicine was extraordinary.

But did the medicine cure the patient? Yes and no. Thankfully, the global economy avoided depression. The immediate free fall in global aggregate demand was arrested. Stock markets rebounded.

But then, beginning in 2010, the world economy progressively slowed, and the question is, why? The global growth rate dropped from roughly 4.3 percent in 2010 to 2.5 percent by the middle of 2015, according to World Bank data. Growth has slowed further since. If China's true growth rate is, as some analysts believe, not much more than half of its announced official rate, the world economy is barely growing at all.

Back in the United States, the economy could also never quite regain its momentum on a sustainable basis. Something always held it back. Despite a few months here and there of striking economic improvement, each time the sugar rush faded. Young people still couldn't find really good, full-time jobs, and many still can't. Income growth for average working families ticked up slightly here and there but, for the most part, remained unimpressive. There is a good reason people are angry.

The Federal Reserve was a kind of fall guy in this unfolding drama. True, there was an immediate need for action. But that should have been for the short term. Instead, the Federal Reserve's emergency rescue policy of massive injections of liquidity into the banking system became the primary policy for achieving long-term economic growth.

But the policy brought with it ugly unintended—and unfair—consequences. When Federal Reserve officials brought America's short-term interest rates down close to zero percent, they produced a great tool for helping the Wall Street banks repair their balance sheets damaged as a result of the crisis. The big banks borrowed at next to nothing. Then they purchased longer-term, higher-yielding debt on the open market. The result: a guaranteed profit stream on the spread between the two interest rates. Financial insiders call this the "yield curve play."

The central bankers followed up with an additional policy of massive bond buying called "quantitative easing" to keep long-term interest rates low. The zero interest rate policy was a special boon to Wall Street's private equity firms. Quantitative easing salvaged the damaged balance sheets of the companies in which they'd invested. These troubled companies were allowed to refinance. When the stock market recovered, the private equity executives took their freshly refinanced companies public. Isn't life great?

But the policy that brought back giant profits to Wall Street banks was a disaster for Main Street and its smaller banks. With near zero percent interest rates, average working families lost income from their money market funds and savings accounts in what amounted to the greatest wealth transfer from Main Street to Wall Street in the history of the country. Even worse, the policy helped produce a collapse in Main Street confidence about the future. The feeling was that Washington, D.C., had a list of priorities. At the top of the list were the large Wall Street banks. Working families and small firms and their smaller banks (because they were not considered "systemically important" to the overall financial system) were at the bottom of the list. Today large parts of the American workforce are so angry that the long-term future of American politics is beyond prediction.

Hedge fund manager and former Yale adjunct professor Scott Bessent adds an additional concern. When the Federal Reserve engaged in its policy of quantitative easing, a huge amount of consumer spending and borrowing that would have happened in the future was moved to the present to take advantage of the attractive low-cost financing. At the same time, the low rates encouraged corporate America to take on more debt. Now U.S. corporations could be a time bomb because of their dangerously high levels of debt. Argues Bessent: "We were assured the corporate CEOs were optimizing their balance sheets. In financial history, optimal is rarely robust. The next downturn will be worse because corporate balance sheets are now a lot more fragile."

Meanwhile, the American elite were experiencing a new gilded age while average working families were left out of the party. Even at the turn of the century, the incomes of average American working families were beginning to stagnate. After the 2008 financial crisis and the Fed's rescue policies, income inequality worsened. The richest 1 percent in America received almost 60 percent of the growth in wealth between 2009 and 2014, according to Emmanuel Saez in "Striking It

Richer." Why? The Federal Reserve's rock-bottom interest rates were a boon to the stock market. The richest in society owned the most stocks to begin with. As the equity market tide rose, the top had the most boats floating in the harbor. During the Obama Administration, in the rescue operation from the financial crisis, the Americans with the highest incomes ironically were handed the winning lottery tickets.

The frustration of middle- and working-class families came to a head in the 2016 U.S. presidential primary campaigns. Both Donald Trump and Bernie Sanders rode the wave of post–financial crisis anger.

The great mystery is why the central bankers let Congress and the Obama Administration off the hook. During a severe economic slowdown, monetary, fiscal, and regulatory policies normally work in tandem to try to right the ship. With Washington, D.C., in stalemate, fiscal and regulatory reforms, the normal avenue to achieving higher levels of economic growth, were taken off the discussion table. So initially was any effort to examine the role of currency manipulation and nontariff trade obstructionism. Instead, monetary stimulus became the magic pill for curing everything wrong with the patient. But the medicine hardly turned out to be the miracle drug. The definition of "money" turned out to be a lot more complicated. And the reason: Money cannot be separated from the unpredictability of human behavior.

So now the U.S. economy has stumbled into a swamp of mediocre long-term growth. Politically, socially, and racially, the United States is tearing itself apart. People are desperate for answers and direction. There is still a sense of helplessness and futility in the air. It is a feeling that America is a sitting duck, vulnerable to domestic and international dangers beyond our control.

Don't get me wrong. The United States has not yet fallen back into recession. For many elite families, the economy is doing fine. The official unemployment rate has dropped steadily. For average middle-income families, however, it still feels economically like waking up each day with a migraine headache and the intense need for a root canal procedure. The suspicion is that the future is not going to be good. That is why, when the price of gasoline plummeted during the second term of the Obama Administration, working families initially saved this energy windfall rather than increase their consumption of goods and services. Average folk were fearful of the future. And they still are.

Working- and middle-class families have reason to be concerned. Many forecasters project a dismally weak U.S. economic growth rate for the next decade or two. The theory is called secular stagnation—that the economy is facing headwinds that are all but impossible to overcome. It suggests that the U.S. economy's medium- and long-term potential is limited regardless of our actions. A slowdown in population growth and the slow pace of transformational technological innovation have fostered resistance to expanded investment in new capital goods. The economy's ability to produce is, therefore, hamstrung by declining rates of capital formation and a deterioration in employee skills. Overall, the economy saves too much and invests too little. The bottom line: We are bogged down for the long term.

The U.S. Congressional Budget Office predicts, for example, that from 2016 to 2026, the U.S. economy will grow by an average annual rate of roughly 2 percent a year. Other experts suggest an even weaker long-term growth rate, closer to 1.5 percent. Either way, such an outcome would be catastrophic for America's future.

Growth rates have startling long-term implications. These numerical differences sound trivial, but they can have huge exponential ramifications for the livelihood of average folk. Since the year after the United States was founded in 1789, for example, U.S. real GDP has grown by an average annual rate of a much higher 3.73 percent. Had America throughout its history grown instead by an average of roughly 2.3 percent (slightly higher than today's U.S. Congressional Budget Office forecast), its per-capita income today would be lower than Papua New Guinea's, according to the *Wall Street Journal*. In other words, America's per-capita income would not reflect the output of the most powerful economy in the world. Instead, it would be lower than the per-capita income in a relatively poor country in the southwestern Pacific Ocean.

What that says about America's future is this—growth is everything. Or, if not everything, it's almost everything. During Bill Clinton's presidency (1993–2001), the economy grew by nearly 4 percent annually, an impressive achievement. The *Wall Street Journal* points out that had the economy under Presidents George W. Bush (2001–2009) and Barack

Obama (2009–2017) continued to grow at that healthy rate, the U.S. government today would have an annual $500 billion budget surplus. Instead, under the lower average growth since 2001, the United States has an annual budget deficit of roughly the same amount.

Here's a view from another angle: Between 1952 and 2000, the U.S. economy grew at an impressive average annual rate of 3.5 percent. As a result, real income per person in America (adjusted for inflation) jumped by more than 300 percent, from $16,000 to $50,000, according to economist John Cochrane. This is the kind of growth the *Wall Street Journal's* William McGurn describes for average working families as "like getting a raise year after year." Had the American economy instead grown at today's subpar growth rate of, at best, 2 percent, real income per person today would be $23,000, only a 70 percent increase.

Here's an even more stunning conclusion: Coming into office, the Obama Administration faced the worst recession since the Great Depression of the 1930s. Still, the rule of thumb in the past is that the steeper the drop, the sharper the rebound. After the bitter 1982 recession, for example, during the first 11 quarters of the recovery and expansion, the U.S. economy grew by an average of more than 6 percent. Sadly, after the 2008 recession, that sharp rebound never happened, in part because of the freezing of the distribution of credit. Had the U.S. economy after the 2008 financial crisis rebounded by the higher GDP growth rates of other post–World War II recoveries, a typical middle-class family since then would have taken home more than $11,000 in additional income per year!

It is easy to see why America's middle and lower-middle classes are so angry. The exponential nature of growth matters. Average folk can feel in their bones that they are losing out. For generations, inequality was tolerated because people at all income levels were becoming better off. Yet now the working and middle classes have realized their wages have been stagnating or falling for decades. This frustration leads to the fundamental question of this book: Why can't the economy perform better to help American working- and middle-class families protect themselves from a dangerous world? Why are the economic actors holding back?

The economic experts are grappling with a number of questions related to today's low U.S. growth rates. Is the problem the weakness of the rest of the world economy? That weakness is fostered by economic disappointment and financial uncertainty in emerging markets like China, which have threatened to put the world in a disinflationary or even deflationary stranglehold. (Disinflation is when the rate of price inflation slows. Deflation is when price levels actually fall. Stable prices are essential for small companies in particular. They hire new employees and expand plant and equipment based on confidence in the price stability of their products on the open market. If prices drop, these companies are crushed. The floor falls out from under their business plans. They can't earn a profit. People lose their jobs.)

Or are people holding back because of the rise of ISIS and the sense that no one's running a world that has become geopolitically dangerous? Or is the reason today's enormous debt? Is it the result of bad international deals on trade and currency relationships?

Is the problem sociological? As high-tech investor Marc Andreessen put it, sometimes people simply feel, "I can't take more change."

Is the problem America's own fiscal, regulatory, and monetary policies, including the way the economy currently generates growth, which squeezes the middle class between the lower- and upper-income segments of society? In other words, some families move up, but many move down.

Is it the fact that Washington, D.C., has become captive to the partisan hacks, so nothing ever gets done? Is it that our policymakers naïvely still believe in top-down economic design even as the rest of the world, whether because of the appearance of Facebook or the rise of ISIS, is in the midst of a bottom-up revolution?

Or is it an attitude problem? Have Americans themselves lost the courage, daring, and optimism toward the future that has traditionally made the United States the world's hothouse of innovation? And is our current innovative dynamism too limited to glitzy information technology breakthroughs in relatively rarified places such as Silicon Valley that are less than transformational for most of the population?

What's holding us back? The truth is, all of these elements have some bearing on the problem. They all make up the stiff headwinds that are impeding America's GDP growth.

If 1 or 2 percent long-term GDP growth is unacceptable, how do we raise the long-term growth rate to, at a minimum, 3 percent? How does technological innovation play a role? And to what extent do human behavior and attitude make a difference if the economists' macroeconomic tools, led by interest-rate policy, are no longer working as effectively as envisioned? Would confronting today's enormous debt make a difference? In short, what are the paradigm shifts that could motivate the American people to have greater hope for the future? How does our new president change the public's attitude toward the future?

As this book will demonstrate, the most important paradigm shift is a return to what I call a Main Street Capitalism mindset fixated on achieving massive business startups and innovative daring, all taking place on a level playing field. But that requires a change in expectations. The genius of Presidents Franklin Delano Roosevelt, Ronald Reagan, and Bill Clinton was that, to varying degrees, they were able to change people's expectations. They convinced average folk that things were going to get better. So people invested their savings, companies expanded hiring, and innovators started new businesses. The difference today is that these people and firms in the current climate need to engage in these activities in more of a bottom-up way, and policymakers must make bottom-up economic advancement a lot easier.

Sadly, millennials (Americans aged 18–35 who make up more than 25 percent of the population) don't remember the U.S. economy much before the year 2000. Bill Clinton's robust economy is ancient history. For millennials, when talking about the impressive growth rates of the 1980s Reagan era after the dismal 1970s, you might as well be discussing the economy during the Lincoln Administration. All today's young people have known is an economy under George W. Bush and Barack Obama that has not performed up to its potential.

It is not surprising that this is the first generation that, when asked for its list of priorities, puts solving the problem of "income inequality" at the top of the list. Nothing wrong with that. Millennials also insist that economic growth be achieved in a carbon footprint context of combating catastrophic climate change. Yet the goal of "higher economic growth," of enlarging the economic pie, is almost never mentioned. Why? The millennials have never experienced a fully robust economy. As a result, they have lost confidence in capitalism. They have never known a capitalism that was geared to the aspirations of average working families.

None of this is intended to denigrate an entire generation. Sensing the economic system is rigged against them, many young people have redefined GDP, particularly given their observation that economic growth by traditional means is going to be limited. They look for a broader sense of justice in the companies that provide their consumer purchases. Such thinking is hardly new. In the 1968 U.S. presidential campaign, during a period of deep national anxiety, Robert Kennedy sought to reshape our definition of what it means to be "rich" as a nation. His words were inspiring and still are:

> The gross national product does not allow for the health of our children, the quality of their education or the joy of their play. . . does not include the beauty of our poetry or the strength of our marriages, the intelligence of our public debate or the integrity of our public officials. It neither allows for the justice in our courts nor the justness of our dealings with each other. [It] measures neither our wit nor our courage, neither our wisdom nor our learning, neither our compassion nor our devotion to country. It measures everything, in short, except that which makes life worthwhile; and it can tell us everything about America, except why we are proud to be Americans.

There is a lot to this notion that a nation's "wealth" is a complex concept. The goal of economic achievement is hardly the mere acquisition and collection of things. We are not economic determinists. The ultimate economic goal is to create something bigger than ourselves, to create something that transforms society for the better.

In 1973, the British economist E. F. Schumacher's book *Small Is Beautiful* appeared. At the time, many conservatives dismissed the book as a return to nonsensical Luddite thinking (Luddites were the English workers in the early 1800s who destroyed mill-related machinery because they believed technological progress was dangerous for the common man). Many liberals embraced the book as the gospel of a new economics that de-emphasized a "philosophy of materialism."

Today, rereading the book, I can't embrace all of Schumacher's thinking, but I see that he was quite prophetic on a number of fronts. Early on he expressed skepticism toward the power of global multinational and financial institutions and the lack of "human scale" in the workings of the economy. As Madeleine Bunting wrote in 2011 in *The Guardian*, "Small is beautiful is an idea that keeps reappearing—the latest incarnations are farmers' markets, and local cafés baking homemade cupcakes—because it incorporates such a fundamental insight into the human experience of modernity. We yearn for economic systems within our control, within our comprehension and that once again provide space for human interaction—and yet we are constantly overwhelmed by finding ourselves trapped into vast global economic systems that are corrupting and corrupt." In many ways, Schumacher was describing today's debate between Corporate Capitalism and Main Street Capitalism.

Schumacher insists that the "philosophy of materialism" be de-emphasized in modern society. Although he is correct to a point, it does, however, give one pause that a majority of average working American families today lack the means to handle even an unexpected $500 emergency bill, say for car repair or a trip to the emergency room, according to a January 2016 national survey by Bankrate.com. At least 54 percent of Americans aged 15–34 earn less than $30,000 a year. More than a third of young adults aged 20–39 are saddled with student loans. So the low level of income growth matters. It is not some abstract theoretical construct. It is a reality in the lives of millions of families. The rich and upper-middle class have experienced income growth, according to a study by the Urban Institute's Stephen Rose. Middle- and lower-middle–class and poorer households have not. Material well-being matters. It matters a lot.

The most striking thing about U.S. millennials is their apparent lack of awareness that they live in a world about to become a lot more competitive. In China, in contrast, 78 percent of young people aged 20–29 are optimistic about their nation's future. In the United States, that figure is only 26 percent. In China, the best students are fiercely determined to make their country the best in the world. They have the U.S. economy in their mental crosshairs.

China's youth are determined someday to lead the world. They want to complete China's destiny as the world's economic, technological, and cultural leader. They have been taught that this role was sidetracked by

Western influences four centuries ago. Achieving their goal won't be easy in their corrupt, state-run economy. But China's youth, nevertheless, desperately want to win. They want to beat America's millennials in the battle for control of the world economy.

Meanwhile, in the United States, in the debate over children's participation trophies in athletic events, a majority of college-age millennials believe all kids should receive a trophy just for showing up, according to the results of a Reason-Rupe national survey. Everyone should be rewarded equally regardless of effort or accomplishment. That does not portend well for America's economic future.

Given everything that has unfolded since the 2008 crisis, American society is fundamentally changing. Polls show that more Europeans than Americans today believe the free-market capitalist system is the best system for the future. It is ironic that Americans lack confidence in capitalism at this time. In the developing world in recent decades, a creative capitalism has pulled more people out of poverty than all the efforts by governmental institutions such as the World Bank. In 2006, Surjit Bhalla, a former World Bank official and Goldman Sachs partner, conducted a study that concluded that between 1980 and the 2008 financial crisis, the globalized capitalist system moved a billion people out of poverty (with poverty defined by the traditional dollar-a-day measure). By contrast, from 1950 to 1980, when the World Bank, United Nations, and other international support agencies flush with money were in their heyday, global poverty actually increased.

Perhaps most troubling is the changing attitude of many young people toward capitalism. In the summer of 2014, a poll found that almost 60 percent of Americans aged 18–29 say they would happily support "socialism" as an alternative to the free-enterprise system. Only 16 percent of those individuals fully knew the definition of socialism, according to a CBS/*New York Times* poll. Be that as it may, the surprising interest by millennials in the campaign of U.S. Democratic presidential candidate Bernie Sanders, a self-described Democratic socialist, was a case in point. There is now a new and unexpected American infatuation with the perceived benefits and joys of a European-style system of democratic socialism with government a lot more integrated into, and in control of, the free-market economy.

The European approach sounds reassuring: capitalism with a heart, with large corporations and banks heavily influenced by competent government managers who predictably guide the economy forward. Contrast this with America's often derided "cowboy-style" capitalism of take-no-prisoners entrepreneurial daring that continually threatens the status quo with countless business startups and failures. The dark side of cowboy capitalism, critics also charge, was precisely the kind of free-wheeling thinking that led to the 2008 financial crisis. The Wall Street bankers lost any understanding of the valuations of the assets on their own balance sheets—and didn't care. And the critics are correct. More of those reckless bankers should have been aggressively prosecuted.

The more stable European model sounds preferable, offering safety and predictability. It all sounds reassuring, except for one thing: The facts tell a remarkably different story. Since 1990, the American economy under a U.S.-style innovative capitalism more than tripled in size. And how about Germany and France—world headquarters for committee-led managed capitalism with a heart—for the same period? Growth of their economies was a paltry 40 percent. Since 1980, U.S. employment jumped 50 percent, according to the Organisation for Economic Co-operation and Development (OECD). Amazingly, Europe during this period experienced only an 8 percent increase in new jobs. Meanwhile, American families on average have over 60 percent more disposable income than families in Italy, and almost 30 percent more disposable income than German families, according to the OECD.

Venezuela is the latest country to experiment with outright socialism as an economic model. How did things turn out? Disastrously. Socialism, combined with an overdependence on the oil sector at a time of plummeting oil prices, turned the Venezuelan economy into a basket case. Even sugar, clean water, and toilet paper have been in short supply.

And what about the Chinese system of government-managed, central committee–led free enterprise that is supposed to be the new model for the world? Don't pack your bags yet. Because nominal wages have swiftly risen in recent years, China's overall manufacturing cost advantage has largely vanished. Producer prices are dropping while nominal wages are rising. That troubling combination makes it tough for most Chinese companies to have a profitable future. That explains the Chinese leadership's almost reckless attempt to drive the economy through hyper-investment in urban infrastructure and housing/business complexes, not to mention its desperate efforts to use the central bank to try to pump up Chinese stock market prices as an alternate source of prosperity.

As its economy has weakened, China's total debt load, once relatively modest, has now grown to almost two and a half times the size of its economy, according to the *Financial Times*. Unofficial forecasts suggest economic growth is significantly lower than officially stated. And that doesn't factor in a pollution problem that is making London's Great Smog of 1952 look like a clear and sunny spring morning by comparison. In China, 4,400 people die from air pollution every day.

Look around the world today and what do you see? A deep frustration among millennials is setting in. Young people worldwide can't find jobs. They are not starting businesses at the same rate they did several decades ago. Significant parts of the world, including Europe and many Asian countries, have rapidly aging populations and shrinking labor forces. The combination is a recipe for a future of endless economic frustration.

And here's the point: Those capitalist, or semi-capitalist, economies most heavily government-managed, led by Europe, Japan, and China, are faring the worst, by far. Their failure to meet economic expectations is contributing to a hellishly unpredictable worldwide geopolitical environment. Perhaps that's why former U.S. Vice President Joe Biden wisely said of Senator Bernie Sanders: "He calls himself a 'socialist.' I recommend that he become a 'realist.'"

Main Street Capitalism is less a predetermined, cookie-cutter formula for economic success and more a mindset. But it is a mindset that has been around a long time. On December 10, 1966, Robert Kennedy, with captains of industry and hopeful black housewives around him at a press conference, helped launch the Bedford-Stuyvesant Restoration Corporation. Looking back, what was important was less the details of the organization and more its founders' mindset. As journalist Evan Thomas described it, "The Bedford Stuyvesant Corporation was [Robert Kennedy's] kind of organization: small, anti-bureaucratic, seemingly democratic but in fact tightly controlled, operating outside the mainstream and proud of it."

So here's a counterintuitive, non–politically correct suggestion: Maybe the answer to combating the decline in the global economy's growth rate is not less American-style cowboy (or cowgirl) innovative capitalism, but more of it. True, ending today's rampant currency manipulation and trade obstructionism is essential. But the ultimate solution to the economic problem of working- and middle-class families is a world with less Corporate Capitalism and more Main Street Capitalism.

Okay, I realize that all this talk of different forms of capitalism versus socialism can be confusing. So consider the differences in economic systems as reflected in the amusing descriptions once offered by a mythical social philosopher.

Under SOCIALISM, you have two cows. You give one to your neighbor.

Under COMMUNISM, you have two cows. The State takes both and gives you some milk.

Under FASCISM, you have two cows. The state takes both, shoots one, milks the other, tries to sell you some milk, forgets, and then throws the milk away.

Under CORPORATE OR WALL STREET CAPITALISM, you have two cows and engage in financial engineering. You sell three of them to your publicly listed company, using letters of credit opened by your brother-in-law at the bank, then execute a debt/equity swap with an associated general offer so that you get all four cows back, with a tax exemption for five cows. The milk rights of the six cows are transferred via an intermediary to a Panamanian company secretly owned by the majority shareholder who sells the rights to all seven cows back to your listed company. The annual report says the company owns eight cows, with an option on one more.

Under INNOVATIVE OR MAIN STREET CAPITALISM, you have two cows. You sell one and buy a bull. Your herd multiplies, and the economy grows. You sell them and retire on the income.

So why has the U.S. economy been held back? Why are average folk so angry? America has had too much financial engineering, or Wall Street–style capitalism, and not enough innovative, or Main Street, capitalism. The latter is the kind of highly innovative capitalism driven by entrepreneurial daring from the bottom up that multiplies jobs and opportunities.

By Main Street Capitalism, I am referring not to a libertarian view of markets in which anything goes and government oversight plays no role. Witness the failure of regulatory oversight of the reckless Wall Street bankers that led to the heartache of the 2008 financial crisis. I mean entrepreneurial, risk-taking, business startup capitalism, as opposed to the Corporate (or status quo) Capitalism that has descended on the world in recent years. That latter form of capitalism is the great de-equalizer, stifling economic growth to the detriment of average working families.

Innovative capitalism fixates on the small and daring centers of high-growth economic reinvention. It is the kind of capitalism that challenges status quo thinking and empowers even those at the bottom rungs of the economic ladder. Some analysts, including James Pethokoukis, call this "empowering capitalism."

By contrast, Corporate Capitalism fixates on survival by dominating the government's levers of power to protect the status quo. Main Street Capitalism would have the United States dominate the world as a broad-based innovative powerhouse. Main Street Capitalism means higher growth but a lot of disruptive, sometimes nasty creative destruction of the existing corporate establishment. Unimaginative firms with famous names fall. More imaginative new firms rise up to take their place, expanding the market for goods and services in the process of creative destruction. Think of the names Google and Facebook overshadowing previously more famous names such as IBM, Intel, and Hewlett Packard.

Corporate Capitalism is consistent with today's modest 1 to 2 percent growth in an economy of seeming predictability, but with actually a lot of personal destruction and heartache for those less fortunate because of the economy's lack of economic mobility. Under Corporate Capitalism, political interests fight over pieces of a shrinking pie. As I'll later show, they desperately use legal, political, and financial influence to protect market share. Under the empowering influence of Main Street Capitalism, the pie expands, allowing all to rise higher on the economic ladder of success. There's little time for fighting over pieces of the expanding pie.

Under today's status quo–oriented Corporate Capitalism of diminished economic expectations, corruption has become an epidemic. Trade agreements are bastardized. Currency manipulation is rampant. Entrenched bureaucracies and special interests choke off the initiative of the risk-takers and of small and mid-sized firms. The big win out over the small, the established over the new. As a sign of this trend, look at the direction of financing. In 2014, America's ten largest banks issued small business loans of only $45 billion, down nearly 40 percent from 2006, according to PayNet, Inc., a research firm that tracks small business financing.

At the same time, the Fortune 500 corporate community has borrowed massively, but not to invest in new plant and equipment. They borrowed to buy back their own stock. Buying back stock pumps up the value of the company's stock price. The executives become more prosperous. There is nothing wrong with that if the corporate executives are using the company's own cash. But the situation is different when they use the central bank's extraordinarily low interest rates to accumulate unheard-of levels of debt to pump up their share price for the short term instead of investing in America for the long term. And while this was happening, medium-sized and small businesses were being denied credit, left to financially suffocate while the policy community in Washington, D.C., including the Federal Reserve, remained detached on the sidelines.

It will become clear as you read this book that I have a strong bias toward business startups. And why are startups so important? *The Atlantic* magazine's Derek Thompson makes the crucial point: "One good reason to care about startups in America is that they tend to *start . . . in . . . America. . . .* The vast majority of job creation at large multinational corporations—as much as 75 percent of new jobs—takes place overseas."

In the United States, both political parties have sided too much with the corporate capitalists. That is why, in the 2016 presidential contest, the outside candidates performed far beyond expectations. Average folk know that both political parties "change shape to fit the zero-sum contours of the moment," as *New York Times* columnist David Brooks put it. Both have contributed to an environment of policy stalemate. As a result, a new, long-term era of mediocre global economic performance looks to be irreversible.

But is such a dismal economic future really permanently set? It doesn't have to be. Maybe our real problem is not *secular* stagnation. Maybe it is *policy* stagnation combined with a stagnation in human creativity and courage, and the unfairness of a less-than-level playing field.

Let me state again: Nothing about economics is predictable. An economy's health depends on behavioral elements that don't always fit on a spreadsheet. Economies are not just a collection of abstract statistics about monetary velocity, aggregate demand, trade imbalances, and output. Economies are a consensus of the hopes, dreams, and fears of people, the emotions that drive consumer confidence and that lead people to start new firms or expand existing ones. In an economy, the behavior of people matters. That's why there is reason for hope. Changes in human attitudes in the collective driven by effective leadership can change the world. The notion that economic success is cosmically predetermined—that it is all just a matter of luck—is nonsense. True, luck factors some into the equation of success. But the notion that the economic power of a new idea and individual initiative (hard work) are minor factors in success, as an increasing number of social theorists insist, is a cop-out. In determining economic success, the motivation and initiative of people matter.

Several years ago on Father's Day, Peter, one of my sons, gave me an unusual gift that illustrated this point—a copy of *Easy Rider*, a movie from my youth that has become a cult classic. The film got me thinking about the role people play in the success of an economy. We are not only consumers but entrepreneurial producers and, in some cases, dreamers of breathtaking innovation. Many economists prefer to look at abstract data detached from any human element. But when all is said and done, it is people who are essential to achieving vibrant levels of economic growth. The economics profession needs to better understand what motivates the behavior of people. And today, fear of a world economy of unknowns and a Washington climate of stalemate and ugly partisanship is robbing Americans of their hope in the future.

Easy Rider was crudely made in 1969 for a surprisingly low $400,000. It is about the journey of two young drug-culture motorcyclists on a multistate trek from Los Angeles to New Orleans. The movie is significant if only because it showcased young actors—Jack Nicholson, Dennis Hopper, and Peter Fonda—who went on to big-time Hollywood fame.

In its most memorable scene, two of the protagonists sit around an evening campfire, musing about the evolving state of America. "You know, this used to be a helluva good country," says the character George Hanson, played by Nicholson, the now famous Academy Award–winning actor (while sounding exactly like the older Nicholson in today's films). "I can't understand what's gone wrong with it."

Across the campfire, Hopper, playing the character Billy, sits back in momentary silence. In deep thought as the crackling sound of the fire intensifies, he prophetically answers: "Man, everybody got chicken, that's what happened."

Today's economy is being held back for reasons that are to a significant degree behavioral. The problem is us. Americans "got chicken" about embracing the future. We lost our nerve and our verve. And we have worsened the problem by allowing ourselves, in the midst of this timidity, to become hyper-partisan. All of which has contributed to Washington's inability to get anything done.

In early 2013, for example, *The Hill* newspaper produced a stunning article written by the Democratic pollster Mark Mellman. He wrote about the results of an experimental poll (conducted with Republican pollster Whit Ayres) in which it turns out the only factor that seemed to matter in determining a person's opinion on any topic was party politics. Two groups of respondents were asked to respond to two different education plans, which were actually the same plan, with one labeled "Democratic" and the other "Republican." The plan dealt with familiar issues—class size, teacher pay, and the like. The conclusions were startling. When the plan was presented and described in detail as the Democratic Plan, Democrats by huge margins loved it and Republicans hated it. When the exact same plan was presented and described in detail to a second group of similar makeup as the Republican Plan, Republicans preferred "their party's plan" by an overwhelming majority. Democrats hated it. The upshot: Partisanship in America has reached such a poisonous level of absurdity that our economic future has been hijacked. And the great irony is that we are the hijackers.

The drive to foment partisan division has been relentless. In late 2015, a Democratic political analyst, appearing on a cable television news outlet, suggested that economically the status quo of modest 2 percent growth is just fine. The economy is prospering. He pointed out that for those Americans living in the tech-savvy, Democrat-oriented urban areas concentrated on both coasts (cities such as New York, Washington, D.C., Boston, Los Angeles, and San Francisco), the economy in recent years has fared reasonably well. So what's the problem? It is only those hapless souls living in suburban and rural America, the so-called Republican fly-over states, he said, who continue to economically suffer.

Such an analysis was not only meanly partisan, but inaccurate. Real median income for African-American households across America dropped 13 percent from its peak in 2000. This is four times worse than white households, according to the Census Bureau. Black household median income rose by 30 percent between 1992 and 2000. Since then, the livelihoods of African-American families, particularly since the financial crisis, have been crushed regardless of their place of residence. For working-class white families not part of the tech-oriented services economy, the picture has not been that much better. And that is true wherever they live. The life expectancy of working-class whites is dropping, according to research by Anne Case and Angus Deaton.

Notice the relationship between partisanship and prosperity. During the high-growth, big jobs–producing presidencies of Ronald Reagan (1981–1989) and Bill Clinton, both political parties, when forced to, and despite their differences over the proper level of taxation, worked together for the benefit of the nation's economic welfare. (Reagan lowered the top individual tax rate from 70 percent eventually down to 28 percent. Clinton later raised the top rate on the affluent to 39.6 percent but also signed legislation dramatically cutting the capital gains rate.) During the subsequent deeply partisan years of George W. Bush and Barack Obama, policy stalemate reigned, the economy underperformed, and for average people, the American Dream began to vanish. The deglobalization of the world economy and rise of nationalism of course also contributed to this trend.

Let me state right off that this is no "back-to-the-future" call for a return to the policies of the past. In today's information economy of global disinflationary pressure, the economic problems are different from the situation that existed during the Reagan and Clinton years. Back then,

America dominated the world economy while China and India were not yet major economic players, as they are today.

Globalization, the integration of the world's financial markets and markets for goods and services, turned out to be an imperfect good—a great, flawed, sometimes disappointing wealth-creating machine that raises real questions about the fair distribution of economic benefits and the potential for producing financial panics.

The Reagan and Clinton years, nevertheless, offer an important lesson. The willingness of both presidents to compromise provided an essential certainty and stability for economic and financial decision makers in the private economy. In 1983, for example, when the Social Security system was in trouble, President Reagan and Democratic House Speaker Tip O'Neill agreed on a compromise plan to save the system. That's what political leaders are supposed to do with problems that concern the country's vital interests. Just the opposite unfolded under Presidents George W. Bush and Barack Obama. The coming entitlement nightmare is almost never mentioned. Indeed, President Obama, who once publicly bemoaned the fact that the Medicare program is on the road to insolvency, in his last year in office called not for reform, but for a massive expansion of the existing vulnerable program.

To be fair, the presidency of George W. Bush began in unfortunate circumstances for the nation with the voter recount in the state of Florida. Half of the American voting public ended up thinking their man, Democrat Al Gore, had won. And he had won—the popular vote, but not the Electoral College. After the U.S. Supreme Court stopped the Florida vote recount, a lot of my Democratic friends became convinced the election was stolen. Washington, D.C.'s climate began to change dramatically for the worse. There were no more Washington dinner parties per se. There were "Republican dinner parties" and "Democratic dinner parties." The result, sadly, was the beginning of a period from 2001 on of nasty, blind, destructive partisanship by both political parties. During this period, coincidentally or not, the public's hope for the future soured, the economy underperformed, and the American Dream began to vanish.

The Reagan and Clinton years were hardly perfect. Policymakers made their share of mistakes. Some, including the Clinton era's elimination of the Glass-Steagall Act's separation of banks from investment firms without thinking through the risks of such a change, given the weakness of the capabilities of the regulatory system, contributed to the 2008 financial crisis. There were moments of deep partisan nastiness (the Clinton impeachment vote). But the relative bipartisan cooperation of that era, driven by the willingness of Bill Clinton and then–House Speaker Newt Gingrich to resolve differences when it really counted, provided certainty to consumers, investors, and entrepreneurs. Take a look at the actual data. The economy boomed. The budget went into surplus. True, the Clinton economy lucked out with the rise of the Internet revolution. But a bit of luck is always essential to successful policymaking. During his presidency, Bill Clinton achieved impressive GDP growth rates of roughly 4 percent.

Many economic analysts mock the Reagan years as little more than a time of all-consuming greed. But during that period, the economy achieved five years of 4.5 percent average growth. That's far more than twice today's economic growth rates. For nearly 18 months, the economy produced the equivalent of 450,000 new jobs a month (adjusted for the larger size of today's economy). That's more than twice today's monthly new jobs average. But, to be fair, the national debt also tripled as defense spending soared.

Just the opposite unfolded under George W. Bush and Barack Obama. A hateful partisanship reached its zenith and covered Washington, D.C., like a thick, suffocating blanket of stalemate. For sure, the Bush Administration supported efforts to achieve stronger business investment and greater foreign investment. Nevertheless, the economy since 2000 has progressively slowed. Had there not been home equity loans and other temporary and illusory fruits of the bubble economy, the annual GDP growth rate during the nearly seven George W. Bush years before the financial crisis would have averaged 1 percent, economic historian Niall Ferguson calculates. The U.S. economy under Barack Obama achieved a paltry average annual growth rate of roughly 1.4 percent.

One reason for this stark difference in performance, argues former Clinton Administration economist Rob Shapiro, is that both Bill Clinton and Ronald Reagan "supported stronger rates of business investment, public investments to modernize infrastructure and to support basic research and development, greater measures to liberalize trade and direct foreign investment and measures to bring about higher productivity growth" than occurred under George W. Bush and Barack Obama. When forced to engage in bipartisan compromise, they did so. As a result, stresses Shapiro, throughout the Reagan and Clinton years, "U.S. households of virtually every type experienced large steady income gains, whether they were headed by men or women, by blacks, whites or Hispanics, or by people with high school diplomas or college degrees." Not so after 2000.

Hard-line conservatives (not to mention their counterparts on the left) have a difficult time swallowing the concept of policy compromise. They should look to Ronald Reagan. In 1967, when he became governor of California and delved into the give-and-take with the Democratic-controlled legislature, many of Reagan's hard-line campaign supporters urged him to adopt an all-or-nothing negotiating style. To their disappointment, Reagan chose to compromise. And he was good at it, no doubt as a result of decades as an actor negotiating movie contracts and as head of the Screen Actors Guild. So was Bill Clinton, who benefited from having been governor of a state where bipartisan negotiations were essential. In his negotiations with a Republican U.S. House of Representatives, Clinton often got more than he gave. But he negotiated, and that's in part why he presided over a successful economy.

I experienced Ronald Reagan's sentiment toward bipartisan compromise firsthand. In January 1980, I was among a small group of economic strategists who spent three days with then-Governor Reagan developing an economic recovery strategy for his 1980 presidential campaign. I had never before met the candidate. As he briskly walked into the small conference room of the Los Angeles Airport Marriott Hotel the first day of our discussions, two things surprised me: The first was trivial. Each day Governor Reagan wore the same brightly colored sports coat made up of a series of multicolored patches. It looked as if the candidate had just left his day job selling used Dodges off the car lot. His stylish wife, Nancy, must have been mortified. And, when he took off that jacket, he had the biceps and forearms of a 25-year-old, though he was 69 at the time.

But second, and of course more importantly, as the days of discussions unfolded, I was struck by the degree to which Reagan was not interested in partisanship. Instead, he was intensely interested in policy ideas with blue-collar appeal that would be attractive to reasonable folk across party lines. It became clear why, against all expectations, Reagan had been a successful governor with a Democratic legislature. He could engage in bipartisan deal-making.

As President Reagan reflected later in his autobiography *An American Life*, "A lot of the most radical conservatives who had supported me during the [gubernatorial] election didn't like it. 'Compromise' was a dirty word to them and they wouldn't face the fact that we couldn't get all of what we wanted today. They wanted all or nothing and wanted it all at once." What Reagan sought instead was what he referred to as "the highest batting average possible" without ending the negotiations. In policy-making, the perfect can be the enemy of the good.

In 2013, the rock star and political activist Bono gave a telling interview on *Charlie Rose* about the poisonous political culture in Washington, D.C. The musician was being asked about his work to promote better medical care and enhanced economic prosperity in Africa. In Washington, D.C., Bono charged, extreme conservatives want no government involvement with Africa's economy, which is unrealistic. Extreme liberals distrust private market forces entirely, which is just as naïve.

Then Bono uttered a provocative phrase that seemed to sum up America's fundamental economic problem—and opportunity—at a time of extraordinary global risk with a domestic crisis of confidence. He said it is time the extremists obsessed with purity, on both the right and the left, move aside. It is time, he said, to unleash "the radical center"—the majority of the American people open to common-sense compromise in a dangerous world.

Bono was right on point. The world is a boiling cauldron of uncertainty, chaos, and danger. The American people, despite being forever tempted by the allure of partisanship, recognize the enormity of today's problems and are finally beginning to wake up. The hold of political parties on the electorate is steadily weakening. People are beginning to yearn for pragmatic change—anything that works, regardless of political label. The essential point is this: Out of anger comes opportunity if our political leaders are wise enough to pay attention to the nation's mood of anxiety.

It is easy to cynically conclude that in public policy, things never change. So why bother? The forces of the status quo seem to remain forever intractable. But that is not altogether true. Change can happen—and quickly—sometimes from completely unpredictable sources. Particularly in a democracy, leaders have the ability to send a powerful message to private markets that a positive paradigm shift is underway. And markets have a history of responding positively to perceived paradigm shifts. A nation's mood can suddenly be transformed. This happened in 1981, less than seven months after Ronald Reagan entered the Oval Office. This is an example of a Republican leader, but history is full of leaders of all partisan stripes who brought about important change as well.

The decade of the 1970s had been a period of economic malaise, hyperinflation, and double-digit interest rates. The national psyche seemed to have lost any sense of purpose. British historian Paul Johnson went so far as to sum up the 1970s in his book *Modern Times* as "America's suicide attempt." America's bloated corporations were international laughingstocks. German and Japanese corporate juggernauts were the supposed new models of global excellence. The U.S. economy seemed forever doomed to failure and mediocrity. The failed Ford Pinto, the small, quality-compromised compact car that was the subject of a massive lawsuit over safety issues, was the poster child for America's hapless 1970s industrial predicament.

Early on in his presidency, Reagan triggered a surprise paradigm shift by doing something highly unusual and enormously risky. On August 5, 1981, he fired most of the members of the Professional Air Traffic Controllers Organization (PATCO), a total of 11,345 people. They had tried to shut down the nation's airports with an illegal strike. The irony is that the PATCO union liked and supported Reagan. On the surface, the president's actions seemed mean-spirited.

Almost all the president's advisers warned Reagan of the pitfalls of firing a union (just as many political experts today warn of the dangers of bold, bipartisan economic reform). The potential for a European-style labor transportation shutdown across the board in response, they argued, could bring all U.S. transportation systems to a halt. That would have crippled the American economy, quickly throwing tens of thousands of workers out onto the streets. To me, the risks of such a gamble far outweighed any potential upside. Yet after offering a last, and unsuccessful, ultimatum to go back to work, Reagan fired the PATCO members. The entire world held its breath. No economically devastating European-style labor shutdown occurred. Thankfully, a lot of organized labor knew what was at stake.

The episode represented a political turning point for America, a powerful and unexpected paradigm shift. In the early 1990s at a breakfast with then Federal Reserve Chairman Alan Greenspan, I asked America's chief central banker about the air traffic controller incident. Greenspan said that in his former life in the private sector at that time as an adviser to many large U.S.-based multinational corporations, every CEO was fixated on the air traffic controller outcome as a potentially transformative event. Their increasingly dinosaur-like corporations would now face a new climate of political and economic flexibility that would enable the restructuring necessary to compete in a world of aggressive global competition. Former Democratic President Jimmy Carter (1977–1981) had cracked open the door with his deregulation proposals in trucking, railroads, finance, and other industries. Now, Reagan completed what Carter had started by forcing a change in market expectations. The issue was not that unions were evil or lacked a role in a modern economy; the question was whether a broad political consensus existed to allow bloated American companies to aggressively restructure. The outcome sent the message of American toughness, commitment to the rule of law, and belief in the future. Most of all, the message stated clearly that the policy forces of the status quo were in retreat. Positive change was coming.

Foreign governments immediately took note. William Brock, America's lead trade negotiator at the time, told me that in his first official trip to Japan (which occurred before the firing of the air traffic controllers), his Japanese counterparts were rude and dismissive in the discussions, showing no willingness to compromise. During the next trip (which occurred just after the firings), the attitude of the Japanese negotiators had radically changed. Suddenly, they were respectful and willing to compromise on trade issues. America was getting tough; it was going to allow its bloated corporate infrastructure to be restructured. The stagflation dragon was about to be slain. It is frustrating that a lot of those revitalized corporations have of late been lured overseas by more generous tax treatment than in the United States.

Greenspan made the argument that Reagan's action with the air traffic controllers contributed to a broader renewal of American self-confidence and a can-do spirit of optimism. Our new president needs to implement a new set of similarly bold actions. One should include a policy that, in an effective and an equitable way, brings back to the United States those highly competitive U.S. corporations that now do business from offshore.

Today many economic experts continue to insist that a mediocre U.S. economic future is baked in the cake, that America's economic future is limited. But picture for a moment this scenario, and ask yourself if the experts' strategic advice can be fully trusted. Imagine the U.S. economy has really stumbled. A full-fledged economic stagnation with a lot of human heartache has touched every working American family. The unemployment rate has doubled. Interest rates have soared to double-digit levels. The good news: U.S. Treasury securities now yield double-digit returns. The bad news: The inflation rate has suddenly jumped sky high. Your retirement investment account, after inflation, is treading water. Retirees are eating their seed corn.

In foreign policy in this scenario, the Russians worldwide are on the march. Washington's difficult negotiations with Iran reflect a profound distrust by both negotiating parties. Then, because of perceived American weakness, the Iranians suddenly take an action that proves to be, day in and day out, globally humiliating for the United States. Nightly TV commentators announce that America's global leadership role is fading. Suddenly, energy prices are rising swiftly. The entrepreneurial community is in despair. The American Dream is dying.

Sounds like the stuff of a second-rate cable TV commercial with a pitchman selling investments in gold and silver. Actually, that description was America's predicament in the late 1970s. I know. I was working on Capitol Hill at the time. I spent my working hours at Ground Zero in what was then the national politics of despair. Americans had a feeling that their country was seriously slipping. People felt hopeless. There was a sense of futility in the air. Everything that could go wrong was going wrong. The entire nation felt vulnerable to global events beyond anyone's control. Republicans heavily blamed Democratic incumbent Jimmy Carter, but the truth is some of America's predicament was simply the result of bad luck.

But here's the point: Within several years, the American people under new leadership turned things around. They turned their anger and anxiety into something positive. They shifted expectations in a more positive direction. They can do it again. But where to begin? The first step in the journey is to reboot capitalism itself for more robust growth rates. The first move is to launch a series of initiatives to rediscover a Main Street form of entrepreneurial capitalism that bolsters American attitudes. The first challenge is to reset the American people's mindset toward capitalism itself.

The view of the experts is shortsighted. The American Dream is not necessarily over. The future is unknowable. It is what we make it. What the rest of this book will show is how America, despite global and domestic obstacles, can build a higher-growth economy. The experts got it wrong. In economics, human behavior under daring, imaginative, and creative leadership can change the world. Expectations can shift toward a brighter future. The dreamers and discoverers can move to center stage. But it is time the experts begin to better know what they don't know. As the next chapter will show, the road to a more robust economy begins with humility.

TWO

The Illusion of Certainty

Growing up, I had a favorite uncle named Vernon who owned a small roofing company. He was an avid fisherman and taught me to catch rockfish and blues on the Chesapeake Bay. Whenever Vernon came up with a memorable line or witty phrase, he had this striking habit of repeating the phrase over and over, year after year, to the point of annoyance or amusement depending on how you saw the dynamic of family gatherings. Nearly a half century later, my children accuse me of the same practice.

Vernon's favorite, oft-repeated witticism was this: "Know the definition of an expert? You have to break it down into two parts. First, what is an 'x'? Mathematicians say an 'x' is an unknown. Second, what is a 'spurt'? Webster's Dictionary defines a spurt as a drip under pressure."

Then my uncle paused, preparing himself to deliver his grand punch line we had heard dozens of times. He sat back and proudly proclaimed: "An expert is nothing more than an unknown drip under pressure." The joke might have been amusing the first time, but no one can remember.

Yet my uncle was prophetic. Today we live in an age when our economic experts have unprecedented access to information. Yet we have so little understanding and wisdom despite the fact that we claim to know just about everything. To compensate, too many of today's economic policy experts do not exercise their curiosity or investigate; instead they posture using a form of techno-speak demagoguery in the name of partisan cheerleading. Their sense of certainty about the way the world works often reaches the level of farce. Nobel Prize–winning economist Joseph Stiglitz says economists' forecasts are wrong between 60 and 70 percent of the time. Yet the profession's claim to precision in knowing what the future holds knows no bounds. The progressive economist Robert Johnson, in an unusually frank instance of professional self-reflection, admitted this: "Economists, who were recently at the core of power and leadership in society, are no longer trusted. Today, economics is a discipline in disrepute."

Perhaps the experts' greatest flaw is their inability to predict the timing of financial panics. Our brains are hardwired for the short term. We're still like the prehistoric hunter-gatherers just trying to survive the day. We bask in the illusion of the certainty of the present. As the physicist Stephen Hawking prophetically put it, "The greatest enemy of knowledge is not ignorance. It is the illusion of knowledge." The great enemy is the illusion of the permanence of short-term stability—that things will never change.

In the years prior to the 2008 financial crisis, most economic forecasters were brimming with confidence. All was well. The global financial system was sound. Soaring domestic housing prices were hardly a threat. A U.S. housing bubble was unlikely because housing prices largely reflected strong economic fundamentals. The giant Wall Street banks knew what they were doing. They were rationally efficient in their approach to measuring financial risk.

One minute, everything looked okay. Then suddenly, catastrophe. The financial markets struck with brutal force. The problems compounded exponentially. The economic forecasters themselves fell into crisis.

Since then, economic forecasting has come to be seen increasingly less as a science and more as an art form. It is the art of understanding something intangible: the unpredictability of human behavior. It is the art of persuasion. And it is also the art of coming to terms with a world in constant flux.

After all, what does it mean in the coming analytical world of highly computerized Big Data if the marginal cost of many services and products (an example already happening: paralegal advice) through greater efficiency drops to near zero, as some futurists are predicting? Do the monetary tools of our central bank economists become even less effective than they already are? What does it mean for the goal of full employment? Does this mean the end of capitalism as we know it, when manufacturing jobs largely vanish, service-oriented jobs dramatically decline, and a shared or barter economy becomes more of the norm? Does the job of government become one of managing a population of almost 325 million people, many with nothing to do?

The economy continues to amaze and perplex. Why is it that in 1998, during the Asian crisis and Russian default, falling energy prices (including the price of gasoline) for the U.S. economy spurred consumption and, to everyone's amazement, kept the U.S. economy from falling into recession? Yet today's fall in energy prices initially produced no big consumption boom. Instead, a fearful American consumer initially saved, rather than spent, more than 40 percent of the "tax cut" provided by the recent spate of extraordinarily low gasoline prices.

The economics profession's anxiety today no doubt also stems from the fact that bottom-up innovation is almost impossible to quantify through modeling. The economists have historically demonstrated an inability to gauge the power of technological breakthroughs to solve seemingly intractable problems or to create new ones. The concept of Main Street Capitalism, in particular, is an annoyance because the dynamic of grassroots innovation is difficult to model.

Economic forecasting has had a troubled history. In the years leading up to the 2008 financial crisis, the experts suffered from knowledge limitations that proved disastrous for average folk. Crucially, the experts failed to see before it was too late what had become the mispricing of almost every asset almost everywhere in the world.

A lot of the problem stems from an overconfidence in mathematics. On September 25, 2014, the *Financial Times* published a remarkable editorial arguing that the field of economics is suffering from the illusion of "a growing bias towards mathematical elegance," with forecasts that should "not be taken too literally."

In the natural sciences, particularly in the field of physics, a similar suspicion toward the perceived precision of mathematical techniques is growing. As far back as the late 1950s, Eugene Wigner, the Nobel Prize winner in physics, argued that our mathematically determined "laws of nature" describe only a small part of our knowledge of the inanimate world. He added that attempts at predictions using such mathematical precision "may not prove their truth and consistency."

Therefore, the collapse in the credibility of forecasting is not limited to the world of economists. It may be intimately related to a collapse in the mathematical basis of knowledge in general. In a world of illusion, the experts had allowed numbers to become more like abstract symbolic gestures, manipulated to achieve a sense of precision. The approach created an artificial world of certainty detached from the real world of roiling chaos, imprecision, and human behavior that was anything but certain.

In this world, the experts assumed that the future global economic and financial landscape could be predicted. They were overconfident. They blew the call. Now the world needs a game plan to reboot the economy, but too many economists cling to the illusion of certainty, including ideological certainty.

In the economics profession, the ideological battle lines are indeed drawn. Everyone thinks he or she has the corner on truth. The economists, right and left, are too often engaged in a kind of trench warfare over policy. And their hubris is contributing to dysfunction in Washington, D.C.

The great irony is that the profession's historical track record is not comforting. The record is one of missed calls, misplaced certainties, and abysmal forecasting failures.

In 1929, for example, the economist Irving Fisher, considered by many the most important financial market theorist of his era, famously assured the world: "Stocks have reached what looks like a permanently high plateau." Three days later, Black Tuesday produced the greatest stock market crash in history. (Fisher learned from his mistake and went on to develop a theory of debt and deflation that was used by some to predict the 2008 recession.)

In 1982, two of America's leading young economic minds wrote a paper warning that rip-roaring inflation was a certainty in the near future. Within less than four years, inflation had dropped to only 1.6 percent.

In 1989, Nobel Prize–winning economist Paul Samuelson said this: "The Soviet economy is proof that, contrary to what many skeptics had earlier believed, a socialist command economy can function and thrive." Not long thereafter, the Soviet Union ceased to exist.

In 1999, a couple of Republican economists thought the dot-com stock bonanza would never end. They proudly predicted the mother of all stock rallies, suggesting that the Dow Jones Industrial Average would rise to the level of 36,000. The dot-com bubble burst.

In 2010, 23 economists signed an open letter to then–Federal Reserve Chairman Ben Bernanke predicting that the Federal Reserve's quantitative easing policies would lead to swiftly rising inflationary expectations, if not hyperinflation. Wrong call.

The Federal Reserve employs more than 300 Ph.D. economists. Each January, as if they are in the movie *Groundhog Day*, these experts confidently predict the economy's annual growth rate. Using sophisticated economic modeling, they almost always offer predictions far rosier than the actual outcome.

University of Pennsylvania psychologist Philip Tetlock studied the predictions of 284 experts in economics and political science. His perhaps too-over-the-top conclusion, published in 2005: The experts performed not much better than "a dart-throwing chimpanzee."

Yet there seems to be no limit to the certainty offered regularly by the economics profession. In his impressively researched 2016 tome, *The Rise and Fall of American Growth: The U.S. Standard of Living Since the Civil War*, economist Robert Gordon argues that the future is set in stone: U.S. labor productivity growth will be 1 percent and medium-income growth below 1 percent for as far as the eye can see. Game over. The American Dream is dead.

Yet his critic Tyler Cowen, writing in *Foreign Affairs*, offered the uncomfortable fact that in 2004, just before U.S. productivity growth really began to collapse, Gordon predicted U.S. productivity would continue to grow between a robust 2.2 and 2.8 percent, and perhaps as high as the blockbuster rate of 3 percent. Now we have a dilemma. Asks Cowen: Which Gordon do we believe? The one who was ultra-bullish on America? Or the new one, a proponent of the secular stagnation theory?

Bill Gates, the founder of Microsoft, piles on:

How do you calculate the value of millions of pages of free information at your fingertips? How do you calculate the impact of the entire hospitality industry flipped on its head? In the future, GDP may not grow as fast as it did in the past—or, for all we know, it may—but that alone doesn't tell you whether people's lives are going to get better.

Implicit in Gordon's analysis is that nearly all the big problems have been solved, and any improvements over the coming decades will be at the margins. Gordon's refrain, referring to automobiles and refrigerators and telephone systems, is "These achievements could happen only once." This is true—but it's true for things in the future, too. By Gordon's definition, a robot that's better at seeing and manipulating things than humans will only happen once. A cure for Alzheimer's will only happen once.

None of this criticism is meant to demean the thousands of good people engaged in worthwhile economic research and analysis. As Dino Kos, the former head of the New York Federal Reserve's foreign exchange department, notes, "Economic forecasters have a difficult time pinpointing last quarter's GDP—that is, the past. How can we expect them to predict the performance of the economy a year or two ahead? Much less five years ahead?" What all this criticism boils down to is that in economic forecasting, humanity's knowledge limitations are considerable. Expect the unexpected. Even in finance, a situation with which I am familiar, the best Wall Street financial traders are wrong nearly 50 percent of the time. And most have high-priced research departments to back them up. Time will tell whether real-time data sets as a result of the Big Data revolution improve the performance of the forecasters.

It is only the truly courageous who are willing to attempt to predict the future. For example, in the spring 2016 issue of the magazine I started in 1987, *The International Economy*, I asked 50 experts to look ahead ten years at what outside-the-box developments could shock the world. Experts in general, I said, have had a poor track record of such forecasting. They missed the Arab Spring. Most never saw the 2008 global financial crisis until it hit. Most missed Brexit. What surprises will we see a decade from now? What will the experts today fail to anticipate?

The 50 top experts offered some fascinating insights. Even more interesting were the dramatic differences in their forecasts. For example, a well-known senior Japanese banker suggested the Bank of Japan, Japan's central bank, will have gone bankrupt. The yen will have lost its status as legal tender. Yet a respected Japanese professor predicted Japan instead will rebound to become the world's infrastructure leader.

One foreign policy expert predicted the fall of the Kingdom of Saudi Arabia. Another expert, a well-known commentator on Middle East affairs, predicted that the Saudi's archenemy, the Republic of Iran, will be overthrown.

Many experts predicted a British economic decline as a result of the United Kingdom's decision to exit the European Union (Brexit). A think tank expert countered, however, that Britain ten years from now will have become the big economic winner relative to continental Europe.

One expert predicted the continuation of ISIS and its terror network. Another predicted ISIS will have faded.

An expert from the Carnegie Endowment suggested the taxation of climate pollution will have been one of society's great breakthroughs. A former Bill Clinton energy official suggested it is possible, though not certain, climate change will turn out to have been less severe than expected.

Many predicted the breakup of the European Union. The chief economist for an important investment fund, however, suggested a European revival and no breakup. The former head of a European central bank predicted the millennial generation will have reformed Europe.

Some suggested more economic disappointment in China. But by default, China will gain a greater Asian role. A former Chinese official predicted his country in ten years will have become very religious.

A Russian expert predicted more global bubbles, weaker growth, and strained fiscal policies worldwide. Yet a think tank economist predicted U.S. GDP growth could be faster than expected. Another think tank expert suggested that a decade from now, the entire world will be better off. Other experts countered that the global risks are enormous, and that the world economy will have undergone major negative structural changes from the realm of technology. Yet in the midst of such pessimism, a prominent Democratic budget expert was relatively sanguine. He suggested the possibility that a decade from now, a President Paul Ryan will have struck a Grand Bargain—a bipartisan deal—that fixes America's fiscal problems.

My point in all of this? The views offered were highly insightful and sometimes shrewdly counterintuitive. But what struck me as odd was how many times one expert said "up" and others on the same subject shouted "down." The future is beyond prediction. Yet the survival of the world financial system depends on an elaborate game of confidence. The size of the markets, relative to the governments, has become so monstrously huge that there is no other means of maintaining stability. The game of confidence offers the illusion that the experts, particularly our policy officials, have a handle on knowing the future. If need be, governments can act. The experts' superior insight into the future can provide financial market stability. But it is all just a game, an exercise in illusion. Yet the stability of the entire world economy depends on this game of confidence.

Despite the difficulty of predicting not only the future but the recent past, consider the almost manic grasp at economic certainty and precision that has engulfed the two main schools of modern economics—the neo-Keynesian and the neoclassical. Many of their advocates seem to think the schools are religions with sacred texts, anointed saints, and one-size-fits-all solutions to economic disappointment. The first group continually quotes John Maynard Keynes with great reverence. The second group invokes Milton Friedman and Friedrich Hayek with equal fervor.

Actually, the two schools are merely imperfect (sometimes highly imperfect) ways of examining human economic activity: the neo-Keynesians from 30,000 feet up to get the big picture concentrating, in particular, on the level of the economy's aggregate demand, and the neoclassical school looking more through a microscope to take a measure of individuals and their responses to incentives and disincentives. Both schools offer useful but imperfect measurements and understanding. Both offer the illusion of certainty. Both at times underestimate the uncertainty of human behavior. The schools were never intended to become cults of belief, fundamentalist bastions of intolerance. But that, sadly, is what they have become.

Neo-Keynesian and neoclassical economists continue to clash over how best to guide the economy. Their arguments have grown tiresome because, when all is said and done, neither school seems capable of predicting something absolutely central to the workings of the economy— the velocity of money. Money velocity is the measure of the rate at which people and companies circulate money back and forth among themselves as they engage in economic activity.

Central bankers can expand the money supply and make credit more available, but if money velocity stays the same or declines (because both working families and CEOs remain discouraged and fearful of the future), the economy's health stays the same, or worsens. The central bankers' tools fail. The new money fails to circulate adequately. The velocity of money is one of the economy's great mysteries precisely because, again, attitude is everything.

Given the uncertainty of human behavior in a world where people don't always act logically, economic policymaking has no choice but to be a process of trial and error, of compromise, and of honest debate and assessment of results. Instead, policy seems increasingly driven by political bumper sticker slogans, nasty blogs, and snide newspaper columns— anything that can be quickly tweeted to destroy the opposition in a kind of sad game of ideological grade school tag by professionals who should know better. Honest pursuit of truth is in too short a supply.

With my background growing up in a working-class neighborhood, everything in my heart says policymakers should double the U.S. minimum wage. Now! In today's gilded age, why wouldn't such a change be the right and just thing to do? My head, however, perceives the situation as more complex.

The issues surrounding the fast-food giant McDonald's are a case in point. McDonald's was one of the first mass consumer businesses to go into inner-city areas. And the company was damned for this effort (the restaurants have also been criticized for contributing to childhood obesity). But here's the thing. It turns out that more than 60 percent of the owners of McDonald's franchises once flipped burgers in their youth. Talk about an amazing chain of upward mobility. Double the minimum wage, and one thing is certain: Sooner or later as the technology of fast food preparation advances and labor costs increase, those hamburger-flipping jobs will be gone. They will be outsourced to machines. The chain of upward mobility will break. But then, of course, what about the hamburger flippers who don't go on to make it big? Can they really live on today's low minimum wage? The point here: The reality on the ground is lot more complex, and often in conflict with, the simplicities of conventional certainty of the academy's ideological debates.

The greatest challenge for economic theorists is to factor the role of human behavior into the macroeconomic equation. Human behavior often runs counter to conventional assumptions. Indeed, the notion that human behavior should play a more significant role in our economic understanding is nothing new. In 1759, in his treatise *The Theory of Moral Sentiments*, Adam Smith began to explore the psychological reasons behind economic behavior. So, a few decades later, did the early economist Jeremy Bentham, who, in describing how economic actors attempt to achieve the economic state of "utility," acknowledged the foundation of psychological motivation.

In the 1960s, as we deepened our understanding of how the human brain sorts information, the field of economics began a subtle shift. A major question emerged: Why do normally rational people often make irrational decisions that are not in their best interests? And if financial market participants can make mistakes that are "irrationally systemic," how can we trust the field of economic modeling?

In 1978, Herbert Simon became the first non-economist to win the Nobel Prize in Economic Sciences for his work suggesting that people lack "unlimited information-processing capabilities" and instead are limited by "bounded rationality" in their economic decision-making and problem solving. Throughout the 1960s and 1970s, Daniel Kahneman used psychology to explain economic decision-making that seemed to part from rational neoclassical assumptions. In 1968, Nobel Laureate Gary Becker published an important article in the *Journal of Political Economy* entitled "Crime and Punishment: An Economic Approach," which explored the role of psychological motivation in economic decisions. Behavioral economist Robert Shiller, another Nobel Prize winner, has been a powerful force in questioning the hyper-rational economic models that purport to explain the economic future.

My intention is hardly to besmirch neoclassical economic thinking. To do that would mean, as the University of Chicago's Richard Thaler put it, "throwing away a lot of stuff that's useful." Neither is my point to suggest that the level and direction of an economy's aggregate demand are irrelevant. In other words, in the days and weeks after the 2008 financial crisis, with global stock markets plunging and aggregate demand collapsing, I don't believe the Federal Reserve should have sat on the sidelines allowing market prices to "clear." Market prices might have "cleared" all the way to a second American depression in less than a century.

My intention is simply to suggest that humankind is fallible. We see, as even the radically fervent St. Paul described the human condition, "as through a glass, darkly." We have knowledge limitations based on the often unpredictable behavior of humans. Yet we suffer from the illusion of certainty. Today, concerning the folks who run Washington economic policy, the description "the best and the brightest" should not be used as a compliment.

This drive for certainty has led to confusion among our political leaders. For decades, going back to the period when Yale's James Tobin and other proponents of top-down economic management enjoyed major influence, policymakers have been fed the myth that the economy is somehow easily controlled—like a giant machine that can be operated with expert precision. In other words, economic growth and job creation supposedly occur at a uniform rate like a massive factory predictably spitting out candy bars or loaves of bread. In this make-believe world, the economic masterminds fiddle top-down with fiscal, monetary, and regulatory policy knobs to try to predetermine economic growth and to control with precision the degree of innovative startups. The level of prices is also supposedly formula driven. The masterminds think the destructive forces of innovation can be easily controlled. It is as if the economy is a mathematical abstraction, devoid of any association with the emotions of people.

Actually, the workings of the economy are a lot more chaotic, complex, and uncontrollable precisely because of the role of people and their expectations of the future. The economy is more like a countless collection of living organisms of unpredictable movement and confusing direction regularly engaged in what the pioneering economist and political scientist Joseph Schumpeter called "creative destruction." Just as with any organism, where millions of cells grow and die on a continual basis, the economy each year both creates and loses millions of jobs and countless businesses. Innovation both surprises and disappoints.

Businesses fail and business owners retire, but new ventures start up to replace them. Sometimes this dynamic occurs because new and better ideas replace old, inferior ones. Keynes's "animal spirits," both positive and negative, appear and disappear, sometimes in cycles, sometimes haphazardly as people's level of confidence changes. The question is, what motivates the innovators who are at the center of this chaotic process?

None of this is to suggest that consumption is unimportant to the economy's growth. Consumption is tied to income, which is usually influenced by employment. But looking at consumption from a height of 30,000 feet is not the only way to view the economic problem. We also need to look at things up close. Or as Willie Sutton answered when asked why he robbed banks: because "that's where the money is."

A large reason for the lack of really good, full-time job opportunities, particularly for young people, may relate to this seminal problem: There are simply not enough businesses starting up and hiring people relative to the number of businesses that are shutting down. People are afraid to start new firms. Those starting up firms, moreover, are finding it painfully tough to survive in today's rigged financial and regulatory environment. The central banks have tried to help. But zero percent interest rates mean little to a potential risk-taker who cannot get credit, has lost confidence in the future, or is dubious of the fairness of the economic system. Attitude matters. It matters a lot.

I have always thought that at the heart of today's economic frustration is that Washington, D.C., has no policy for enterprises yet to be born. There are no startup lobbyists working to ease the way for business ideas that are still the dream of some passionate inventive individual and that could upend the status quo.

And now I would like to introduce an important concept: the 80 Percent Rule: At least 80 percent of new jobs come from relatively small firms that are new—less than five years old. At least 80 percent of the jobs produced come after a firm goes public and receives a flood of investment capital. And, since 2000, the number of initial public offerings (IPOs) has plummeted so far that investor Marc Andreessen proclaimed: "The IPO is dying." The decline came about to a significant degree because legal and regulatory costs had become so high in the wake of the 2002 Sarbanes-Oxley Act, passed in reaction to the Enron scandal. Policymakers need to make it easier for companies in need of capital to go public. Many small companies find the cost of complying with the act's auditing and internal controls to be onerous. Why not resort to the proposal championed by the Kauffman Foundation? Let shareholders themselves decide if their firm will comply with some, if not all, of the legislation's provisions. Remember, it is not small businesses per se that create jobs. It is new small businesses less than five years old that become publicly financed that create the bulk of new job opportunities. Today that financing, when it is occurring, is being done privately by wealthy insiders.

Here's the upshot: When Main Street Capitalism is working, it produces an explosion of success and failure, of reinvention, dynamism, and growth, all happening on a level playing field where the winners and losers are difficult to predict. The dreamers continually come up with new, creative, commercially viable ideas that, in some cases, are transformative for the economy. This climate of dynamic reinvention and equal opportunity to achieve moves the economy to new highs. It empowers people at all levels of the income ladder. Lose that bottom-up climate of risk-taking, and the economy is doomed to mediocre growth. The notion of a reinvigorated economy propelled forward by the engine of grassroots innovation and reinvention, the kind of economy that existed for large parts of the post–World War II period, becomes a faint memory.

In the short term, we can use stimulus to try to boost consumer demand. Central banks can try to increase liquidity to reduce the cost of finance. But without this behavioral climate of entrepreneurial risk-taking, the results are never going to be satisfactory. We'll achieve a mediocre 1–2 percent annual growth ad nauseam—in what *Washington Post* columnist Robert Samuelson labels "Muddle-nomics." We'll muddle through. We'll risk becoming a less extreme version of another Japan—a long-term scenario of mediocre growth, zero or negative inflation, zero interest rates, record low unemployment rates (because so many people have stopped looking for work), a majority of millennials still living at home, and overall general malaise.

In the United States, the anxiety of many economic forecasters also stems from one other question: With the diminishment of Wall Street as a wealth-creating source of overwhelming magnitude, what sectors will drive U.S. economic growth through the next several decades? How will we reinvent an economy when half of the public is now living paycheck to paycheck with virtually no liquid savings?

At its peak strength prior to the 2008 crisis, Wall Street accounted for an absurdly high 40 percent of U.S. corporate profits and 30 percent of the U.S. stock market's gains. The U.S. economic engine, powered by a dangerously leveraged and unsustainable financial casino, was running on all cylinders. (Leveraging means that you initially decide to invest $1,000 in the stock market. But if your banker is willing to lend you another $9,000, you then invest ten times more. All fine and good. If the stock market continues to rise, your returns are ten times greater than they would have been with the mere $1,000 investment. If the market falls, you're in trouble. The bank wants its money back.) Today, the U.S. financial sector is limited to total leverage of about 12 to 1. At the time of its collapse in 2007, the Wall Street firm Bear Stearns was deploying leverage of 36 to 1 and Lehman Brothers 31 to 1.

In today's new era of restricted financial leverage, will there be new products and new industries that help the economy achieve its full potential level of growth? Or is there no choice but to accept a future of central bank–induced financial bubbles? Is terrifying financial volatility our only choice, despite the hardships that it poses for average working families who, when the bubbles burst, suffer the most economically?

Note that there are two reasons why insecurity reigns supreme in the economics profession. First, the notion that central banks can predict the future of inflation or deflation is increasingly a myth. Very few economists predicted that today's price levels would remain so low despite the central bank's cheap credit and massive ocean of new liquidity. The seven-year period after the 2008 financial crisis also demolished the notion that the relationship between inflation and unemployment, the so-called Phillips Curve trade-off, is an accurate guide for policy.

In the view of many economists, today's huge excess capacity (of labor and plant and equipment) should have made the inflation rate go negative. It did not. The problem is that economists have traditionally focused on macro variables (employment, output, etc.) and ignored variables including banking and market factors. The economists' models fail to contemplate things such as excess leverage, dot-com busts, mortgage bubbles bursting, and all the rest of the economy's surprises.

Commenting on today's low trend in inflation (which, again, many experts failed to predict), Adam Posen, the respected head of the Peterson Institute for International Economics, admitted to the *Wall Street Journal*: "Macroeconomics is in the era of Kepler and Copernicus and Tycho Brahe. We built Ptolemaic models and thought we were doing quantum mechanics."

Indeed, the American economy can send confusing and frustrating signals. For example, for the 12-month period between mid-2015 and mid-2016, the economy grew by an anemic 1.2 percent. The surprise is that the economy during the same period produced 2.5 million new jobs—not great but better than expected given the low rate of growth. Wages (average hourly earnings) firmed up a bit.

So which numbers reflect the true picture of the state of the economy? The dismal growth numbers suggested the economy was at risk of recession. The jobs numbers suggested the economy, while hardly robust, would muddle through. Were the growth numbers reflecting a mismeasurement of productivity growth (that is, the economy was growing at a faster rate than the official data suggested)? Or were the productivity growth measurements accurate, but the level of potential economic growth was simply reflecting a low ceiling? The truth is no one really knows the answer to these questions. Then there's the anecdotal argument: If the economy is booming, why are so many working- and middle-class families so frustrated and angry? What we know for sure is that the U.S. economy since 2008 has experienced a series of impressive but brief takeoffs followed by one disappointing leveling off in economic growth after another. No one or two pieces of monthly data have been able to constitute a trend.

A second reason for the economists' insecurity is that nobody is entirely sure that a global financial crisis won't happen again in the relatively near future. The 2008 global financial crisis came about because of a perfect storm of causes. But mostly, global markets declared a buyers' strike against the big banks' less-than-transparent financial architecture. That, again, was the sophisticated, securitized, "trust me" paper assets that Wall Street and other global financial institutions used to measure risk and deploy capital. Despite a lot of lip service about reform, that financial architecture is still largely in place.

Yes, the big banks have been forced to put aside more "rainy day" capital for emergencies. But there is still less than complete information about the estimated prices of securitized assets. Collateralized debt obligations, for example, the financial instruments that disastrously collapsed in price during the 2008 crisis, are still sold in private placements with confidentiality agreements. The system still lacks full transparency. The incompetent credit rating agencies (Standard and Poor's, Moody's, the Fitch Group, etc.), the institutions that blew the call in the period leading up the 2008, remain in operation.

Financial risk, as it was before 2008, is in jeopardy of again becoming dangerously underpriced. Why? Today's global ocean of capital, lacking alternative investments elsewhere, continues to pour into the U.S. financial market. This flood drives U.S. market interest rates lower (or keeps them from rising as much as they normally would as the economic data modestly improve). From time to time as a result of capital inflows, stock and real estate prices have all zoomed in jagged progression to far higher levels than many of the experts expected.

The difficulty of predicting asset prices seems never-ending. In a climate of low interest rates, the Federal Reserve forces mom-and-pop investors to purchase relatively risky assets that they would have never considered if the interest rate returns on their money market funds and savings accounts had regained their higher, historical levels. In other words, to survive, average investors, including the elderly, are being forced to move further out onto the risk curve just to achieve enough of a financial return to supplement pensions and Social Security payments. No wonder anger in American society is raging just beneath the surface.

And it is not just individual investors who are moving onto the thin ice of excessive risk. In 2013 and 2014, U.S. corporations issued 50 percent more debt than in 2006 and 2007. And here's what's troubling: More than 75 percent of this new debt was only B-rated. Investor Stan Druckenmiller points out that 80 percent of today's IPOs are unprofitable. The only other time a similar situation unfolded was in 1999, just before the dot-com stock market crash. Adds Druckenmiller: "In 2014, U.S. corporations increased their debt by the same amount they bought back their stock. Their book value stayed the same but their total debt soared."

Washington reformers assure us all is well. The Federal Reserve and other central banks have now been granted more centralized power in bank oversight. The era of big leverage is over. But weren't they the same folks in the period leading up to 2008 who blew the regulatory call in the first place? And then there's this question: Who will come to the rescue in the event of a crisis now that the world's central banks, led by the Federal Reserve, have all but run out of monetary stimulus ammunition? The watchdog Financial Stability Oversight Council (FSOC) created by Dodd-Frank's Wall Street Reform and Consumer Protection Act? That would only provide false comfort. Or will the central banks be forced to resort to even more unproven and unconventional monetary policies of which the outcomes are hardly certain and the potentially ugly unintended consequences are troubling?

The global landscape is as confusing as ever. The world is beginning a slow but steady retreat away from full-throated globalization, even as the globalization of information and ideas is exploding. The world's financial architecture, including the role of the dollar, is in question. A giant ocean of cheap capital (what professional money managers call the "global carry trade"—that is, money borrowed in U.S. dollars and invested in other assets) has the power to overwhelm the effect of an individual country's monetary policy as the cheap carry-trade capital appears and then disappears, at the whim of an army of hedge fund investors. Now the carry trade is receding, creating a potentially dangerous dollar shortage for emerging markets, which has the same effect as a massive Federal Reserve–induced global monetary tightening.

Even more troubling, some experts can't seem to decide whether America's near-term problem is inflation or deflation. These terms can be confusing, so think about a giant harbor with a tide (the price of goods and services) that regularly rises and falls. Inflation results when the tide rises. Inflation is good for those income earners at the top with a lot of debt. That's because the price of things they own (houses with big mortgages, for example) rises while the value of the debt to be paid back magically drops. Under inflation, the incomes of the affluent tend to be more flexible and adjust (increase) with the rise in prices. By contrast, inflation is devastating to the wage earner and renter. The rental price of their apartment, as well as the prices of the consumer items they purchase, quickly rises. Yet their wages are slow to rise.

Deflation occurs when the tide of prices in the harbor drops. For the affluent, deflation is a disaster. The value of their debt rises. In other words, in real (after-inflation) dollars, the cost of the mortgage to be paid back increases. For the wage earner, deflation should be a good thing. Rents don't go up and sometimes go down. The cost of commodities such as food and gasoline drops. But falling prices themselves are not the issue. The issue is whether dropping prices cause consumers and business executives to reduce their spending in anticipation of prices falling further. Put another way, it is tough for small and medium-sized businesses to survive in a deflationary economy. Business plans, which assume a certain stable minimum price for a good or service, suddenly see the price drop. The business shuts down. Average folk lose their jobs.

Here's the thing. Economists seem reasonably confident they know how to deal with inflation. Federal Reserve Chairman Paul Volcker broke the back of inflation in the early 1980s. As for handling deflation, that's uncharted territory. A worldwide deflation scenario is the thing that keeps economists up at night. As the 1930s demonstrated, massive deflation is usually associated with economic depression.

In this challenging environment, a policy of trial and error to arrive at a new economic narrative would seem to make prudent sense. So would the practice of humility, given the enormous uncertainties surrounding the economic challenge. In a republic, the heart of effective trial-and-error policymaking is compromise. And what is essential to compromise? Empathy. Empathy entails the understanding of your opponents' hopes, needs, and fears. Empathy and compromise are virtually nonexistent in today's economic policy arena of mass hubris. That is one reason the economy has performed below potential for so long. Policy experimentation is impossible. America's political and economic leaders have lost any sense of empathy, and the public knows it.

In the mid-1980s, my then business partner, the late Richard Medley, acknowledged something startling about Ronald Reagan's large individual tax rate reductions enacted in 1981. A progressive Democrat, Richard had been an economic analyst on Capitol Hill. He also worked in the 1984 Mondale presidential campaign. One day, Richard admitted to me the following:

"We Democrats were never thrilled about Reagan's tax cuts, which were too slanted to the rich. But I believe the reason our party did not engage in all-out guerrilla warfare to kill the Reagan tax proposal was tied to Paul Volcker's tightening. Volcker was on a mission to crush [the 1970s hyper-]inflation. But his monetary crunching via high interest rates was devastating for average people. Volcker's policy may have worked, but the policy was heartless. As Keynesians, probably somewhere in our subconscious we had a sense that had Reagan's tax cuts not been scheduled, the U.S. economy might have gone into a depression. Instead, the effect of Volcker's monetary crunching was limited to a deep recession."

Medley was talking about the fine line between inflation and deflation. He saw a theoretical (Keynesian) basis for the big tax cut package that was significantly different than the fiscal arguments used by the Reagan Administration.

Such a pragmatic, win-win approach to policy analysis, where political opponents are willing to look for common ground in a climate of intellectual humility, would hardly be tolerated in today's environment of hyper-partisanship. Instead of seeking effective compromise, economic strategists today engage in partisan food fights for victory at all costs. This is the new scorched-earth economics. And here's the great irony: Even some of our best economists have been sucked into the pie-in-the-face game, played out in social media and in op-ed columns. It is a food fight that would make John Belushi's character in *Animal House* blush.

It is time for economic forecasters to reacquaint themselves with some intellectual humility. Raghuram Rajan, the highly respected former governor of the Reserve Bank of India, India's central bank, and former IMF chief economist, was one of the few economists to anticipate the 2008 financial crisis. He summed up the economic environment most sensibly.

"Economic behavior," he wrote, "is complex and can vary among individuals, over time, between goods, and across cultures. Physicists do not need to know the behavior of every molecule to predict how a gas will behave under pressure. Economists cannot be so sanguine. Economic policymakers require an enormous dose of humility, openness to various alternatives and a willingness to experiment."

Throughout his career, my friend and former boss in the late 1970s and early 1980s, the late Jack Kemp, was fond of repeating President Kennedy's dictum that "a rising tide lifts all boats." Kemp was a New York Republican congressman. In 1988, he ran for the GOP nomination for president. He lost and became secretary of Housing and Urban Development (HUD). In 1996, he ran as the vice presidential nominee with Senator Bob Dole at the top of the ticket. But back in 1989, as Kemp waded into his new job at HUD and began working closely with inner-city residents, he became convinced that "some boats are stuck on the bottom" and can't rise without considerable government help.

Kemp demonstrated a willingness to engage in honest intellectual discovery. In the problem-solving process, he was an honest broker (a practice that probably hurt him politically). It was not that Kemp gave up on his convictions. The poor, he said, don't need just a "safety net" as many Democrats propose. They need a "safety net in the form of a trampoline" so they can rise to higher levels of prosperity in the private economy. He was merely saying that, within limits, all options should be on the table for fair consideration in an honest discussion.

Today, more of those of the left-of-center perspective, as well as others on the right, need to show the same spirit of compromise and willingness to explore in the problem-solving process. In public policy, nobody bats a thousand. The economic profession's pie-throwing brigade needs to stand down. The world economy faces the risk of a series of "unknown unknowns" of potential financial destruction. The matrix of debt, growth, and interest rates is as confusing as ever. Debt, in particular, is a great unknown. Today's extraordinary levels of debt may be something we can live with. Or we may be living on borrowed time as well as on borrowed money. Which conclusion is it? Nobody knows. Humility should be the order of the day simply because of the unpredictability of human behavior. We need a policy climate in which the experts can freely acknowledge that they are always searching for better understanding. They are human. They are sometimes wrong.

We also need to make sure our economic measuring system is not slanted toward the interests and needs of the elite. It is amazing the degree to which elite interests override working people's interests in the compiling of data. Some analysts argue that the government's measurement of inflation has been understated by a number of statistical adjustments (fudges) made since the 1980s. Do these changes make the official inflation rate appear lower than it actually is? If that is true, then several other things are true: GDP growth has been wildly overestimated. And if official GDP growth today is artificially high, then one other thing is certain: U.S. public debt is even larger than the official statistics suggest. We could be at greater risk than we think.

The jobs situation creates similar confusion. Certainly, in recent years, the U.S. employment situation has improved. The official unemployment rate has been halved. Total nonfarm payrolls jumped by 8.8 million during President Obama's second term. But have we truly entered employment nirvana? The true unemployment rate, the rate that encompasses the entire workforce (including the masses of workers who have given up looking for jobs), is still astoundingly high, far higher than the official rate. Almost one out of ten Americans in the workforce is either unemployed, underemployed, or has given up looking for work entirely.

Indeed, the percentage of Americans working, the so-called labor force participation rate, has not been this low since the late 1970s. The rate, particularly among males, is surprisingly low. Some of this drop is tied to baby boomers retiring. Yet almost half of the decline in the unemployment rate since its peak in the dreary years after the financial crisis is tied to declining labor force participation, not to baby-boomer retirements. Many Americans are disillusioned. They've stopped looking for work. Their kids still can't find really good jobs. Some lack the skills for the jobs that are available. From an employment standpoint, America is increasingly a part-time nation. Because of Obamacare's unexpected high costs to businesses, both large corporations and small businesses increasingly prefer part-time employees and consulting-style employee arrangements to skirt the healthcare and other expenses of hiring full-time employees.

And here's the perverse catch. As the employment pool shrinks, oddly the official unemployment rate comes down. But this has been a less than satisfying route to achieving statistical employment success. Why not have every American worker quit his or her job? Then there would be no employment pool. The official unemployment rate would theoretically be at an all-time low: zero percent. Washington policymakers could take a

bow for eliminating unemployment entirely even as the American people's current anger would likely morph into a call for revolution in the
streets.

It is time to have a bipartisan economic discussion to seek common ground. The world has become a paradox of terrifying change and
breathtaking opportunity. Annual growth of 1 percent to a little more
than 2 percent is not good enough. Although the U.S. jobs situation is not
as horrible as Republicans claim, it is hardly the return to employment
paradise the Democrats suggest. It is time to get to work. Our economists
should begin with this thought: The world's central banks have assumed
the role of savior of the world. Political stalemate has taken fiscal and
regulatory policy off the table. But do central bankers have the appropriate tools and firepower to fully complete the job? Their most prized tool
seems to be a policy called "financial repression." With financial repression, the central bank implements a policy of negative real interest rates.
Central banks and large commercial banks continue to buy debt for the
purpose of increasing inflation. And why such an approach? Inflation
reduces the value of debt. But be assured, inflation, which erodes purchasing power, is a disaster for the folks on Main Street. Plus, inflation
increases the cost for society of entitlement programs such as Medicare
and Social Security, which face a troubled future without reforms.

Central bankers are supposed to be the good guys in white hats who
come to the rescue with great wisdom when the economy or financial
system is in trouble. And today the economy is certainly plagued with
problems. Between 2005 and 2015, the average growth of U.S. total factor
productivity (which is an important measurement of innovation) was a
scant 0.3 percent a year.

Yet central banks worldwide are being criticized for their low interest rate policies intended to increase business investment to drive up
productivity. The Economist magazine goes so far as to label the central
banks the global economy's new "distorting presence." Now, in the irony
of ironies, the Bank for International Settlements (the world's club of central bankers, which is headquartered in Basel, Switzerland) argues that
the central bankers got the policy wrong. Specifically, the reason for the
world economy's pathetically slow growth is not a global savings glut and
lack of demand after all, as the disciples of the secular stagnation theory

have maintained. Instead, the world faces a supply problem. The problem is also the central bankers' actions themselves. Zero percent interest rates to boost demand, these critics charge, create a devastating boom-bust effect as the credit bubbles grow and the economy's producers are distracted by less transformative business ventures, including real estate. The credit bubble itself contributes to the economy's loss of dynamism.

I know. This all sounds strange. The world's central banks have a policy that their own club officially thinks is a medicine that's killing the patient. But to stop giving the medicine (that is, to raise interest rates) could risk a collapse of the world's entire banking system (because the banks are loaded with debt, a lot of it government debt). Raise interest rates, and the value of the debt on the books of the banks could collapse (when rates go up, bond prices go down). The balance sheets of the global banking system would become a horror show. Lending could pull back. The global economy could tank. So the central banks have no alternative but to muddle through with a policy that, according to their own official club, is killing the economy's dynamism. Talk about being caught in a financial trap.

Perhaps the even greater threat to central banks is technological. The complexities waiting just over the horizon are extraordinary. A revolution in communication and information technologies, as measured in terms of bandwidth and price competitiveness, appears to be doubling in impact every 12 months. What will policymakers do if the world economy's output grows exponentially but with few increases in the human labor market—that is, few new jobs? Think of the revolution in agriculture a century ago. More than half of Americans worked on farms. Now, because of technological advances, 1.4 percent are employed in agricultural jobs. Could the same happen with many other sectors of the economy? Are average working families the sitting ducks of the future? Will advances such as 3D printing eliminate the need for mass production?

The wave of new information technologies keeps coming and coming, but there is yet no clear endgame to such change. What happens if economic analyst Jeremy Rifkin's theory is correct: that a "formidable new technology infrastructure—the Internet of Things—is emerging with the potential to push much of economic life to near zero marginal cost over the course of the next two decades?" What happens to employment

if, because of the digital revolution and the advancement in what computers can accomplish (not to mention the further effect on pricing of a
world with continued excess supply capacity), the marginal cost of many
things produced moves in the direction of zero? In coming years, two
billion Chinese and Indian workers will go from being barely educated to
being educated at a high school or higher level. Donald Trump and Bernie Sanders asked the appropriate question: What does that mean for the
future of American working families?

The good news is that we are living in a world where information is
now the main engine of economic advancement. Unlike the economies
of the nineteenth and twentieth centuries, when economic growth faced
physical limits in converting natural resources into goods and services,
the twenty-first-century economy will not experience such boundaries.
In 2010, Google's Eric Schmidt estimated that "every two days we create
as much information as we did [throughout history] up to 2003." And
these two days may now have shrunk to hours. For economists, the traditional measurements of GDP are likely to become meaningless. The economics profession may also have to redefine the role of employment in a
successful economy. As Erik Brynjolfsson of the Massachusetts Institute
of Technology has written, "We're moving to a world where there will be
vastly more wealth and vastly less work." There is no certainty, however,
about any of these conclusions, but the potential for such an outcome is
sobering.

Some theorists suggest that some form of shared economy will take
hold, completely redefining the concept of gross national product. But
the truth is nobody knows the answers to these questions. The president
of the United States should immediately call a global summit on economic growth, technology, price stability, and financial risk. This should
be a gathering that begins with the premise that we are living at a time
of enormous economic uncertainty. All assumptions are fair game for
questioning. Among the subjects for discussion: the global macroeconomic effect of new information technologies, the relationship among
currencies and the significance of new outside currencies such as Bitcoin, the effect of global capital flow movements on financial risk, the
relationship between monetary policy and debt, the role of global excess
supply capacity on worldwide pricing, and the challenge of spreading the

benefits of the high-tech world across all sectors of society—of making every man and woman a potential wealth-creating entrepreneur. Invite a spectrum of experts to the summit—liberal, conservative, and middle-of-the-road.

In coming years, one of the economic profession's great unknowns is likely to involve the issue of today's massive global debt projections as they relate to both price levels and levels of economic confidence. Today, some experts suggest debt doesn't matter. Yet, after the financial crisis, many of the same experts grossly underestimated the role of *personal* debt in the souring of the outlook of most American families. To the surprise of many experts, American families chose debt deleveraging over consumption despite the George W. Bush and Barack Obama Administrations' near trillion-dollar combined fiscal stimulus intended to address the huge drop in domestic demand. People's fears carried the day, even if basing economic decisions on them was detrimental to the goal of recovery. Debt influenced human behavior.

Are the experts today misinterpreting human behavior by overlooking the threat represented by today's enormous *public* debt? And is the fear of debt holding back the economy? Or is debt irrelevant, at least in our lifetime? No one knows for sure, and that uncertainty makes charting our economic future so challenging. With today's extraordinary levels of debt, are we once again living in a world captured by the illusion of certainty? At least one thing seems certain. As economist Larry Summers has put it, "It is difficult if not impossible to remain the world's greatest power while also the world's greatest borrower."

For policymakers, the order of the day should be humility. In 1975, when I first came to Washington, D.C., as a staff member on a U.S. Senate committee, I attended my first hearing on the economy. I was 22, practically in short pants. The subject of the hearing was the threat of inflation. A whole host of brash young economists, right and left, gave their opinions. They did so with great certainty, many with bravado. Everybody had an angle. All of them were sure they had the corner on truth. This was my introduction to policy hubris in action. The level of intellectual pomposity was striking.

Then the great economist Arthur Okun stood up and went before the committee. One senator began by asking Okun about his views of

inflation. I'll never forget his forthright response. The eminent economist belted it out of the park: "We don't understand inflation and never
have."

Economists, like all human beings, are flawed. They swing back and
forth, one minute offering unrealistically optimistic recipes for policy
perfection, the next minute rhetorically machine-gunning down their
ideological opponents with reckless abandon. Many are spurred, I believe,
by a deep insecurity about their profession's understanding of something
as amorphous as the nation's self-confidence and sense of purpose. And
why should people today feel confident? American working families hav-
en't seen much in the way of sustained increases in real income since the
late 1990s. They live in a world threatened by radical uncertainty. Why
should average folk not be apprehensive about the future?

Thankfully, intellectual property is now the most valuable property
in today's always changing economy. Even though the economic system favors the elites, we are living at a time when the communications
technology revolution is still within the grasp of all sectors of society.
Innovative breakthroughs can appear unexpectedly. Some will turn the
status quo on its ear. For the U.S. economy, there is just as much reason
to be optimistic as pessimistic. The American economy has traditionally been the world's premier incubator for innovative breakthroughs. As
the saying goes, "Nobody ever got rich betting against the United States
of America." Historically, the country's ability to reinvent itself, to draw
on its inner core of spirit and optimism and new ideas, has known no
bounds. There are many reasons to be positive about America's future.

Though the world is a scary place, high-tech investor Christopher
Schroeder makes the point that even the global economy has enormous
potential for growth: "We are witnessing a major shift that could benefit
all human beings worldwide. In less than five years, two-thirds of the
world will be walking around holding the equivalent of today's smartphone, a device with more computing power than NASA had in the
1960s." There is no way, therefore, of measuring the world's creativity as it
is deployed worldwide through this powerful technology. Stated another
way: At the turn of the century, only 400 million people worldwide used
the Internet. Today that number is over three billion with a collective
computing power that boggles the mind.

The rise of women as a powerful global economic force should also not be underestimated. In India, for example, women currently contribute only 17 percent to the country's official GDP and make up only a quarter of the workforce, according to the McKinsey Global Institute. But things are changing as the gender gap in education, use of digital technology, and access to finance are narrowed. McKinsey researchers estimate that women could add $700 billion to India's GDP in 2025. Some of these women, now being held back, will start new businesses and become entrepreneurial leaders with big-time global reputations for their smarts and daring.

It is impossible at this stage to measure the economic multiplier effect of a global innovative culture more tolerant of risk, firing on all cylinders on a million fronts. When the electric motor replaced the steam engine, it took more than a decade for this change to have a positive influence on productivity data. We may, therefore, already be in the early stage of the information revolution's positive effects, but not know it. Or the situation may be just the reverse. We don't yet know.

The world's potential economic downside is surely evident, but its potential upside could be extraordinary. The question is whether the political establishment, the defenders of the economic and financial status quo, allow this creative destruction to freely unfold. It all comes down to our attitude toward risk and our willingness to reject both short-termism in policymaking and today's blind devotion to bigness.

As the late Joel Kurtzman, the former *Harvard Business Review* and *New York Times* editor, captured so succinctly, "There are no facts about the future." Despite an ugly world, there is still room for optimism. After all, as the investor Christopher Schroeder asks, "What country today is the number-one per-capita consumer of YouTube on planet Earth?" As odd as it sounds, the answer is not the United States, the United Kingdom, or even China. It is Saudi Arabia. And Saudi women, because of societal restrictions, make up the largest group of viewers. What are their most popular viewings? Answer: Anything dealing with education.

The experts argue that an American scenario of slow economic growth is baked in the cake. But what happens if nearly 325 million Americans all collectively become inspired to re-engage and reinvent their economy behind a bipartisan leadership that removes obstacles to growth and changes today's negative expectations toward the future? How do you model the economic effect of the arrival of bold and effective leadership that brushes aside the ideological extremes and charts a new course? There is no algorithm that can factor in the thing that has always made America exceptional—its boundless joy and can-do optimism toward future possibilities. Americans are the problem, but in a climate of empowering Main Street Capitalism, they can also overnight become the solution. The central bankers fixate on whether the economy has enough liquidity. What they should be more concerned with is another type of liquidity—the liquidity of confidence. Indeed, when all is said and done, confidence creates liquidity.

The innovators are the secret to long-term prosperity. But the stifling hand of Corporate Capitalism is already squeezing the neck of the innovative economy hard. There is already an effort by the big high-tech firms themselves to consolidate market share and control future economic progress through platform delivery services. As former Clinton Administration Labor Secretary Robert Reich argues, "Big Tech's sweeping patents, standard platforms, fleets of lawyers to litigate against potential rivals and armies of lobbyists have created formidable barriers to new entrants. [Average folk] end up paying more than they otherwise would, and innovations are squelched." So, in the irony of ironies, even the new high-tech innovators of daring are at risk of stumbling, this time by their own corporate capitalist forces of the status quo.

Steve Jobs once famously described innovators for an Apple ad campaign as "the misfits. The rebels. The troublemakers. The round pegs in the square holes. The ones who see things differently. They change things. They invent. They explore. They create. They inspire." But what they do is also confusing and, at times, threatening to the established economic order. And, as strange as it sounds, at this late stage of the game, many economic experts can't seem to agree on the answer to even this basic question: Does the U.S. economy have too much innovation—or not enough?

THREE

The Economy's Turbocharger

Despite a world of economic chaos, financial risk, and geopolitical uncertainty, the Silicon Valley high-tech crowd is resilient. The high-tech innovators move forward anyway. They are the ultimate optimists, explorers, and pioneers. They seize the moment. They are the perfect embodiment of Main Street Capitalism.

What we don't yet know, however, is whether, with the label "Main Street," we are talking merely the Main Streets of the tech centers of Palo Alto, Cambridge, Santa Monica, and Austin, or Main Street, U.S.A. In other words, we don't know whether today's innovative breakthroughs are as transformative for all of society as the innovations of the past. Is the economy being held back by the lack of the kind of empowering innovation that can really turbocharge an economy and transform life for ordinary people? In one form or another, innovation has affected all parts of society. The question is whether all parts of society are able to participate in a process AOL founder Steve Case calls the "rise of the rest." Will all of society have the opportunity to innovate, build, and create jobs as part of a groundswell of super-charged dreaming and discovering?

The tech world's enthusiasts counter that the development of 3D printing alone may lead to an entire new industrial revolution. Look around the country in places such as Pittsburgh, Detroit, Denver, Akron, and Cleveland, they say. There is some amazing creativity unfolding. But is it absolutely certain that these developments will transform the lives of average working families? Nothing is certain.

This notion of "seizing the moment," nevertheless, is reminiscent of an amusing, and admittedly trivial, incident that happened to me in early 1981 after Ronald Reagan became president. I was still working on Capitol Hill and received a call one day just before the inaugural celebrations from Reagan adviser Lyn Nofziger. He thanked me for my after-hours help providing policy advice to the campaign.

Nofziger was a bearded, middle-aged man who was always sloppily dressed. He was disorganized, but he had a big heart. That day he did something foolish. He asked if there was anything Reagan could do for me, to which I replied: "Yes, Lyn, there is something, but I doubt it can be accomplished. I have one-on-one photographs of myself shaking hands with Reagan. How about one where I'm working with the president side by side on some project in either the Oval Office or the Cabinet Room? Someday I may want to run for public office. You never know. That kind of photograph could prove useful."

Nofziger moaned. Then grunted. Then he let out a long ten-second exhale, so I quickly changed the subject. Clearly this was not something acceptable under the constraints of an incoming president's schedule.

Eight months later, on the hottest day of August, my wife, Vickie, and I were moving out of our small home in the Maryland suburb of Kensington. I stood outside drenched in sweat, wearing boat shoes, shorts, and a t-shirt, watching as the exhausted movers loaded the last box into the moving van. I gave the van driver a check for the cost of the move and slowly walked back into our empty bungalow.

Suddenly, the phone rang. "This is the White House," the female voice at the other end of the line said. It was just after noon. "Your photograph session with President Reagan is set for two this afternoon, so enter at the southwest gate," the woman said. "What photograph?" I asked in complete astonishment. "The one Mr. Nofziger set up for you," she answered. The one he never told me about.

I quickly called Nofziger. "Lyn," I said as he came to the phone. "How about tomorrow or any time other than this?" To which the senior presidential adviser responded: "Dave, this is your main chance. Better seize the moment."

"Hold that truck!" I screamed half a minute later, racing out the front door and down the street to the van, which was slowly pulling away. The moving van driver stopped and kindly opened the back door of the truck. I climbed on top of various cardboard wardrobe boxes looking for one that contained a suit. I was scrambling. The heat inside the truck must have exceeded 105 degrees. "Found a suit," I said to myself. "Got a clean shirt too and a pair of dress shoes, but no belt, no clean underwear, no tie, and no socks. I'm running out of time!"

I raced inside. It was now approaching one o'clock. Little more than one hour to go, and I lived at least 25 minutes away from the White House in non–rush hour traffic. Luckily, in our packing we had mistakenly left a ten-inch-square washcloth and an old, plastic razor in a bathroom. I showered and shaved and dried off as best I could.

Within minutes I was racing down Connecticut Avenue in the direction of the White House. Off in the distance I spied something important—a drugstore, fortunately with a parking space right out front. Racing through the store's front door, I asked the sales clerk, "Do you sell socks, ties, belts—anything like that?" To my good fortune, while socks and belts were out of the question, the drugstore sold ties, the clip-on variety. Wearing my red clip-on tie, with no belt, no socks, underwear that felt as if I had just come from a dip in a swimming pool, having just tried to shine my shoes with the remaining washcloth from the house, I walked into the West Wing of the White House.

President Reagan was gracious. Even White House Chief of Staff James Baker and Counselor to the President Ed Meese sat behind us in the photo in the Cabinet Room for good measure. Several years later, I decided to run for a seat in the U.S. Congress. I was not a particularly compelling candidate, and the primary would be rough against an opponent who had nearly won the seat two years before. Six weeks before voters went to the polls, I had only 15 percent support. But then hundreds of thousands of postcard-sized copies of that photo of me working with Ronald Reagan were sent all over my Baltimore-area congressional district. Television commercials presented the same image. I lost by about 1,000 votes out of about 16,000 cast during a heavy, all-day rainstorm and went on to launch my macroeconomic advisory firm. But the situation taught me an important lesson: Sometimes in life, no matter how awkward and frustrating, you have to seize your moment. And that lesson applies to America seizing the moment to cut the tough bipartisan deals allowing the country to continue its global preeminence in innovation and to make every man or woman the potential founder of a new business enterprise. This is the time.

Incidentally, running for public office is a brutal process. It requires a large degree of courage and daring. It is not for the emotionally thin-skinned. But this political experience probably gave me the confidence to start a financial advisory firm in which I am regularly asked to walk the high wire—to provide judgments about possible future geopolitical, economic, and financial events based on incomplete information. Not being ultra-partisan or blindly ideological in my outlook, I would have not fit in as a pol in today's Washington, D.C., anyway. Too many in Congress and the White House are obsessed with short-term, partisan tactical victories and oblivious of the longer-term issues facing America, including the conundrum of technological change just over the horizon.

America's technology sector is, indeed, changing. It has become extraordinarily nimble. The industry is undergoing an explosive period of new innovation convergence. True, the disciplines of robotics, 3D printing, artificial intelligence, genomics, blockchain, biosciences, aerospace engineering, and others are facing tipping points where anything can happen. Yet these disciplines are all interrelated. Their convergence has the capability to produce further advancements beyond our imagination. The tech world is using that convergence to seize the moment. On top of that, governments, research firms, and universities collectively plan to spend $1.4 trillion on research and development to build on today's breakthroughs in Big Data, nanotechnologies, stem-cell transplants, gene therapy, and further worldwide applications of smartphone technology, according to *The Economist* magazine. In the tech world, despite the financial markets' fits and starts, what a time to be alive!

But here's the thing: How does this amazing world with its quantum leaps in technological advancement square with the American workplace, where not all jobs are mind-numbing, but most don't involve quantum leaps in anything? How does the world of angry supporters of Donald Trump and Bernie Sanders relate to the world of Mark Zuckerberg and Elon Musk and their acolytes? Or to Google CEO Sundar Pichai, who earned $100 million in total compensation in 2015, and Apple CEO Tim Cook, who took in $10 million in 2015, not including stock? A median-income worker in the high-tech world earns more than $80,000 a year, according to the U.S. Bureau of Labor Statistics, but half of American workers earn less than $30,000.

Don't get me wrong. Innovation is the key to a successful economic future. It is the ultimate source of sustainable economic growth, as Nobel Prize winner Robert Solow famously explained in 1957. Innovation is the economy's turbocharger. Innovation that leads to productivity growth (doing more with less) is the only way to increase broad-based prosperity that improves a wage earner's quality of life. It is the magic formula for growth. It has the capability to be the economy's Great Equalizer.

In the two decades between 1990 and 2010, innovation within a system of Main Street Capitalism cut extreme poverty in half throughout the world. As a result of innovation in communications alone, people with the most minimal of Internet connections today have unprecedented access to health-related information. The forward march of malaria, tuberculosis, and HIV/AIDS has been slowed, even as antibiotic resistance is a new problem. There is no doubt that the interconnectivity between the Big Data computer revolution and medical research is transforming the medical field, quickening the pace of lifesaving breakthroughs.

The leaders of America's technology sector also make a case that innovative breakthroughs have had a multiplier effect far beyond tech centers such as Silicon Valley. Some call it the "PayPal Effect." When PayPal, the online payments system, succeeded, it made its founders and original employees rich and then spun off those fortunate few, who went on to invest in the next generation of entrepreneurs. PayPal executives have gone on to launch more than 500 startups, including Elon Musk's Tesla and SpaceX and Max Levchin's Yelp and Affirm. The benefits to the U.S. economy of this multiplier effect have been tremendous.

High-tech investor Christopher Schroeder calls this virtuous circle/network effect the "flywheel effect." The concept begins with the notion that virtually every company in the world is, or eventually will be, a software company. As Schroeder puts it, "Buy a cup of coffee? That's a software transaction. Buy a car? The same. We can no longer tinker under the hood anymore as our cars are sophisticated computers. We no longer just have the familiar automobile manufacturers. Tesla, Google, and Apple are now car companies."

Moreover, when a company such as Apple hires "x" number of people, its requirements for operation as a tech company alone create the need for four times "x" in supplier firms. Eighteen times "x" in other jobs are also created by smaller firms that now have access to Apple platforms through the app development community. In the political world, people fixate on tech innovations' tendency to destroy jobs. But there is also a platform multiplier effect at work that allows thousands of innovators to start new spin-off firms that expand the job base.

Here's an important glimpse into the future. A renaissance in high-tech innovation in a high-growth global climate of Main Street Capitalism is not just a nice goal if the world were a perfect place. It is the only way the world can save itself from a coming tidal wave of social chaos and violence associated with joblessness and debt. The facts are startling. Over the next 25 years, three billion more people worldwide will enter the global middle class. This growth will require the creation of 750 million new jobs. For many countries, within a quarter-century nearly half of their populations will be under the age of 30, all desperate for a better life. Talk about an economic challenge and a potential global political powder keg. An innovation renaissance is the only means of avoiding a global political calamity of economic hopelessness dropped someday into the laps of our kids.

But notice the complexity here. Even as innovation is the secret to high levels of growth, innovation itself is a powerful disrupter. As Jeffrey Garten, author of *From Silk to Silicon*, has observed, "We may have much higher levels of unemployment and underemployment, and we may rue that day. We may prefer a time when most people could find something to do."

What Garten is referring to is the rise of artificial intelligence (AI). If computers increase their IQ by just 1.5 points per year, in less than a decade computers will be smarter than 90 percent of the U.S. population, according to *Harvard Business Review*. AI has the capacity to be an awesome economic disrupter. Both theoretical physicist Stephen Hawking and investor Elon Musk have suggested that unless controlled, AI could be disastrous for average folk. Some estimates suggest a loss of seven million U.S. jobs in the next five years alone as a result of biotech, AI, robotics, and other technology changes, with the creation of only two million new jobs.

And then there is what I call innovation's greatest conundrum. Despite the dazzling nature of today's high-tech innovation in a world of Big Data, is today's trend in innovation actually on a quality decline in terms of its transformative nature? Is it, in other words, transformational enough to benefit all of society? Is this decline the reason for the drop in recent decades of the U.S. economy's productivity performance? Is this quality decline the reason for the economy's inability to produce sustained increases in real income for average folk? Or are we misreading the nature of technological innovation? In the Information Age, is the new goal to "do more with less," as the economist John Quiggin put it? Or is it to do more with more, as many tech enthusiasts counter?

The recent history of American productivity growth is revealing. In the late-nineteenth century, U.S. productivity growth increased as the United States became a great global economic power, enabled by huge productivity growth in agriculture, which freed labor for other uses. Productivity growth then rose to new highs in the twentieth century. But since the early 1970s, except for a brief period from 2000 to 2002, productivity growth, as officially measured, has been on the decline. That is, unless one thing has happened: Our official statistics are under-measuring the effect of innovative developments on growth in the information economy. That could be. Everybody has a suspicion regarding the potential for mismeasurement. In early 2016, I asked former Treasury Secretary Larry Summers for his opinion on this matter. His response: "We may already be seeing the mis-measuring effect in healthcare."

But short of some massive, across-the-board mismeasurement problem, it is difficult to find any technological advancement today that has empowered daily life, and led to a more productive economy, as much as the two big breakthroughs of the nineteenth century: steam power and the application of electricity (with the democratization of learning in the year 1455 as a result of the arrival of Johannes Gutenberg's printing press perhaps the premier historic advancement). Both nineteenth-century advancements exponentially expanded the power of human and animal strength. But they were much more than technological innovations. As the historian John Buescher writes, "These technologies seemed to erase the primeval boundaries of human experience, and to usher in a kind of Millennial Era, a New Age, in which humankind had definitively broken its chains and was able to 'annihilate time and space.'" They were particularly transformative to the lives of everyday folk.

Electricity, of course, enabled a lineup of revolutionary communications breakthroughs, from the telegraph to today's email. Without electricity, today's globalization of finance, trade, news gathering, and industry would not have come into being. Today's information age would not exist.

To be sure, the evolution of the Internet has been impressive. A star lineup of geeks in the rarified atmosphere of northern California and other high-tech centers will continue to upend the economy while applying the digital revolution—including communications, information sharing, Big Data, and the Internet of Things—to virtually every mundane aspect of our lives. Who cannot be impressed by the Mark Zuckerbergs, the Elon Musks, the Kevin Systroms, the Jack Dorseys, the David Karps, and the Evan Spiegels of the digital world? Most showed up with nothing. They saw enormous potential in the application of the microchip. Now they are all members of the young tech overachievers club. Who cannot be overwhelmed by the masterful work of Andrew Grove at Intel, who for decades was an organizational visionary in the global high-tech world? And women such as Kiran Mazumdar-Shaw who founded Biocon, Weili Dai of Marvel Technology Group, and Cher Wang of HTC are just a small sampling of an emerging female revolution in business startups. Over the last decade and a half, women have been launching businesses at a pace 1.5 times faster than that of any other group. In 2014, women started businesses at a rate twice as fast as men, according to the *Harvard Business Review*.

But can any of these individuals, male or female, really be compared to individuals such as Alexander Fleming, who in 1928 discovered penicillin? Or Louis Pasteur and Joseph Lister before Fleming, who were first to identify and appreciate the importance of combating bacteria? During World War I, one out of every three soldiers who died did so of some form of bacterial disease. During World War II, after the development of antibiotics, that death rate dropped to less than 1 percent. Before the technological breakthrough of antibiotics, infections such as syphilis and bacterial meningitis killed millions.

Today's technological innovators would counter that with the quantum leaps in the amount of data that can fit on a computer chip, we are now near the doorstep of a new age of "wearable" computers. Someday soon, they say, tiny sensors inserted throughout the body will be able to detect the first sign of disease, dramatically increasing the length and quality of the human lifespan. Or, as some optimists have put it, we will see "technology that will allow human beings to live forever." With the emergence of genomics, robotics, AI, and all the rest of today's innovative breakthroughs, society may be entering an era of multiple "steam engines" all interrelated.

Yale's Jeffrey Garten argues that one thing that is different about technology is that it is not going to reach a plateau, as it did in the past. Technology will feed on itself. Argues Garten: "Take artificial intelligence. Once it begins to spread, once there are robots that actually can learn or that have some intuition, it's inconceivable to me that this will not amount to a transformational technological change of the kind that people referred to in the twentieth century."

The greatest challenge is to figure out how to make the entire economy, not just Silicon Valley and the dozen other tech centers, the innovative economy. In this debate over the quality of today's innovation, a lot of major issues remain unresolved. One side of the quality argument suggests that the effect of the digital economy and information revolution on productivity growth is already happening big time. It is just, again, that the government's tools for measuring the effect of such advances are inadequate. Proponents of this view argue, for example, that when the electric motor was invented, it revolutionized many industries. Tasks that before required a hundred workers could suddenly be done by several employees. Yet it took more than a decade for the official statistics to fully measure the powerful effect the electric motor was having on productivity growth. Garten argues that real change in productivity comes after the technological miracle is "diffused into a wide swath of the economy." It takes time.

There is something to this argument. Today's advances in information technology, as Larry Summers argues, clearly already seem to be having a powerful effect on the healthcare field. Yet those benefits have not yet been reflected fully in the official statistics. Some analysts argue that it is impossible to predict the result of the computing power of the smartphone soon to be in the hands of billions of people and brains worldwide. The result could be one of the biggest bottom-up revolutions in the history of mankind. But it is too soon to know for sure.

Those on the other side of this quality-of-innovation argument suggest just as vigorously that there is an innovation gap. Peter Thiel, the original financier of Facebook, believes that the world's efforts at innovation may be on an economically counterproductive quality decline: "The technical achievements of the last quarter century culminated in the production of the iPad and smartphone. But that was small potatoes compared to the achievements of the previous quarter century, which landed a man on the moon. The quarter century before that produced something even more revolutionary—the atomic age. And so on. There may be an emerging innovation gap underway."

Thiel talks of innovative advancement in terms of the exponential revolution in travel. First the steam engine in the 1830s, then the internal combustion engine in the 1860s, air flight in 1903, landings on the moon, and, by the early 1970s, supersonic travel with the Concorde. But what's happened since? The travel revolution has had its ups and downs. The Concorde was mothballed in 2003. In the 1970s, experts predicted that the individualized form of flight transportation as presented in the *Jetsons* cartoon program—a kind of personal hovercraft—would arrive by the turn of the century. It never happened. Instead, the world got the Segway. But then again, Sir Richard Branson's Virgin Galactic is planning passenger flights to space, including Mars.

Opponents add that within a decade the world will see driverless cars. The number of deaths and injuries from accidents will plummet (but so too will the economic future of the insurance industry). Decades from now, we probably won't own cars, but we'll be using them. Uber could be combined with driverless cars, completely changing the way we think about transportation. The dark side of the "gig economy" could be that few have true economic security. This sense of vulnerability is what unnerves and scares many Americans.

Whether the United States is experiencing an innovation gap could take years to determine. In the meantime, our most immediate challenge to expand the innovative revolution is to make it more "democratic." The challenge, in short, is to create an environment that inspires every man or woman to become potentially the operator of some type of enterprise, no matter how small. As it is, it is not clear that today's new "Uber Capitalism" will produce huge rises in real income. For the relatively few owners, yes. But it is not certain how the army of drivers will financially benefit.

And that's the essential point. An economic renaissance requires something of enormous challenge: the wholesale transformation in attitudes of *existing* society. Innovation needs to occur in the way we use *existing* workers, place *existing* investment dollars, and manage *existing* approaches to knowledge. The goal is a bottom-up narrative that not only seeks the best of the world's future entrepreneurial breakthroughs but also seeks to transform all elements of *existing* society. Changing the public's expectations toward the future is a huge part of this process.

True, there is an ugly slice of the tech sector that argues for the "ultimate exit"—a world where the folks who explore technological innovation stand apart, ultimately separate from the United States and other industrialized nations. Some Silicon Valley theorists have suggested the inevitability of "sea steading," the eventual establishment of floating cities that become islands of physical isolation. The tech geniuses cut themselves off from the rest of society in a world in which the only thing that matters is the technological revolution.

Such thinking reflects a weird combination of arrogance and naïveté. It is as if these theorists think the industrialized world governments would sit back powerless, allowing disruptive technologies to cross borders unimpeded in a world they believe will always allow the free flow of information. In the event of "sea steading," just the opposite is likely to be the outcome: Governments will mobilize in joint opposition to try to eliminate the downside of technological change. They will, in effect, attempt to close their borders. That is why the leaders of Silicon Valley need to make the "democratization" of the innovation revolution a top priority.

Indeed, Edmund Phelps, the Nobel Prize–winning economist who now teaches at Columbia University, argues that such "democratization" is not only tactically important for the tech sector from a political perspective; it is the secret to innovation's ability to raise an economy's per capita income. In examining the unfolding of the modern Western economies, he noticed something unusual about the phenomenon of economic innovation as it relates to improvement in real income for average working families. Phelps said, "Despite impressive discoveries by navigators like Columbus, the freeing up of capital and land, the rise of global trade, and the explosion in knowledge, the Western economies saw little progress in real wages from the Middle Ages through the Enlightenment. Between 1500 and 1800, output per worker remained flat."

Now understand what he is saying. When Leonardo da Vinci (1452–1519) and Galileo (1564–1642) were in full creative force and explorers such as Columbus (1451–1506) were roaming the world, life for the average person remained economically stagnant. There were no gains in per-capita income. Huge royal families and the Church fundamentally drove a rudimentary form of crony capitalism that existed primarily to keep others down. But then came an astonishing turn of events, according to Phelps: "From the 1820s to the 1870s (and then continuing into the early twentieth century), four countries—England, France, America, and Germany—broke away from the pack. Productivity soared and real wages jumped."

Phelps believes that the huge post–Middle Ages increase in the stock of capital and land explains only a small fraction of the improvement. The rise of trade and the creation of railroads and canals also don't fully explain the economic breakout. Neither does the improvement resulting from an increase in productivity alone. Productivity increases don't always guarantee wage increases.

Something else was at work. What made the difference was a change in attitude and expectations. A narrative of a new way of life was being written. Prosperity resulted from the broad involvement of average people in the process of innovation. Behavioral elements were at work. A motivating economic culture turned England, France, the United States, and Germany into modern economies driven by a Main Street Capitalism mentality. Average people who were close to the economy became investigators and experimenters. All sorts of people were turned into "idea people." "Financiers became thinkers, producers became marketers, and end-users became pioneers," argues Phelps.

Out of this motivating culture came a high dynamism of aspiration, curiosity, self-expression, and audacity to venture into unknown territory—to veer off into directions not supported by conventional thinking. History shows it wasn't just a handful of well-known genius inventors—that era's version of Apple's Steve Jobs or Facebook's Mark Zuckerberg—who transformed those breakout economies from the top down. It was also average folks going against the grain, questioning conventional wisdom from the bottom up, with enormous creativity. Corporate values that prized the role of the state and large, private institutions led by the Church increasingly gave way to values that favored the individual. These values centered on behavioral elements such as people's material well-being, job satisfaction, and personal growth. Ordinary people won out.

The secret to those successful breakout economies was what Phelps calls "mass flourishing." A new grassroots dynamism set in. People began to salivate for the future, to aspire, and to imagine. Average people on Main Street turned into what Phelps calls "idea machines." Ordinary people reinvented ordinary products and services. In other words, a Main Street Capitalism mindset was born. "From the 1830s to the early 1960s, Americans were in a frenzy of creating, tinkering, exploring and testing," argues Phelps. They were, as Abraham Lincoln recognized at the time, gripped by "a rage for the new." It was innovation by the masses on steroids. What exactly was that mindset? States Phelps: "Thinking for oneself, working for oneself, competing with others, creating and exploring the unknown [with] the gumption to stand apart from community, family and friends." Phelps believes that to return to that mindset, Europe and America will need to "reconquer the medieval demons" and "reaffirm the individualist and vitalist values that were fundamental to the dynamism of the West's brilliant past." Put another way, attitude is everything.

To be sure, most of today's government policymakers are aware of the unique role of innovative change in creating prosperity. The historical lessons are clear. Policymakers are simply at a loss for what to do to nurture the process. They try to centrally manage the process. It is extraordinarily difficult. It is like trying to nail Jell-O to a wall.

The think tank McKinsey Global Institute conducted a study to try to gauge the difficulty of predicting innovative success. The results were instructive. Out of ten thousand brilliant ideas—the so-called game changers—that number of ideas generally leads to the founding of only a thousand firms. Of those, the venture capital industry picks about a hundred to finance. Of those, about twenty go public—that is, they are listed on a stock exchange and thus are candidates for explosive financing and growth. But only two go on to become leading, trend-setting companies. Talk about long odds.

The idea, therefore, that a collection of omniscient professors, government professionals, and corporate planners can somehow identify the two promising ideas out of ten thousand is an exercise in hubris on steroids. If they could do that, they'd all be as financially successful as Warren Buffett.

True, you can bring together bright people and hope that their collective imaginations produce something amazing. You can build the entrepreneurial "ecosystem" with the academy and the financiers, let the government offer prizes for innovators to do things like design more fuel-efficient cars or improve cleanup techniques for oil spills. But don't be surprised if you end up with the Segway or the Concorde. Innovation, of course, has the capacity to produce positive unexpected consequences. When cotton clothing came along and replaced wool clothing for the masses in Britain in the period between 1750 and 1800, for example, the level of disease unexpectedly, and happily, plummeted. Cotton can be easily washed in hot water, unlike wool, killing typhus and the body lice that carried the disease. But such surprises are difficult to predict.

In understanding the dynamic by which innovation appears, even the experts have knowledge limitations. The venture capital startup industry entails a difficult, hands-on process in which 1 percent of investments make it big. In the world of entrepreneurial creativity, sometimes the person coming in seeking funding who appears almost crazy turns out to be the big success story. Crazy like a fox.

Identifying successful innovation is tricky. Nokia and BlackBerry executives at first dismissed the significance of the iPhone. When they came to their senses, it was too late. Sometimes success is less dependent on a brilliant idea than on the brilliant entrepreneurial abilities of the people trying to commercialize the idea. Success can depend on their persistence, audacity, and deep faith in pursuing their ideas despite initial rejection. Remember when VHS beat Sony's Betamax and Microsoft's Windows beat Apple's operating system? In both cases, the losers had the better technology, insists technology analyst Joe Kennedy. But the winners had the product that initially met consumers' overall needs better, including ease of use. (Of course, the two "losers" had far different afterlives: Sony ended production of Betamax in 2015; Apple galloped from triumph to triumph of innovation and quality.)

There is a certain amount of chance in evaluating and selecting winners. As startup investor Marc Andreessen admits, "There is a sense in which all of this [picking of winners] is math—you just don't know which Tuesday Mark Zuckerberg is going to walk in." It is like winning the lottery. You have to buy some lottery tickets, but only a certain tiny percentage will be winners. But the odds are increased by the network, or flywheel, effect as the best talent coalesces in a kind of backyard gathering. The best want to be around the best.

It is not clear that America's new product and method innovations can be rejuvenated by massive government funding for scientific research. I do believe that funding for the National Institutes of Health and other government research should be dramatically increased. It is a point of reform on which America's common-sense political middle should come together in agreement. Yet it is important not to oversell the potential commercial results of this spending. Some economic historians argue that a large number of innovations appeared *before* the major scientific advances of the nineteenth century. In the big growth period 1820–1960 of rising per-capita income, Italy and the Netherlands, largely through their governments, produced what at the time were some of the world's most amazing scientific breakthroughs. Yet these countries never made it into the Rising Per-Capita Income Club. Their existing societies failed to be transformed via mass flourishing. The truth is a lot of the new products we celebrate today are based more on new commercial ideas and applications by average folk than on new brilliant scientific advances themselves. Think of the movie *Joy,* in which the protagonist lifts herself out of poverty with something as simple and essential as the self-wringing "Miracle Mop."

It is a great mystery why entrepreneurial innovators even strike out on their own, often at enormous personal financial risk. They start new enterprises, sometimes leaving good, stable jobs, when statistically the chance of failure is high. They max out their credit cards, mortgage their homes, and drain family and friends of investment capital to the point of discomfort.

A few do it for money, so the financial reward matters. They want to make a killing. Some do it for the love of creating and inventing, the love of the new. Most do it for pride and with little concern for financial reward, at least in the beginning. But fairly soon they realize the idea has to be financially viable. Others have personalities that make it difficult for them to fit into large companies. Many are immigrants, seeking the entrepreneurial freedom and rule-of-law protections of the U.S. economy.

Entrepreneurs often have an almost metaphysical sense that despite enormous obstacles, the new enterprise must be started based on the new idea. As investor Christopher Schroeder puts it, "They want it so badly they can feel it in their teeth." Therefore, the entrepreneurial sector is, as strange as it sounds, a bit delusional. Entrepreneurs overwhelm common sense with an overriding confidence based on unrealistic expectations. But thank God they do!

Entrepreneurs take the risk even though only a small percentage make it from the startup to the scale-up phase. There is a lot of concern about the recent lack of business startups, and rightly so. But we also need to understand the problems that a business has after it has been founded, of marshaling the forces necessary to scale up the enterprise. Apple, for example, had been around for years before it made it to the big time. Today small firms are finding the scale-up phase difficult to a significant degree because of the scarcity of educated, skilled talent in the workforce and the problem of gaining access to markets.

Until now, this discussion has only briefly explored the disruptive, at times frightening, social aspects of ever-advancing technological change. Innovation is one of the economy's great paradoxes. Henry Ford once showed Walter Reuther, the head of the United Auto Workers, around a new automated production plant. The head of Ford tweaked the union boss, asking, "Walter, how are you going to get those robots to pay your union dues?"

Reuther instantly replied, "Henry, how are you going to get the robots to buy your cars?"

Today, what would Ford and Reuther think of the new, emerging automobile world of self-driving cars, driverless cars, electric cars, and

Uber? Traditionally, the automobile business model has been built on a sense of romance in the context of consumerism. For the baby-boomer generation, what better consumption experience could there be than to drive along a seaside coast in a red 1965 Ford Mustang, convertible top down, with the soft purr of the engine in the background? It is doubtful a driverless car owned by Uber, one of hundreds of thousands that all essentially look alike, will be able to replicate that magical experience that in the post–World War II period has played such a dominant role in the American consumer's psyche.

Innovation's destructive force is undeniable. The year 2012 produced a startling contrast. The pioneering camera company, Eastman Kodak, founded in 1888, once had a payroll of 145,000 employees, but in 2012 filed for bankruptcy. The same year, Facebook bought the photo-sharing business Instagram for a billion dollars. It had only 13 employees at the time of the sale.

Iconic, dominant firms like AT&T, Control Data, and Pan American World Airways all at some point stumbled, and two disappeared. Why? In large part, they failed to keep up with the destructive innovative process, Joseph Schumpeter's famous concept of "creative destruction." Decades ago, Xerox replaced the mimeograph industry. Then Xerox lost its footing. Microsoft software derailed the IBM mainframe, but then Microsoft became a little long in the tooth.

Even the most seemingly cutting-edge businesses, Silicon Valley's venture capital firms, are vulnerable to new forces of creative destruction. A firm called AngelList, for example, now connects accredited investors directly to online startups. A decade from now, venture capitalist firms as we know them today may largely no longer exist. Dozens of other crowd-funding portals are already in operation. Soon there will be thousands. The democratization of startup funding has begun. Instead of a handful of venture capital clearinghouses holding the power over funding decisions, eventually millions of funding sources will finance the future of innovation from the bottom up. This is a powerful and positive development. Why have a few brains picking winners and losers when millions of brains can collectively drive the process?

In 2013, Oxford scholars Michael Osborne and Carl Benedikt Frey produced a study of the likely effect over the next several decades of increasingly sophisticated computerization on American workers. Their prediction was radical: Two decades from now, nearly half of the U.S. workforce could be replaced by machines. It is easy to see how they arrived at this conclusion: In the period between 2005 and 2015, the United States has experienced a mini–manufacturing boom. Factory production has jumped by a third. Sounds encouraging. The facts are not. The actual number of manufacturing jobs has not dramatically increased despite today's much larger economy (even though many argue the economy is near full employment).

Change is scary. The computer is an extraordinarily powerful machine. The potential for dramatic increases in processing capability, algorithm development, and data manipulation is literally beyond our ability to predict. The public's fear that the exponential growth in technology could radically displace both blue-collar and white-collar middle-class jobs, therefore, is understandable. A lot of people worry less for themselves than for their kids. Could their offspring eventually be replaced in the workplace by a robot, a machine, or a computer chip? It is not surprising that two out of three Americans, though optimistic by nature, today lack the confidence that their children will have a better life than they do.

The experience of innovation's creative destruction, while beneficial to society as a whole, can be heart-wrenching to those in the crosshairs of change. Some economists call new technological innovations that lead to productivity increases the economy's "job killers." But does anyone bemoan the jobs lost 80 years ago when the automatic bowling pin-setting machine was invented? Are we in tears over the crushing effect on the blacksmith and saddle-making industries with the invention of the automobile? Here is where today's policymakers face a great conundrum. In the years leading up to the 1980s, Americans endured double-digit inflation and interest rates, rising joblessness, the dysfunction of the U.S. corporate sector, whole cities in disrepair—arguably conditions worse than today's overall. Yet back then there was no Donald Trump–Bernie Sanders effect questioning the foundational pillars of free enterprise, free trade, and capitalism itself. Why today? Is it because the mysteries and uncertainties of technological change have instilled in the public an inherent fear that the train of advancement is leaving the station, and they are not on it?

Today we have firm evidence that technological revolutions also create new industries that have also employed millions of workers. Eighty years ago, occupations such as nuclear medicine specialist and computer programmer, and jobs in a host of other new technical fields, didn't exist. The future could produce new occupations beyond our imagination. Tech companies such as Honor (geared to in-home elderly homecare) and Udacity (which provides online programming training that could alter the whole college educational experience) are already examples of new Internet-based innovations with the potential to be significant net job creators.

The process of innovation—though it often entails creative destruction—propels the economy forward with new products and services, and possibly with new ways of living. Australian economist John Quiggin has observed that the "full implications [of today's new economy] will be hard to discern until we break with the mental categories of the twentieth century, and develop new ways of thinking about the information society." He notes, "Much of the value in the information economy is generated by informal interactions through various forms of social media. Combining this trend with steadily increasing productivity makes it possible to envisage a massive reduction in formal working hours, perhaps to the 15 hours a week envisaged by Keynes nearly a century ago. [It will be a world] in which people interact in many and complex ways, largely unconstrained by location."

In a sense, what is required of today's policymakers is a kind of leap-of-faith attitude that maintains that the future will turn out okay. Human ingenuity and creativity, as they have done in the past, will save the day.

What seems obvious is that in this uncertain environment, a lifetime of skills training for the workforce will be essential. Online education is beginning to fill this gap as more educational options open to adults. This process of professional reinvention will become essential for the entire workforce. The key point is that the information economy is transforming the way we spend our time in an organized workspace. As Quiggin argues, value will increasingly stem from interaction and steadily improving productivity. The information economy has the potential to "break the link between improving living standards and unsustainable growth."

There is an additional reason why, despite innovation's role as an economic disruptor, the world still needs an explosion in innovation and higher productivity growth rates. The reason relates to the world economy's extraordinarily loose monetary policies and mountains of public and private debt. When central banks slash interest rates to near zero percent as they have all over the world, economic activity that would have happened in the future is moved forward, attracted by the lower cost of financing. But this shift creates a trap: the need for ever-lower interest rates to keep the engines of the global economy running.

But how can interest rates be reduced if rates for large parts of the world are already near or at zero percent? Let me repeat: The risk is the creation of an endless series of boom-and-bust cycles in stock market, real estate, and other sectors as central banks buy bonds to keep the world economy afloat. The escape from this trap of low-interest-rate/bond-buying dependency is to dramatically increase the rate of productivity growth as fast as possible. The hope of avoiding future financial dislocation is counterintuitive. It results from an explosion in productivity-enhancing innovation. And for America, that requires a change in attitude and a recognition by its leaders of the headwinds to growth holding back the innovative economy.

America's recent declines in productivity growth (again, assuming productivity is being measured accurately) are a troubling barometer of the future. The economy seems to be suffering from a growth-stunting disease. Finding the magical environment for entrepreneurial risk-taking, again, is extraordinarily difficult. But a dynamic climate of innovation is without a doubt helped by what former U.S. Ambassador to Italy David Thorne calls "an effective ecosystem" with an ease of connection between entrepreneurs and the academic and funding communities, all in a climate that tolerates failure. Many countries suffer from poor innovative performance because their labor laws make closing down failed enterprises (and laying off employees) almost impossible. So innovators don't take the risk of starting new enterprises, sensing there is no easy exit strategy in the event the business proves to be unsuccessful. In many countries, failure leads to complete loss of reputation. Some countries still have debtor prisons, which is insanely counterproductive for economic growth. Startups seldom appear in an environment where failure is illegal or socially repugnant. And failure is a fact of life in the startup world. Only a small percentage of startups succeed.

So why did business startups in the United States, the land that tolerates failure, occur in 2015 at a rate one-half of the rate for 2005? Why the lack of interest among young Americans in starting new enterprises? Outside of high tech, young people in the United States have little tolerance for risk. The share of people under 30 who own private companies has dropped to a 24-year low, according to the Federal Reserve. Why the slowdown? Why the failure to build more firms that offer commercial applications to today's technological breakthroughs? There are a number of reasons why people are afraid.

First, people may assume that all the major technological advances have appeared. But such thinking is flawed. As Erik Brynjolfsson and Andrew McAfee argue, "If all technological progress in the economy stopped today, would productivity growth grind to a halt? We don't think so. On the contrary, we believe that there are decades' worth of potential innovations to be made by creatively combining inventions that we already have in creative ways."

Second, people believe the game is rigged in favor of existing firms. There is a lot to this charge. Look at the way financing of small and medium-sized firms has become skewed. Twenty years ago, firms went public at the early stages of their existence. Microsoft, IBM, and Hewlett Packard, for example, all went public before their valuations exceeded even a billion dollars. Large segments of the investing public benefited. These firms came out of nowhere to competitively challenge the existing economic order to the betterment of society. Average folk, through mutual funds, could participate in this economic success.

Today, for a host of legal, financial, and regulatory reasons, companies are not going public in the same fashion. They are often financed behind the scenes by a private club of big investors. Then they go public. As a result, the American financial order is a lot less "democratic." The small investor has been largely cut out of the process of investing in new ideas. The small-scale innovators look at this trend and at their lack of big-time financial connections to this elite investment club, and they hold back. Thankfully, crowdfunding is now helping to make access to financing more available for everyone.

As I'll later show, incumbent firms rig the rules against the new-comers. This is happening at the same time the young challenging firms are facing a mountain of bureaucratic red tape and oppressive taxation (example: the self-employment tax) from government at all levels.

Third, even though society has always been fearful of the new, in today's high-tech world of commercial application of innovative advance-ment, people are fearful not only of the new but also of the new coming at them with terrifying speed.

Fourth, although today we have more transparency and access to information, people ironically are overwhelmed with the quantity of that information and lack the sorting process to determine what's relevant.

Fifth, because technology allows people to verticalize, we associate only with people of similar preferences and views. As investor Christo-pher Schroeder observes, "We tend not to see opportunities that are not relevant to our current, narrow environment. That verticalizing trend makes us more risk averse, fearful of the new."

Sixth, the world has become a terrifying place of radical uncertainty and unknown unknowns. It is an extraordinarily difficult environment in which to operate any business with full confidence in the future. There is no safety net in the event of business failure.

Seventh, Washington policymakers make clear that they are too often unaware of their macroeconomic blindness. One minute, Federal Reserve officials send the message that the economy is about to take off and much higher interest rates are coming. A week later, the central bankers' mes-sage is just the reverse.

And finally, we are witnessing government policy overreach and cor-porate misbehavior at its worst. Dean Baker, a progressive economist, argues that legal maneuvering associated with technology is often "used as a weapon to benefit some groups in society at the expense of others." He estimates that drug patent law manipulations alone, in which corpo-rations deploy legal maneuvers and lobbying pressure to extend a patent's termination date, involve a cost to Americans of $360 billion a year. That's more than a third of a trillion dollars each year!

So the number of business startups is way down, and those who operate small and medium-sized businesses are not expanding their companies. The big and the powerful continue to manipulate the process of innovative creativity to their advantage. All over the world, the corporate capitalists use government connections to produce instruments for creating monopolies and for impeding the spread of knowledge and the transfer of technology. The spirit of an empowering Main Street Capitalism is being crushed.

The question is whether the United States is different. Can America, with its innovative engines firing on all cylinders, economically decouple from a world increasingly beset with financial and geopolitical uncertainty, mistrust, mercantilism, centralization, international financial dysfunction, and pessimism?

Americans have historically been unique in the world. Their unbridled optimism and sense of mission have made them exceptional. Even during the Great Depression, America's optimistic dreamers built the Empire State Building in a mere 410 days. Americans began work on the Golden Gate Bridge in 1933 and finished it four years later. The original Twin Towers in New York City took three years to build, begun in August 1968 and completed by July 1971. After 15 years, the World Trade Center in New York is still yet to be completed.

Better policy is essential for America to succeed, and this book lays out various suggestions for reform. It is a call for unleashing a new attitude of common-sense compromise. But the United States is also in need of something more fundamental. It needs massive national therapy with the goal of developing a transformation in the public's attitude. That requires the new president to write a new bipartisan economic narrative of optimism and hope for the future. The narrative needs to be one of daring innovation. My greatest fear is that in today's climate of global disorder, governments, including our leaders in Washington, will resort to heavy-handed, top-down efforts to try to increase prosperity.

Still, there are many reasons to be optimistic. In his 1983 book *History: The Human Gamble*, economist Reuven Brenner went so far as to argue that it is not uncommon for periods of gross income inequality to be followed by periods of massive innovation. Perhaps the reason is the human instinct to avoid being left behind. People take risks, sensing the economic train is leaving the station.

Investor Marc Andreessen makes this case: "To argue that huge numbers of people will be put out of work [by robots] but we will find nothing for them—or us—to do is to short human creativity dramatically. And I am long on human creativity."

America's reputation for creativity is, indeed, impressive. In 2012, just as he was about to retire, then–Chinese President Hu Jintao offered a remarkably frank insight. His greatest worry with China's long-term growth challenge, he said, was with innovation. China could easily *make* an iPad, he said, but his country's economic system lacked the ability to produce the kind of individual—think Steve Jobs—with the creativity, freedom of thought, ability, courage to fail, and sheer daring and audacity to actually *invent* an iPad. He wanted China to be the world leader in innovation. It was a backhanded compliment to America's legacy of innovative risk-taking and achievement.

In 2015, a year of heightened tension between Russia and the United States, television commentator Charlie Rose asked Russian President Vladimir Putin to name what he admired most about America. Putin paused for a moment and seemed reluctant to answer, but then the tension released. It was as if a light bulb went on. "I like the creativity," he responded. "Creativity when it comes to your tackling problems. Their openness—openness and open-mindedness—because it allows them to unleash the inner potential of their people. And thanks to that, America has attained such amazing results in developing their country."

No one yet knows for sure whether the United States has an innovation gap. But one thing is certain: America's capitalist model needs to be rebooted. America's best young minds need to think less about careers in hedge funds, banking, and private equity, of incrementally moving around financial paper for lucrative fees, and more about a career inventing things. They need to join the world of Main Street Capitalism, the Great Equalizer. Audacious discovery is the goal, the true magic of this capitalism for all.

New breakthroughs in engineering, science, medicine, energy, and technology—and a host of more mundane commercial discoveries and applications—are waiting to be achieved to transform the lives of those in all segments of society. That is the way economics brings across-the-board value as those discoveries are applied to our everyday lives. Unleash the audacious dreamers in all sectors of society. They control the future.

It is time to kick-start a Main Street Capitalism revolution of breathtaking daring. A thriving economy propelled forward by innovative startups is built on something highly amorphous: the more confident and dynamic the attitude of people toward the future, the higher the growth, the greater the number of jobs created, the greater the willingness of job seekers to be mobile. That is innovative capitalism. The behavior of people matters. A confident, dynamic, grassroots sense of purpose toward the future is the secret to creating greater prosperity.

And the question is this: How did America lose that sense of purpose? How did America's once broad-based Main Street Capitalism morph into a false Wall Street/financial engineering–style Corporate Capitalism? And why, in a dangerous world, has it been so difficult to reverse this trend? As the rest of this book will demonstrate, there are several dominant reasons: (1) the economic and financial systems are, again, rigged in favor of the large against the small, (2) the size of the world's enormous public and private debt is terrifying, (3) our economic policymakers have been captured by the forces of partisan stalemate and little reform is ever implemented, and (4) last, but certainly not least, the world economically, financially, and geopolitically has become a frightening place with no one in charge. As former Treasury Secretary Timothy Geithner aptly put it: "It's a messy, dark, sad world that we live in. There's a lot out there that could damage our interests. The only threat to us that really matters over time—and that should scare everybody—is the capacity of our political system to find the will to act."

The 1995 movie *The American President*, starring Michael Douglas in the title role, offered a prophetic insight into America's future. In the final scene, Douglas as the president running for reelection against his opponent (played by Richard Dreyfuss) ended a press conference with a speech that captured what is wrong with American politics on the part of both political parties. Douglas concluded his remarks with this insight:

> We have serious problems to solve, and we need serious people to solve them. And whatever your particular problem is, I promise you [my

opponent] is not the least bit interested in solving it. He is interested in two things, and two things only: making you afraid of it, and telling you who's to blame for it. That, ladies and gentlemen, is how you win elections. You gather a group of middle-age, middle-class, middle-income voters who remember with longing an easier time, and you talk to them about family, and American values and character.

Twice the movie's president uttered this compelling line: "We have serious problems to solve, and we need serious people to solve them." America's need at this time of extraordinary economic challenge could not have been said more succinctly. It is time for America's leaders to stop the nonsense and get to work.

FOUR

Top-Down Frustration in a
Bottom-Up World

I remember the event as if it were yesterday. The date was December 8, 2010. I was attending the surprise retirement party for a friend and client, Stan Druckenmiller, the most successful financial investor of his generation with the best record of returns in the business. At age 57, he had announced several months earlier that he would retire from managing other people's money.

That night was a surprise on a number of counts. Druckenmiller believed he was having dinner with a friend at a favorite neighborhood restaurant called Caravaggio, a small, casual spot on the Upper East Side of Manhattan that specializes in simple northern Italian cuisine. Instead, 50 of his closest friends and associates were secretly waiting quietly in the restaurant's bar to launch the surprise. But as we waited, the chatter was also of an unexpected guest.

As I walked into the dimly lit restaurant's lobby, I thought of the near quarter-century I had spent as an adviser to the lead trading strategists of a number of large, macroeconomics-oriented hedge funds. This was a world in the midst of dramatic change as a result of the financial crisis that had exploded onto the scene two years earlier. For the hedge fund world in particular, and for financial markets in general, nothing would be the same. The same is true for the economy. The massive financial leverage of previous years was now a faint memory. At one time, the Wall

Street banks funneled what seemed like unlimited loans to the hedge funds to take trading positions in various global financial instruments. Not anymore.

That was one of the reasons Druckenmiller (for decades the former chief trader for the mega–hedge fund Soros Fund Management who went on to build a successful fund of his own), was retiring to manage his own family funds. He knew the financial industry was being cut down to size. It would never be the same.

As Druckenmiller's friends were awaiting his arrival, I looked over the crowd and thought to myself: "I may be the only person here not a billionaire." This was not the "One Percent," the target of the then rabid Occupy Wall Street movement. This was the One Thousandth of One Percent crowd. Most of the legendary hedge fund managers and private equity titans of the last quarter-century were there, crammed into the small restaurant bar. Some I knew to be enormously generous in their financial dealings with subordinates; others were truly greedy, selfish, manipulative monsters. But all had one thing in common: Every day, they had "skin in the game"—that is, unlike the big Wall Street bankers, they bet their personal fortunes daily in various global markets based on their instinct for how the world worked. Now these masters of the universe stood there waiting for the guest of honor.

But before that happened, something strange occurred. An unexpected guest arrived: Jamie Dimon, the chairman of JPMorgan Chase. Strangely, it was as if financial royalty had entered the room. A sudden energy was in the air. The cocktail chatter clicked into a higher, louder gear. A striking man of medium height with soft brown hair and wearing a pinstriped suit, Dimon approached the collection of mega-billionaire financiers waiting at the bar with a self-assured look. All I could think of was the image of war-weary British Field Marshal Bernard Law Montgomery (Monty) meeting for the first time his less self-assured, but better-armed, American counterparts in World War II. All eyes were fixed on the confident banker who, compared to his banking competitors, had been the most successful in negotiating around the landmines of the financial crisis.

As Dimon stood there, I also thought of Mick Jagger. For whatever the reason, like little boys these world-class billionaire money managers sheepishly made their way toward the banking star, hoping to achieve some momentary face time. "This is a real badge of honor for Stan," a well-known private equity fund manager strangely whispered to me as he whisked past in Dimon's direction.

Then it hit me. Here was a situation that was completely absurd. What was happening was a perfect reflection of the degree to which the U.S. financial system had become removed from reality. A room full of the world's most successful money managers worth billions of dollars, and who collectively traded trillions of dollars daily, were fawning over a mere banker. Although perhaps the best of the lot, Dimon was essentially the leader of what had become a collection of giant financial zombie institutions that were holding back the U.S. economy.

The situation reminded me how much the human psyche is worshipful of the kind of large institutions that form the core of today's smothering Corporate Capitalism. That night, a room full of the world's most sophisticated financial thinkers and risk-takers seemed strangely unaware that Dimon, after the financial crisis, was really the little man in the room. The system nevertheless worshiped bigness, and governments and central banks stood ready to serve as the bankers' valet, eager to be of help. By the time of the retirement dinner, the big banks were already beginning to repair their balance sheets. Perhaps Bill Frezza of the Competitive Enterprise Institute summed up the situation best when he suggested that the big Wall Street banks "perfected the art of privatizing gains while socializing losses. They tested the limits of moral hazard and won." Yet the rest of the financial system, including the financial heart of Main Street Capitalism—the regional and community banks that finance job creation in the small business sector—remained shattered. Their world was still unhinged.

There is a sense of unfairness about what unfolded. The world has become a collection of winners and losers, and the winners—usually large established institutions—are manipulating the system at the expense of the entrepreneurial newcomers. In 2011, for example, even the high-tech stars of innovation, Apple and Google, spent more money trying to squash or contain technological newcomers (hiring lawyers, extending patents, and purchasing potential rising competitive threats) than they spent on research and development. Tech investor Peter Thiel, who co-founded PayPal, argues that these firms are engaged in "the opposite of innovation; they are monopolies." Main Street Capitalism, the Great Equalizer, the kind of capitalism that demands a level playing field, is under massive assault in this new zero-sum economic environment where the "big" almost always carry the day.

Not convinced of this thesis? After the 2008 financial crisis, large corporations were flush with cash. Their balance sheets were as healthy as ever. That's because, in the years after the crisis under the Federal Reserve's medicine of near zero percent interest rates, the U.S. corporate sector alone sold several trillion dollars' worth of bonds and used more than half of the incoming funding to repurchase their own shares. While corporate debt across-the-board soared, champagne corks popped in corporate board rooms.

This absolute obsession with the big, the established, and the corporate over the small, the new, and the entrepreneurial permeates Washington, D.C. But this bias has come at the expense of economic growth. So has the preoccupation with short-term financial gain over long-term prosperity for all.

As a result, average working families, both in the United States and all over the world, have sunk down into the muck of economic disappointment and heartache. The economic strategists are at a loss. They thought the global economic and financial landscape was under their control. Prop up the Fortune 500 and the big Wall Street banks and all will be copacetic. These giant institutions, the establishment firmly believed, are the dominant financial underpinning of the capitalist system. Corporate Capitalism is king. Yet the truth turned out to be a lot more complicated.

True economic success emerges largely as a result of behavioral changes from the bottom up—not the top down. In his book *The Evolution of Everything*, Matt Ridley points out the fascination by elites with top-down design rather than bottom-up "evolution" when it comes to major achievements in science, economics, and social change. Most breakthroughs evolve without architects and a grand design. They appear suddenly from the bottom up.

Indeed, we live in a world where the elites are constantly being surprised, whether by the rise of Facebook or of ISIS. Observes energy policy strategist J. Robinson West: "The generals always fight the last war.

An example is the U.S. energy surge. It was the independents, not the major oil companies or the federal government, that caused the shale boom, responding to market forces. The generals were clueless because big bureaucracies don't work anymore."

Since the 2008 financial crisis, increased regulation and the zero interest rate policy have made the business models of the big banks obsolete. Those banks, and their global counterparts, have morphed into heavily regulated, relatively risk-averse organizations, not unlike the lackluster town water or electric utility company. The consolidation of the U.S. financial services industry since the 2008 crisis has been a counterproductive development. These sluggish banks have held back the economy.

The big banks have access to capital and are protected and controlled by government. What they no longer have enough of is a risk-taking mindset. The bankers are engaged in a process of liquidity illusion. Instead of the banks providing full liquidity to the financial markets, that liquidity for years has been provided by hedge funds and by private equity firms with hedge fund components. Observes hedge fund manager Scott Bessent: "I am no fan of the big banks, but the Fed and other regulators have developed an incongruous posture toward these institutions, providing a massive amount of monetary easing on the one hand and regulatory overreaction on the other. The new bank fines and other penalties are stifling normal loan growth and hurting the economy. The regulators were asleep during the housing bubble. The banks' bad actors from the 2003–2008 period got away. But now Main Street is being asked to pay the price."

The real concern is that since the 2008 financial crisis, the U.S. banking system has consolidated. Now 80 percent of America's bank capital for investment is controlled by only a dozen giant zombie banks. Before the crisis, the top dozen banks controlled only 45–50 percent of such capital.

America has entered a new era of politicized banking with decision-making held by relatively few banking institutions, the U.S. Treasury, and the Federal Reserve. In a dramatic reshaping of the U.S. financial sector, today four banks alone—JPMorgan Chase, Bank of America, Citibank, and Wells Fargo—now control nearly 60 percent of all U.S. bank assets (all four banks have been fined for illegal banking practices). Armies of regulators camp out in these big banks every day, looking up the bankers' nostrils. American finance has centralized, and that has been a bad thing for the economy. And so has Washington, D.C.'s nonstop infatuation with top-down economic management.

To be sure, after the financial crisis and all its heartache and economic destruction, having a few big banks become the center of credit allocation at initial glance no doubt sounded reassuring. It was Washington's idea of controlling financial risk. Yet if the goal was to restore middle-class jobs lost by a decline in the ability of small and medium-sized innovative enterprises to survive, this new financial architecture was insanely counterproductive. True, some of those bankers should have gone to jail. The justice system failed to do its job. Yet the fact remains that a vigorous economy depends on a vigorous banking system. Banks, big and small, are the nerve center of the private economy. Crush the nerve center, and you crush the economy.

In policymakers' attempts to regulate and restructure away financial risk, however, American working families and small businesses have suffered the most. And unlike in Europe and Japan, the U.S. financial system until now has never been overwhelmingly dominated by big banks. America has traditionally benefited from a vibrant, multilayered system of financial intermediation. True, banks have always been responsible for a large percentage of overall credit allocation. But both large and small institutions engaged in the deployment of credit to the economy. That is one reason the U.S. economy has historically been a robust job-creating machine and hothouse of innovation. Small and regional bank funds, and community banks, joined venture capital funds, turnaround funds, and private mezzanine financing in contributing to the achievement of a brisk growth in innovation.

To one degree or another, these sources of funding were all committed to Main Street Capitalism. That dynamic is now missing from today's consolidated banking system. Big banks take a financial risk on Google only after Google becomes Google, not before. Today the coddled Wall Street banks, in many cases now drained of their best talent (who often moved to hedge funds and private equity firms), have become the central focal point of America's financial universe. Washington, D.C., has become

America's new financial capital. And one more thing: If hedge funds are left as the financial system's private providers of liquidity, that system has a problem. Hedge funds exist for two purposes: (1) to earn a profit for their owners and investors, and (2) to bring efficiency to financial market prices (i.e., to challenge policy officials when they stretch the truth and corporate CEOs when they shade the reality on their balance sheets).

The true shame of the 2008 financial crisis is that the big and the powerful were the most protected because of the risk their failure would pose to the larger financial system. Wall Street banks were allowed to engage in fiction relating to mortgages, particularly home equity lines of credit. They financed second mortgages that often were worthless. Because these loans were not written down, the banks overstated earnings and increased bonus pools for their executives. And, lo and behold, these executives often held fundraisers for politicians. Note that part of the banks' actions stemmed from the insistence by Congress on the subsidizing of home ownership through government-sponsored enterprises (GSEs)—such as the Federal National Mortgage Association (Fannie Mae) and the Federal Home Loan Mortgage Corporation (Freddie Mac).

In response to the financial crisis, policymakers engineered a $700 billion taxpayer-funded bailout. But in this great stare-down between Washington and Wall Street, Washington blinked. Instead of using those resources to confront the problem of toxic waste on bank balance sheets that had forced the banks into this corner of timidity, U.S. policymakers deployed its own version of what the Japanese did in response to their commercial real estate crisis in the late 1980s and early 1990s. Japanese policymakers bowed to political pressure and failed to insist that the toxic assets on the bank balance sheets be immediately marked down in price. Tokyo policymakers "got chicken." They took halfway measures because removing the toxic assets would have been an admission of failure and sign of disgrace. The entire senior management of the Japanese banking industry would have had to have been removed. In the case of Washington after the 2008 crisis, authorities bought the big banks' stock. Washington also "got chicken." Instead of real pricing, the big U.S. banks got Soviet-style Gosplan pricing, based on government-inspired mark-to-market fiction followed by a blind-eyed overregulation by the Federal Reserve.

After the period of consolidation, the big banks began to regain their composure in their new zombie state. But that wasn't true for small and medium-sized companies, or for the thousands of small, regional, and community banks that fund them. These enterprises were all credit-starved right from the start. And, in many cases, they still are.

Local community banks are the workhorses of the financial system. They supply the vast majority of small business loans. Since the financial crisis, more than 500 of these banks have collapsed, struck down by a crisis environment for which they bore little blame. Is it surprising that since 2008, small business startups and productivity growth rates have been disappointing? One solution, suggested by economist Robert Shapiro, is for the Federal Reserve—to correct its too heavy-handed regulatory blunders—to "require or encourage" large banking institutions that draw on the Fed's cheap credit to identify a specified increment of the new credit creation that goes to young enterprises.

Make no mistake, there was something horribly wrong with the post-crisis picture. And it is clear why working families today are so angry. After 2008, if you were a failed, brain-dead Wall Street banker who nearly tanked the world economy, you had easy access to the Federal Reserve's cheap liquidity. If you failed as a giant bank, you were considered special. Your bank could systemically bring down the entire financial system. But if you were a struggling enterprise out there alone with a brilliant idea that could someday employ thousands of people, obtaining financing was next to impossible. The normal sources of risk capital had dried up, but no one from Washington, D.C., was there with your safety net. The too-big-to-fail banks enjoyed a cost of borrowing far lower than other firms because financial markets became convinced government authorities would never let the big banks go under. The fix was in.

To be sure, Silicon Valley has tried to come to the rescue with potentially powerful technologies in the financial sector. The so-called Fintech sector has placed a bull's-eye on the nearly $5 trillion in accrued revenues of today's global banks. Fintech believes it can measure risk, price loans, and reduce the cost of borrowing a lot more efficiently than the zombie banks. New organizations such as Lending Club, SoFi, and Prosper Marketplace are at the forefront of this movement. Apple Pay and Google have also taken a piece of the payments system once the sole domain of the banks. Through new technologies, the tech sector is trying to compensate for Washington's incompetence in mismanaging banking reforms by failing to appreciate the unintended consequences of its policy actions.

There is a larger, and highly important, point here on how Washington, D.C., deals with the economy. In America, there is a dividing line that separates the big and centralized from the small and decentralized. It is David versus Goliath. And in the twenty-first century at a time of enormous economic challenge, the big get all the breaks. Goliath always wins. And that's one reason the U.S. economy is underperforming. Take a look at the Small Business Administration (SBA). The big, ironically, win out even there. Even the definition of the word "small" has been expanded. True, the total amount the SBA has paid out in loans has gone up, yet its loans to truly small businesses (loans of less than $150,000) have dropped by two-thirds since 2005. This is a symbol of a Washington mindset in need of immediate change.

It is the small and decentralized society that will reinvent the economy from the bottom up. If highly centralized, top-down control worked, the Soviet Union would still exist, dominating the global economy. Look at the dumbfounding, corrupt, and incompetent behavior of the big Wall Street banking institutions in the lead-up to the 2008 crisis. Consider the long-running failure of the U.S. government to provide on-time medical benefits to veterans. The benefits of large-scale centralization and top-down control all too often are an illusion.

In the summer of 2009, the first year of the Obama Administration, I had a meeting at the White House with a friend, an economic adviser to the president. The meeting provided a perfect microcosm of the pressure keeping Washington policymakers from producing a bottom-up economic prosperity agenda.

Approaching the outskirts of the White House grounds, I could sense excitement in the air. After checking in at the security gate, I found myself waiting in an elegant room for my appointment. Finally, my friend burst through a door, waving to me to join him in a walk to his office.

Gushing with excitement, he told me a story that was both amusing and telling about the political culture of the time in Washington. He had been delayed because of a meeting to discuss the weak, post–financial crisis U.S. economy. The meeting included the four most powerful domestic policy advisers to the president.

Two of those advisers, chief of staff Rahm Emanuel and political strategist David Axelrod, both longtime Chicago pols, arrived first (other, less important advisers, including my friend, were already there). Within minutes, the other two policymaking powers—Treasury Secretary Timothy Geithner and Larry Summers, director of the National Economic Council—entered the room. Both of these individuals intimately knew the challenges of the global economy. Both had helped promote greater global policy coordination as Treasury officials during the Clinton Administration.

As Geithner and Summers were sitting down, one of the two powerful Chicago pols joked, "Here comes the Aspen Institute, or should we call you two the Davos twins?" This latter name was an amusingly snide reference to the conference of international bankers and corporate leaders held annually in Davos, Switzerland, that U.S. Treasury officials often attend. Immediately, one of the two internationalists shot back, "We're doing fine. How's Tammany Hall?" This was a reference to the backroom corruption and insidious deal-making that plagued New York City politics and government from the late nineteenth into the mid-twentieth centuries (and by extension Chicago in the twenty-first).

This light-hearted exchange was revealing about today's underlying political/economic conflict facing both political parties. On the one hand, the public sees the unfairness of the government racket—Washington's inside deals—that is the enemy of Main Street Capitalism. They prohibit a fair playing field. The compromised economic system plants seeds of doubt about capitalism itself. The Supreme Court's *Citizens United* decision in 2010, which unleashed a flood of special-interest campaign money from the billionaire class, hasn't helped the process. It is not surprising that only one in five Americans now trusts the government to do the right thing.

On the other hand, the public sees elite global economic forces promoting a new, more brazen Corporate Capitalism. Several years ago, the so-called Davos mindset of big-money elites never saw the rise in the global price of wheat and other agricultural commodities as much of a problem. Then the Arab Spring erupted, fueled by rising bread and clothing prices. The rest is history. The Davos mindset missed two other major events: the reckless behavior of the big Wall Street banks in the years prior to 2008 and the Brexit vote in the United Kingdom in June 2016.

To be sure, the folks at Google, Amazon, Apple, Jack Ma's Alibaba Group, and other large, highly creative firms will probably object to this assessment. Their response: "Not so fast! We're not like AT&T or Verizon. Our large corporate platforms work because they allow the basis for spinning off other high-tech enterprises. This process has been essential to decentralization." But the process has also caused a new centralization. And it's not clear that the tech platforms, now controlled by a few, will be able to remain forever free of politics. The select few will use their political connections and legal power to stifle competitive challengers. And why not? The tech world is a hyper-competitive place. Beginning in the fourth quarter of 2015, tech IPOs almost came to a halt. Private and public funding slowed. And when the economic pie stops growing, one thing is certain: A corrosive Corporate Capitalism always rises to the surface to stifle competition. This is happening even in the technology sector.

Robert Reich of the University of California at Berkeley makes the point that because ideas are now the economy's most valuable form of property, centralization always remains a threat to ordinary people. "The most valuable intellectual properties," argues Reich, "are platforms so widely used that everyone else has to use them too. Google runs two-thirds of all searches in the United States. Amazon sells more than 40 percent of new books. Facebook has nearly 1.5 billion active monthly users worldwide." This massive concentration, observes Reich, even as it sounds impressive, actually creates barriers to entry that put both consumers and competitors at a disadvantage.

A top-down mindset aimed at centralization—whether the accumulation of capital in a dozen zombie Wall Street banks or the effort by large bureaucracies to control the economy or even the media (through a small collection of corporate giants)—continues to be a foolhardy Washington fixation. This is a potential point of bipartisan agreement. Both political parties have, at times, fallen for the illusion of centralization and managed control from the top. They should join together to fight this impulse.

Republicans, for example, thought the federal government could "nation build," somehow creating stable democracies in wild and woolly places like Afghanistan and Iraq. Democrats believed enhanced government control of the nation's healthcare system would reduce insurance policy premiums and deductibles for the middle class. Just the opposite has been the case.

Ironically, this illusion of centralization runs counter to the direction of the rest of society, even the direction of popular culture. Or make that *especially* counter to popular culture's direction, which regularly rejects the one-size-fits-all, centralized mindset.

The rest of society is decentralizing from the bottom up fast. Of course there are exceptions, but consider the music business. Pop culture used to move in one mass group. Since 1982, Michael Jackson's *Thriller* album sold an incredible 66 million copies worldwide. That will never be achieved again in today's decentralized music culture. Taste distinctions are highly individualized, and there is far more quality content available now than there was back then.

In television, more than 100 million people watched the character Hawkeye in the final episode of the show *M.A.S.H.* That too is unlikely to be repeated in today's highly decentralized entertainment system. The elite rave about cable television shows like *Mad Men* and *Breaking Bad* as being transformative in nature. Each averaged barely 2.5 million viewers. They are targeted at a highly decentralized audience. The three big network news organizations—CBS, ABC, and NBC—once controlled 78 percent of TV news viewership. Now they control less than 30 percent.

The production of films has dramatically expanded as well. Platforms such as iTunes and Netflix have made them widely available. The movie industry has begun to decentralize.

A similar process is underway in the book industry.

Traditional newspapers are dying. In the new forms of news delivery, like it or not, citizen journalism is taking over via decentralized mobile technology.

Across the world, young people feel confident charting their own tastes and creating their own information without handholding by a centralized trendsetter. A yearning for individualism, for a more decentralized world, is in vogue.

The blogging/Twitter phenomenon is the latest case in point. Everybody's an opinion specialist, changing attitudes from the bottom up.

So everybody sees where the culture is going except Washington, D.C., where policymakers failed to read the "decentralization memo."

By definition, Main Street Capitalism, which empowers individual initiative, is anathema to heavy, top-down, centralized control. Successful innovation requires freedom from control by large institutions, public or private. It requires the freedom to dream and risk failure in order to reap the kind of success that comes from bucking the trend and breaking away from the established norm. Innovation entails the unconventional mindset attracted to bottom-up surprises as new ideas are applied to market opportunities. As Yale's Robert Shiller observes, "Direct government involvement in capitalism is a delicate thing." Committees of experts, even committees made up of the smartest business strategists, have often missed what eventually became big entrepreneurial breakthroughs. Why? As venture capitalist Peter Thiel points out about the information technology arena, "Successful network businesses have initial markets so small they often don't appear to be business opportunities at all."

New wealth and job creation works best in a decentralized environment and on a level playing field that allow individuals to be audacious and crazy. As Steve Jobs once admiringly told a graduating class at Stanford University in reference to the cybernetic revolution and the role of entrepreneurial risk-taking, "Here's to the crazy ones." And that's the essential point: The very thing that gives us comfort during a financial panic—centralized, top-down bureaucratic control to reduce risk—makes up a large part of the headwinds that have lately held back the economy.

Today Corporate Capitalism has wrapped its tentacles around the policy world. It threatens to drown any chance of a return to America's economic potential. It is killing any hope of a culture of grassroots dynamism. I have lived in, and been an observer of, Washington, D.C., for 40 years. The big-money lobbyists run the show to a point almost unimaginable even as late as the 1990s. For all practical purposes, the lobbyists now co-write the legislation. The town is wired. The free market is made to function for them.

If you are not convinced the economic system is often compromised, consider this example based on my own personal experience. In 1987, I launched a policy magazine called *The International Economy*, a nonprofit company separate from my for-profit macroeconomic advisory firm. My idea was to establish a journalistic bulletin board for a wide range of ideas about the global financial and trading systems. My only direction to our editors: the more opinion the better—left, right, and center. I don't need to agree with every article submitted, as long as the opinions are interesting. Owning *The International Economy* has given me an excellent vantage point from which to see the sometimes corrupt way in which Washington, D.C., works behind-the-scenes.

In the spring of 1999, Owen Ullmann, a long-time, part-time executive editor at my magazine (and the managing editor at *USA Today*), mentioned an idea for an article he would write for us about potential problems with the government-sponsored enterprises (GSEs) Fannie Mae and Freddie Mac. Both institutions of course received an explicit guarantee from Uncle Sam to bail them out in the event of a crisis. But were these institutions becoming bastions of a corrupt Corporate Capitalism of political deal-making? Within less than a decade, of course, both GSEs would be in the midst of the global financial crisis. But back in 1999, Fannie and Freddie, as they are called, were considered stable and healthy. Immediately, Ullmann began working on his piece, calling all over Capitol Hill and the administration, exploring the degree to which the GSEs had become nontransparent institutions with little federal oversight. Were they, Owen Ullman asked, like the mythical figure Icarus flying too close to the sun in ignoring the weakness of the housing portfolios on their books? (It turned out the entire Wall Street banking system was also flying too close to the sun.)

But here's the disturbing thing. Roughly a month before its publication, a curious development occurred. A representative from one of the GSEs approached one of the business partners of my separate financial advisory firm. The question: Would my firm be interested in being a highly paid consultant to his GSE? My associate declined the offer. This GSE representative never mentioned the article my separate magazine was planning on the GSE industry, but the timing was just too coincidental. The message seemed to be clear: Back off, please! We'll make it worth your while to do so.

We ran the article as a cover story in our July–August 1999 issue of *The International Economy* under the headline: "Crony Capitalism:

American Style." Owen's article highlighting the GSEs' coming problems turned out to be prophetic. The *Washington Post* and other journalistic organizations subsequently ran similar articles. For me, personally, I caught a glimpse of what may have been Washington at its worst. It is not that influence peddling is illegal (though it can be unethical). It is what people do in an economy that has consistently underperformed. They use inside connections and deploy an ocean of campaign money to keep the challengers at bay. In a world where the economic pie has failed to enlarge, they fiercely lobby to maintain the size of their slice. You get yours before others get theirs. In too many cases, folks came to Washington to do good but stayed to do well. But the economy is compromised as competing interests squabble over pieces of the shrinking economic pie.

Sometimes, the reverse is at work. Often the politicians themselves demand lobbying. For example, for years Microsoft avoided Washington, D.C. The company was forced to reverse course, however, because politicians shook the campaign money tree and demanded Microsoft executives' attention.

This process of "getting yours" is happening all over the world. It is one reason global growth has slowed. The European and Japanese political systems are Ground Zero for the inside deal, with governments a haven for collusive connections with large corporate entities, giant banks, and insurance companies that protect the status quo.

China is becoming the world's headquarters for government defined as a protected club for elites and a haven for outright corruption. A privileged class of only about 86 million Communist Party members dominates a country of more than 1.4 billion people. Now that top echelon of leadership is in political turmoil. Since 2012, more than 275,000 Chinese officials have been hit with corruption charges, according to *China Daily*. The corruption has reached as high as the Politburo's Standing Committee. That is like an American president's senior cabinet secretary being forced to resign in disgrace.

In the United States, the political game is more subtle. It is to enact worthwhile-sounding legislation for needed regulatory reforms. Yet the fine print—the detailed rules of the regulations—are left unwritten. That's so the big-money bidding can begin. The special-interest lobbyists move in and suck the life out of the reforms. The insiders push for exemptions.

As the writer Angelo Codevilla has observed about the American system of government: "Modern laws are primarily grants of discretion." Most members of Congress don't read the laws. They concentrate instead on whom the laws financially empower. Then they move in for their financial piece of the action. To a certain extent, the regulation is designed and operated for the benefit of those being regulated.

In this process of regulatory arbitrage, everybody gets their special deal. Republican supporters receive subsidies for the fuel additive ethanol, a political gift that makes little economic sense. Ethanol costs more to produce than petroleum, removes corn from the food supply, and pollutes more than regular gas.

Democrats offer stimulus money to campaign contributors who own alternative energy companies. Then these unqualified firms go bankrupt, but nobody cares. As venture capitalist Peter Thiel has written, "The clean tech bubble was the biggest flop in the history of 'social entrepreneurship.'" Washington barely noticed. Results don't matter.

But it is in tax policy where the real insider deals are handed out, often to the disadvantage of the entrepreneurial newcomers. For years, private-equity firms on Wall Street paid a low 15 percent capital gains tax rate on all income earned. Yet small and medium-sized businesses (a family that owned, say, three dry cleaning shops and employed several dozen workers) paid taxes at more than twice that rate. Then some of the same Wall Street billionaires who benefited from the special tax loophole set up foundations and ran splashy public relations campaigns. And, incredibly, what was their message? Deficits and debt are ruining the economy.

Washington has fully embraced the culture of the inside deal, the plugged-in exception, the brazen point of inconsistency where nobody bats an eye. The system "is rigged," as Bernie Sanders accurately argued in the Democratic presidential primary campaign. It is less and less fair for outsiders, and most insiders haven't a clue how destructive this culture is to their nation's spirit of, and sense of, fair play. The culture is killing the concept of Main Street Capitalism's level playing field for competition.

Peter Thiel argues that in today's environment of uneven playing fields, the wise choice is to invest in startups run by brilliant and aggressive competitors who control a monopoly either through government connections or the exclusive nature of their patented new technology that their lawyers can then extend to a period beyond reason. Investor Warren Buffett actually boasts of his preference for investing in companies with some type of monopoly advantage—"with moats around them." The Sage of Omaha, the son of a congressman, has a good understanding of human nature—and of how the system works.

This talk of government connections is a sad commentary on America's economic future. Capitalism that entails grassroots innovating requires a level playing field. No inside deals. Average folk need to feel you can come from nothing, but with hard work, determination, extraordinary creativity, and some luck, rise to the top. As corny as it sounds, freedom, fairness, and transparency matter more than ever in creating a culture of grassroots dynamism and social mobility.

That process of winning and losing in a continuously dynamic and competitive playing field is precisely the thing that propels the economy to higher levels of prosperity. Senator Bernie Sanders called for a "revolution." America needs a revolution, but not one of zero-sum division built on a socialist utopian dream. America needs the Great Equalizer, a Main Street Capitalist revolution of dynamism to create an economy more for working- and middle-class families.

This book is not intended to be some philosophical screed against government. Government is important to free markets because it enforces the rules of the road. The Internet itself was the result of government spending. In things such as scientific and medical research, government dollars play an important role in improving a nation's well-being. Those programs need to be better funded. That should be a point of a common-sense bipartisan agreement. Make no mistake. Even though large bureaucratic governmental entities are poor at managing complexity, including the complexity of human behavior in the economic arena, the public sector is important to achieving a thriving society. Without Social Security payments alone, America's poverty rate would be a third higher.

It is difficult to overestimate the degree to which America's rule of law has been essential to its economic success. Tech investor Christopher Schroeder states, "From the perspective of the tech world, the rule of law protecting the free movement of people, goods, services, ideas, and capital may be America's greatest attribute."

The U.S. firm Kentucky Fried Chicken (which changed its name to "KFC" in 1991) offers a useful illustration. At one time, that food franchise was wildly popular in China. Then the state-controlled Chinese media began writing stories that the firm's fast-food chicken was genetically modified and dangerous. The U.S. chicken firm found the Chinese legal system rigged to help local firms. Studies later proved the Chinese media charge to be bogus. But as analyst Todd Buchholz pointed out, the announcement came too late. KFC's China market share had collapsed, but several Chinese firms were able to wing their way in.

Government's role in enforcing intellectual property rights and the right to invest in private property was the absolute foundation of the great breakout economies in the nineteenth and early twentieth centuries. But there is an important distinction between a policy of government help that provides a safety net for its citizens, that protects businesses from absurd market volatility, and that establishes rules of the road, and a policy that, intentionally or not, gives the status quo an advantage within the economic system over the newcomers. Somehow the big corporate status quo interests always seem to arrive at the top of the list of Washington's priorities when government rides to the rescue. The Corporate Capitalists always win. Big business and the politicians have become codependent. The politicians need the campaign cash. The executives need the access.

Therefore, one of the challenges of the twenty-first century is to determine how much government regulatory control of the private sector is enough and how much comes too close to a counterproductive, top-down, futile effort to design economic and social perfection. There is nothing simple here. Businesses bellyache at the mere mention of the word "regulation." But the economic and health benefits from cleaner air and water and safer cars and highways are significant. Just ask the Chinese. Their horrific pollution problem is holding back their economy.

In some cases, the issue is not a choice between more or less regulation, but over how to achieve more effective regulation with the fewest unintended consequences.

But there's no denying that regulation of the U.S. economy intensified under George W. Bush and became downright aggressive under the executive actions and widespread rule changes during the Obama Administration, according to a study by the American Enterprise Institute. In general, if you want less of something from the private sector, regulate it. If you want more, deregulate it. It is not surprising that the most striking years of the American economy's underperformance and heartache came after a period of intense regulation in a post-2008 effort to try to eliminate financial risk. During the first seven years of the Obama Administration, GDP growth zig-zagged up and down but averaged only 1.4 percent per year.

In an April 2016 survey of 22 industries, the Mercatus Center estimated that since 1980 new federal regulations have created a drag on the U.S. economy amounting to a drop in the average annual growth rate of 0.8 percent. Is it really a surprise that the Obama Administration is the first in modern history not to have achieved a one-year GDP growth rate at or above the nation's 3 percent–plus average level? I have many economist friends who insist that the connection between regulation and GDP growth is weak. But ask virtually anyone involved with a small or medium-sized business. The anecdotal tales of suffocating regulatory overreach, beginning under George W. Bush but greatly expanded under Barack Obama, are endless.

I know. There are no simple rules here. Sometimes new regulation is important. High-tech giant Elon Musk argues that the only solution to capping the more dangerous aspects of the artificial intelligence breakthrough—including potentially millions of jobs lost and the vanishing of entire industries—may be through new regulation. Yet Washington's establishment policymakers seem clueless that there is any link between their regulatory actions and today's collapse in business start-ups and mediocre economic growth rates. One reason Silicon Valley and other high-tech centers have replaced Wall Street as the economy's new center of dynamism is that they are now the economy's least regulated large industry. There is a reason the Silicon Valley executives hold so many congressional and presidential fundraisers. They want to hold off the onslaught of Washington's regulatory attack dogs.

When friends ask me to meet with their sons and daughters for career advice, I begin with this question: What is your life's goal: money, power, or social improvement? You can't have all three. If social improvement, become an inner-city public school teacher. If power, become a regulator. If big money, join a high-tech startup. "But what about Wall Street?" they always ask. "Forget it. Wall Street is now a heavily regulated industry."

Again, the problem is not regulation per se. Regulations' ultimate risk is that a well-intentioned process morphs into a process of regulatory arbitrage. Large corporations would prefer no regulation. But they often try to compromise on regulatory solutions in a way that squashes their competition and discourages newcomers. Barriers to the entry of new products and industries rise. Overregulation, therefore, becomes a friend of the big and/or established against the small and/or new. Overregulation too often becomes a noncompetitive enabler, killing the hopes and dreams of most people. By the same token, the elimination of reckless or politically derived overregulation could have the same stimulating effect on the economy as a large tax cut.

Some of America's best Silicon Valley innovators are not that convinced that governmental actions inhibit their activities. Indeed, some such as Elon Musk have used the federal government to their advantage in supporting investments in space and electric cars. But for the rest of the tech sector, time will tell in determining the effect of the government's growing presence.

Uber and Lyft demonstrate that, despite the political clout of the taxi industries, the newcomers are advancing. They are two companies with terrific stories. Both identified a problem—poor taxi service in most cities, including long waits, filthy cabs, and often rude treatment by cab drivers. Both companies came up with an app-based ride-sharing concept that has taken the world by storm. This is a case of some very smart people building a better mousetrap: transportation that is quicker, more reliable, and cleaner than the traditional taxi services, and all at the push of an app on a smartphone.

There was only one problem. Uber and Lyft faced a raft of regulatory onslaughts from governments and politicians intent on protecting the status quo. For example, the South Carolina Public Service Commission tried to shut down Uber from operating statewide (Uber is now legal). In San Antonio, Texas, new regulations relating to driver requirements were promulgated with the clear intent to hamstring Uber's ability to operate. The political insiders tried to game the regulatory system to protect their favored interests, but often failed. But the level playing field is always at risk.

Achieving smart regulation is tough. What has been the aftermath since enactment of the 2010 Wall Street Reform and Consumer Protection Act, otherwise known as the Dodd-Frank legislation, and the Federal Reserve–inspired regulatory measures that responded to the 2008 financial crisis? Again, the big, brain-dead Wall Street banks now control most of America's bank investment capital. The process of policymaking itself has been made needlessly complicated, often as a means of enhancing control over the private sector. Was the intention of the policy changes after the 2008 financial crisis to create a U.S. financial sector controlled by a handful of giant zombie banks? Of course not. It just happened. It was the unintended consequence of well-meaning intentions.

But the page count of the laws themselves gave warning of the financial suffocation about to unfold. When the Homestead Act was passed in 1862, the legislation fit on two pages. When the Federal Reserve Act came along in 1913, the bill was 31 pages long. When Obamacare was enacted in 2010, the legislation took up 2,700 pages. And that was before all the deal-making over exemptions reached full force. The Code of Federal Regulations now exceeds 175,000 pages.

When the Dodd-Frank legislation to reform the financial services industry was enacted in 2010, the act itself numbered some 2,300 pages, not counting the rules associated with it. Shouldn't that fact alone have sounded a warning about the outlook for future lending for economic growth? The regulations resulting from the legislation are described by those dealing with the government requirements as a "20-pound stack and growing." The costs of compliance for smaller financial firms have been enormous. The expense and uncertainty injected into financial decision-making has been destructive to small, regional, and community banks. That's because the legislation's rule-making process, the wheeling and dealing by the lobbying community, is endless. For smaller financial institutions, the cost of hiring so many lawyers, accountants, and lobbyists to deal with the new rules is a killer.

Part of the legislation, the so-called Volcker Rule, is designed to prohibit the big banks from engaging in risky trading practices. All well and good, but the process of compliance for firms down the line is nightmarish. Small and mid-size financial firms face hundreds of questions and thousands of sub-questions. Sometimes one clarification can require hundreds of pages of explanation. Not to be outdone, the European version of Dodd-Frank is expected to exceed 60,000 pages of regulatory rules and details.

As of the summer of 2014, four years after enactment of Dodd-Frank, the Securities and Exchange Commission had completed only 44 percent of the rules the law directs it to stipulate. Talk about freezing the nation's credit system in place by demanding firms know the unknowable. Why this continual delay? The uncertainty was good for political fundraising. Uncertainty is Washington's most effective and least visible campaign money racket. The more corporations and banks face regulatory uncertainty, the more they cough up the fundraising dollars in a culture that has become a cesspool of backroom campaign finance leverage. And because of the lengthy uncertainty of the process, the innovative sectors of the economy wither away. The risk-takers are turned off.

Just after the 2008 financial crisis began, I asked William Seidman, the former chairman of the Federal Deposit Insurance Corporation (FDIC), CNBC television commentator, and a leading guru in the area of financial market regulation, whether Washington policymakers were capable of reforming the economy's financial architecture without the reforms becoming part of the problem. In other words, could the experts arrive at a set of effective "Goldilocks" financial reforms that were neither too soft nor too strong. Seidman's response: "Probably not. Arriving at a proper balance in devising a safety net would require a divinely guided genius, and Washington is not known for its geniuses." Later I asked former New York Federal Reserve President E. Gerald Corrigan how he would devise reforms to confront financial risk. Quipped Corrigan: "You can't eliminate risk. You can't hedge the universe."

Dodd-Frank, a seemingly worthy attempt at control of financial risk, has had so many unintended consequences that even some of the legislation's proponents now quietly nod in agreement that the legislation needs to be reexamined and some parts modified. The legislation set up the Financial Stability Oversight Council with the mandate to target a group of banks and insurance companies considered "systemically important"—that is, potentially dangerous to the entire financial system if they fail. But this approach has already turned out to be problematic. Stanford University's Edward Lazear, who chaired George W. Bush's Council of Economic Advisers from 2006 to 2009, makes the point that financial crises are pathologies of an entire system, not of a few key firms. Thankfully, the Federal Reserve has begun to shift, siding more with an approach based on market rules rather than regulations, that instead requires higher equity capital for banks to protect the financial system.

The Basel Accords for capital adequacy, which the big banks regularly manipulate, similarly need to be reexamined. What is needed instead is a simple rule for the amount of capital (based on a common equity-to-asset ratio) that a bank keeps on hand and for the amount of leverage used. If a big bank falls into trouble, a portion of the bank's debt should be converted into equity. In other words, the era of bailing out Wall Street banking executives is over. But so is the era of misguided regulatory solutions that, sooner or later, do damage to the economic livelihoods of average working families. The regulators assure us the financial system is now safe. But what's the point if American businesses outside the giant corporations in the Fortune 1000 still find it problematic to get credit? The system ironically is frustrating even for the elite. In late 2015, a friend of mine easily worth $80 million co-signed a note to help his daughter purchase a house. They both had top credit scores. "The approval process was a nightmare," he said. "I almost gave up." Think of how tough the approval process is for average folk.

The regulatory process usually begins with a noble purpose: fixing some wrong in the economy or society. But often the regulating exceeds any semblance of common sense and pursues instead an endless drive for perfection. The regulator is never forced to face even the psychological consequences of his or her regulatory actions when working people lose a job or suffer in some other way financially as the unintended consequence of an inept, heavy-handed interpretation of regulatory intent.

The U.S. economy desperately needs greater regulatory certainty. It is time to establish a holiday from all new regulations (except those dealing with immediate issues relating to health and safety), a pause that refreshes, for at least two years and to call for a regulatory summit. Republicans and Democrats can probably never agree on a common regulatory system. Their differences are too great. Still, there are points of common sense a majority of the nation should be able to agree on. That compromise agenda should include the untangling of the duplication in federal regulatory institutions along with steps to enhance the quality and pay of regulators, to find more competent, sophisticated, and less ideological regulators with a true appreciation of the importance of the grassroots entrepreneurial dynamic so essential to the economy's health. Nothing controversial about that. Both parties should agree that the existing antitrust laws need to be more aggressively enforced. Particularly in the areas of healthcare, pharmaceuticals, and health insurance (over 17 percent of the economy), lack of ample antitrust enforcement hurts the economic future of middle-class working families.

But there is an even more important point on which the common-sense middle can agree. The president should set up a bipartisan panel of experts to determine the extent to which American and foreign companies have manipulated the U.S. regulatory process to the detriment of U.S. startup competitors. Call it the Level-the-Playing-Field Panel. If it is shown that a regulatory action or rulemaking was made overwhelmingly in response to an established firm's lobbying arm seeking competitive advantage, that action should be reversed. The organization could use a process similar to that of the Base Realignment and Closure (BRAC) Act, whereby independent defense experts removed largely from Washington politics, as the Cold War was ending, arrived at a list of 350 no-longer-necessary military installations. These were closed in installments between 1988 and 2005.

The Chinese have a saying, "To scare the monkey, kill the chicken." The panel should identify 50 instances in which the regulatory system was thoroughly abused. Call them "The Ugly 50." To send a message to the entire regulatory/lobbying culture of Washington, D.C., kill The Ugly 50. How could any reasonable Republican or Democrat be against a plan that creates a more level playing field? Doing so would call not for a new bureaucracy but for a one-time effort to draw a line in the sand against the ever-advancing forces of Corporate Capitalism. The reversal of these egregious regulatory efforts to gain competitive advantage should be timed so as not to create heightened volatility in financial markets.

Talk about sending a powerful message to the world that America is leveling its economic playing field. Talk about a powerful paradigm, a shift away from a special interest–driven corporate capitalist regulatory system to one more sensitive to the importance of the equalizing force of innovative capitalism. The revolution would be heard around the world. And there is one even more profound change that would send a powerful message of fair play. Financial reform to fix the problems of the Dodd-Frank legislation should provide regulatory relief and exemptions for medium-sized and smaller banks. After all, they played no role in causing the 2008 great financial crisis. It is time to liberate these institutions from the regulatory retribution.

At least two-thirds of the American people know in their gut that the federal government needs to be reinvented. In the private sector, reinvention is a fact of life. For large companies, it is the very lifeline of survival. Guy Kawasaki, an early Apple executive and author of *The Art of the Start*, argues that "there are a lot of large corporations that deliver impressive goods and services. The most effective know there's a downside to bigness, so they constantly reinvent themselves to survive."

Which is exactly what the U.S. government should be doing, but isn't. Government needs to be reinvented and modernized for the challenges of the twenty-first century. That means a reassessment not only of regulatory policies but of tax, energy, education, and poverty policies. One example: Compare the U.S. tax code and the Internal Revenue Service, a grotesque combined system of excessive complication for average working families, with the ease with which the same families can use a credit card at an ATM to get cash anywhere in the world. Talk about a marvel. For starters, government needs to better harness the information tools already being used by the private sector. It is time for a results-oriented policy approach that taps into the wisdom of, and is supported by, the common-sense majority. In 1993, Vice President Al Gore offered his *Report on Reinventing Government*. Such an effort should have opened up a national discussion. It didn't, or at least not with enough sustained magnitude.

In government, there is little penalty for failure, so reinvention hardly drums up much excitement. The Civil Service Reform Act of 1978 makes it almost impossible to fire a federal employee, even for the most egregious of acts. The review process is so grueling for the government manager that firings almost never occur. This is a system without common sense. It is in need of sensible reform.

In the U.S. Congress, there is bipartisan support for legislation sponsored by House Judiciary Chair Robert Goodlatte (R-VA), called the Separation of Powers Restoration Act. The bill includes an important reform that would, through judicial review, curb abusive patent litigation from the "patent-assertion entities" that are really shakedown operations that raise the cost to American consumers by tens of billions of dollars a year. America's common-sense middle should claim this set of reforms as one of the building blocks for reinventing government. The bill passed the House but has been bottled up in the Senate.

In successful economies, reinvention has been the traditional ticket to survival and success. Executives in large established companies know they are always vulnerable to some upstart dreamer working in his or her garage into the wee hours of the morning to come up with a better mousetrap. Look at the way the once mighty Hollywood movie studios are now vulnerable to content delivery services such as Netflix, iTunes, and Amazon. These new entertainment delivery platforms are more nimble and perhaps less blind to alternative solutions to success than the big studios. Now the public has more options more easily attainable, including more original movie content on television. Government needs to adopt the same mindset.

Ask any Washington policymakers today about their greatest concern, and they will say this: In an age of extraordinary debt, they worry about a lack of public resources. Yet the U.S. federal government has trillions of dollars of unused or underused resources waiting to be deployed. As former Clinton Administration economist Rob Shapiro argues, "Governments own more assets than all of their richest citizens put together; but unlike wealthy people, governments don't manage their assets." Other countries such as Saudi Arabia, Singapore, and Sweden use financial experts to manage national wealth funds. The U.S. government should better manage its physical assets.

In their 2015 book *The Public Wealth of Nations*, Swedish economists Dag Detter and Stefan Fölster identify hundreds of billions, and maybe trillions, of dollars of value that could be deployed with a more inventive U.S. government. Here's how their plan would work. The U.S. federal government's non-financial assets are worth roughly $3.5 trillion, or about 20 percent of GDP. If the federal government by being a bit more imaginative was able to raise the annual return on that amount by just 2 percent, the new revenue generated would be $800 billion over ten years. Raise the return by even just 3.5 percent, and that ten-year number jumps to $1.4 trillion.

How to increase the rate of return? Some possible ideas: Reform the Postal Service so that it uses its assets more efficiently. The mail service's productivity gains are 30 percent of those of FedEx and UPS. Raise that performance to 50 percent. The Bureau of Land Management oversees 260 million acres of federal lands. A lot of the land is in Colorado, Utah, and Wyoming. Lease some of the land for energy production. A number of U.S. military facilities (example: the barracks for dress Marines on Capitol Hill) sit on extraordinarily expensive real estate. Move the facilities to less expensive land and lease the expensive land to commercial interests. In short, our leaders in government need to think more like national investment managers, always mindful of the issue of financial return.

On the regulation issue, the United States is like people who, hammer in hand, keep hitting themselves in the head because it is supposed to be the right thing to do—and then complain of severe and endless headaches. U.S. productivity growth is down, the rate of innovative business startups has plummeted, and the American Dream is quickly drifting away. Perhaps it's time to stop hitting ourselves in the head with the hammer. Perhaps it's also time to stop tinkering and to go bold. Send the world a powerful message that the era of top-down regulatory overreach that provides advantage to the big over the small is finished. And so is the economic system's penchant for ignoring the effect of their actions on Steve Jobs's "misfits, rebels, and troublemakers" who challenge the system with new ideas and transformative change. As Jobs added: "While some see them as the crazy ones, we see genius. Because the people who are crazy enough to think they can change the world are the ones who do."

In Washington's policy world of incrementalism, the power of a bold, audacious idea is highly underrated. Yet powerful ideas matter. In the months before the 1986 Tax Reform Act was passed, for example, the entire issue of reforming the American tax code, which was riddled with inefficient loopholes and exemptions, was considered dead (similar to the view of tax reform today). The Reagan White House had produced a tame version of tax reform, which Capitol Hill Democrats declared "dead on arrival." Republican congressional supply-siders were offering their own tax reform plan with the enthusiastic support of the U.S. Chamber of Commerce. The plan not only failed to pass the House of Representatives; it seemed to be an omen that the era of tax reform had not yet arrived. Indeed, with some exceptions, the Democratic Party made clear it saw the idea of eliminating tax loopholes in exchange for reducing tax rates across the board as an illegitimate Republican trick. If there was one certainty as the year 1986 progressed, it was that tax reform was dead.

Yet by the end of the year, tax reform was a reality. It passed both houses of Congress and was signed into law. And it all happened because of an audacious fluke. Here's a lesson on how Washington sometimes works in mysterious ways.

In his first term, President Reagan's Treasury Secretary was a blustery, white-haired, red-faced (when he was angry) Irishman named Donald Regan. Regan was the former chairman of the investment firm Merrill Lynch. I knew Regan reasonably well. Although he may have had his talents as a sales executive in the financial world, he was a political amateur. I would sometimes wince when Regan would, by his comments, demonstrate a startling lack of understanding of how Washington works.

As the Reagan years unfolded and tax reform was dying as an issue, something strange happened at the Regan-led U.S. Treasury. On their own, a band of relatively non-ideological, nonpartisan tax specialists in the bowels of the Treasury tax department offered what was for all practical purposes a radical form of tax reform. The plan was every corporate lobbyist's nightmare. The plan was bold. To achieve dramatically lower tax rates, everybody's ox got gored. The plan was leaked to the Washington press corps.

White House officials across the street went ballistic. They attacked what ironically was officially their own plan. Administration insiders were furious at Treasury Secretary Regan for his political naïveté. How could he have been so stupid as to let some Treasury tax policy eggheads needlessly freelance, offending the administration's own corporate supporters? After all, tax reform was dead.

But then, after the 1984 presidential election, something unusual happened. A new dynamic suddenly took hold. A number of Democratic voices on Capitol Hill suddenly praised the Regan plan (which was also officially the Reagan plan). At the time, I predicted against all conventional wisdom that tax reform would soon become a reality. It was as if the patient had been hit by the electric shock of the two paddles in the hands of the emergency room physician. Against all expectations, the patient revived. Both political sides relatively quickly agreed to a compromise. Declared officially dead, the issue was revived by an unexpected act of audacity.

As the twenty-first century advances, America's new president needs to adopt a similar audacity. It is time to throw the long ball on a grand compromise policy agenda of breathtaking political risk. Wrap the next administration around a new type of thinking—the Main Street Capitalist mindset. The public has seen policy incrementalism at work. It too easily morphs into policy stalemate. It is time to go bold, to reboot the policymaking process entirely. But do it fairly with no partisan agenda. That will send a powerful message of leadership.

Want to create a paradigm shift that moves America into a new, more positive and confident direction? On policy issues, pursue the audacious. Incrementalism is overrated. But time is of the essence. The economy's health hangs in the balance. The American people have reason to be concerned. On issues such as today's exploding debt and currency manipulation, even the experts are not sure of a national game plan to keep us all out of trouble. And, as the next two chapters will show, some of the dangers are downright terrifying.

FIVE

The World's Greatest Wager

While working on Capitol Hill during my early 20s, I was offered a job as a speechwriter for the executives at Chrysler Corporation. I agreed to take the position at the company's headquarters in Highland Park, Michigan, just outside Detroit, for a year. I stayed 18 months. The experience taught me an important lesson: Assume nothing when it comes to threats to your survival.

At the time, Chrysler was enjoying record profits. Yet during this period, American corporations were being ridiculed as dinosaurs. Germany and Japan were the new models of excellence. Within several years of my arrival in 1977, Chrysler would be flat on its back, desperate for a federal bailout.

One of the perks of the job was, despite my junior status, regular access to the executive dining room. Chrysler's dozen most senior executives enjoyed individual private dining rooms. The executive dining room was for the rest of senior management. The room contained round tables for eight. Every day a bowl full of ten-inch-long breadsticks was placed in the center of each table and around the table were several small bowls of soft butter.

I am giving you these details because Chrysler executives in luncheon conversations, particularly when making an emphatic point, had this annoying habit of stabbing the bowls of soft butter with the breadsticks and aiming the armed weapon at the person they were talking to.

"Is that breadstick loaded?" I often joked. "If so, don't point that danger-ous weapon in my direction!"

Several years before my arrival, Chrysler had forged a sales relation-ship with Japan's Mitsubishi automobile firm. Mitsubishi cars built in Japan were being sold in Chrysler's U.S. showrooms. One day, while I was having lunch in the executive dining room, several Mitsubishi executives from Japan were eating at a nearby table. Immediately, the Chrysler exec-utives at my table began quietly belittling the Japanese carmakers. There were racial overtones to the comments. "Look at those teensy-weensy little—," a Chrysler manager named Bruce said, pointing at the Mitsub-ishi executives with his butter-stabbed breadstick. "And their teensy-weensy little cars. They'll never sell. Americans are big people."

I protested that the Mitsubishi cars we had access to in the Chrysler discount sales program were said to be the only vehicles that seemed to work reliably. Everyone scoffed.

A foreign car tidal wave was coming, yet the Chrysler guys hadn't a clue. Months later, I commented to one of Chrysler's group vice presi-dents, who was my boss, that the senior company executives were living in a comfortable bubble of illusion. If a car assigned to them was unre-liable, by the end of the day a man at the executive motor pool named Johnny had exchanged their troubled car for a new one. For Chrys-ler's customers, however, lack of reliability in their automobile meant standing in a cold, long, early-morning service line and then taking the bus and arriving late to work. The veep said the point was well-taken. Given my age, he added that he was "amused at my temerity." "Pretty nervy comments, Dave," he said. "But I can't say I disagree with you entirely."

Around that time, our speechwriting group was asked to write con-gressional testimony for the company's vice president for engineering. A colleague went to the engineering executive's office, expecting a lengthy chat about the company's engineering plans to meet the coming, tough national fuel economy standards. The meeting was delayed for 45 min-utes. "Come with me," the executive said to the speechwriter, suddenly walking out of his office and putting on his coat. "Sorry about the delay. I've got to go over to the Hamtramck plant. We can discuss the testimony on the way."

Hamtramck, closed in 1980 and demolished in 1981, was Chrysler's legendary but almost obsolete multistory, urban production plant. To his shock as my colleague pulled up to the plant, the head of engineering was met at the entry gate by two armed guards. They accompanied the senior executive with great visibility during his entire time at the plant. "What's with the guns?" my colleague asked one of the guards when, after a while, the engineering executive paused to make a telephone call. "On any day," the guard said, "20 to 30 percent of our workforce comes in with an alcohol- or drug-related problem. We are instructed to protect visiting executives at all costs. We've had some close calls." I knew at that moment, despite Chrysler's record profits at the time, that the American auto industry was in trouble. Labor-management relations were in tatters. The labor pool was challenged. Product quality was poor. A global competitive tidal wave was coming. The folks at Highland Park were in denial.

Within less than two years, Chrysler was desperate for a federal bailout. By that time, I had gone back to Washington to become Representative Jack Kemp's chief of staff. Kemp went on to become a member of the House leadership, presidential candidate, cabinet member, and vice presidential nominee. In Congress, the chief of staff has a tiny office connected to the larger office of the member of Congress. Those were the pre–cell phone days. Quite frequently, I would be visited in my tiny, cramped office by none other than Lee Iacocca, Chrysler's new top executive and former president of the Ford Motor Company, along with the head of the company's Washington office (whom I knew from my days at the firm). Why the visit? The executives asked to use my phone to make calls to congressional offices as they desperately sought support for the federal bailout. Each time Iacocca arrived and commandeered my office for ten minutes or so, I could see it in his eyes. It was humbling. He was thinking, "These Chrysler guys failed to see the tidal wave coming. Now I've got to ask this kid [me] if I can use his office to make phone calls."

A similar scenario of failing to see the coming tidal wave could be unfolding with the world's extraordinary level of debt. The economics profession offers two distinct views of today's massive public debt. Either the debt is a potential monster, or the level of debt doesn't matter, at least not in our lifetimes. Which view is true? The truth is, on debt most of the experts have been wrong. Many conservative economists have cried wolf too often, suggesting rising inflation as a result of the debt would swamp America's economy. Wrong call. But does the level of debt have absolutely no significance? Could the American people, despite their lack of financial sophistication, be wary of the future in part because of suspicion that today's rising debt could become a real problem ahead? Could it possibly be that people look at Japan and see that that country's massive public and private debt certainly has hardly made it the world's economic juggernaut?

My concern is that on the issue of debt, the global economic community may have fallen victim to an avoidance phenomenon psychologists call "learned helplessness"—when bad news has been so relentless for so long that people eventually become numb to it. They assume nothing can be done to regain control over their fate. That leads to a subtle, benign optimism. Think of past television news interviews in which the owner of a café, say, in Lebanon or the West Bank, is pictured opening for lunch despite a deadly terrorist explosion across the street several days before, killing dozens of people. There is something in the human psyche that forms a line of optimistic defense in the face of heart-stopping threats. People living this syndrome set up the café tables anyway despite the previous horror.

Projected U.S. public debt has grown to more than $19 trillion, a size exceeding 100 percent of GDP. Debt has been at this high level only one other time in U.S. history, during World War II. But the seemingly really scary numbers are *projections* of unfunded liabilities for entitlements, including Social Security, Medicare, and Medicaid. Harvard's Jeffrey Miron argues that over the next 75 years, the "present value" of all U.S. government expenses, including entitlements, will exceed the value of future revenue by $118 trillion. Put in context, U.S. GDP for 2015 was only $18 trillion.

As the entitlement costs rise dramatically over the next century, certainly the size of the U.S. economy will increase substantially. Whether the economy's performance is substantial enough to fill the funding gap is doubtful. Many politicians are arguing for major increases in entitlement spending. It is as if the current entitlement spending gap doesn't exist.

What is the significance of this funding gap if, as some tech analysts claim, artificial intelligence will eliminate jobs, leaving tens of millions of people hanging around with nothing to do? Asked another way, who will service the expanded debt? Who will fill the gap? A diminished pool of employees?

It is difficult to deny that debt is a major threat to our children's future. In 1970 U.S. entitlement spending was 29 percent of federal budget outlays. As of mid-2016, it is over 64 percent, according to statistics from the Office of Management and Budget and the Council of Economic Advisers. Less than a decade from now, payments for Social Security, Medicare, Medicaid, Obamacare, and other federal health program entitlements, combined with interest payments on America's national debt, could exceed the size of the entire federal budget. Translation: Spending for things like education, childcare, and infrastructure improvements could be at risk. The call by some politicians during the 2016 election season for a massive expansion of Medicare was a reckless act of fiscal insanity and a heartless false promise that can never be kept without risking a massive burden on the backs of the millennial generation.

True, short-term deficits (the annual fiscal shortfall as opposed to the long-term debt) have improved. The congressional spending caps combined with increased payroll employment since the 2008 crisis produced a short-term decline in the deficit. And healthcare costs have come down at least temporarily, which improves the debt picture a bit (although the Congressional Budget Office expects U.S. budget deficits to rise significantly in coming years). The long-term debt picture, however, looks ominous. Roughly 10,000 Americans each day are retiring, according to the Pew Research Center. But under the stranglehold of Corporate Capitalism, our economy can't create enough high-paying jobs for young people to support the entitlement payments to these retirees. The potential for a shortfall crisis is real.

The politics of entitlement reform keep changing, depending on which party controls the White House. In recent years, two groups have emerged—some on the right who seem to use the coming financing gap as a cynical weapon to try to achieve fiscal austerity in all federal spending. Then there are the new deniers—those on the left who suggest there is no funding gap at all. The fact that for every dollar Americans pay now for Medicare they will draw over a lifetime three dollars in benefits is irrelevant. "Don't worry, be happy," the deniers say.

In 2013, at a rally in Washington, D.C., the most popular sign at the protest against Social Security and Medicare reform said this: "HANDS OFF!" But the sad fact is that if policymakers actually do nothing about, for example, challenging the medical cartel that is keeping healthcare costs high, the Medicare program will not survive. So, on the entitlement reform issue, who can you trust? Those with an ulterior motive or the new deniers?

It is, moreover, easy to cynically say that the Social Security funding shortfall can be fixed by eliminating the cap on the amount of income subject to Social Security payroll taxes (as of 2016, capped at $118,500). Sounds simple to do. It's not. Picture a surviving 9/11 fireman living in New York City earning $65,000 a year (not much more than the median income for a New York City fireman), married to a Manhattan public school teacher earning $65,000 (again, not that much more than the median income for all New York City teachers). Despite a joint family income of $130,000, they don't feel rich. This is particularly true given the $30,000–$60,000 cost of their child's college tuition, because at their joint income level, they might not qualify for financial aid. As their representative in Congress, try telling them that they are the simple, quick, and sole solution to America's Social Security funding problem and must accept a stiff increase in their payroll taxes now, with more dramatic tax hikes on any future additional earnings from working overtime or from raises. They'll tell you that you're crazy, and that you may not survive the next election. Any compromise solution, therefore, must involve sacrifice from all parties at the table.

Brookings Institution economist Alice Rivlin has adopted the most sensible and least partisan approach to this issue. A former vice chair of the Federal Reserve, she served as budget director in the Clinton Administration. Her reputation for being fair-minded was so strong that President Obama appointed her to his National Commission on Fiscal Responsibility and Reform. Rivlin believes firmly that there is a coming entitlement shortfall. She has suggested that "fixing Social Security is a relatively easy technical problem. It will take some combination of several much-discussed marginal changes: raising the retirement age gradually in the future (and then indexing it to longevity), raising the cap on the payroll tax, fixing the cost of living adjustment, and modifying the indexing of initial benefits so they grow more slowly for more affluent people."

During the first years of the Obama Administration, when the entitlement funding issue was still being addressed, Rivlin offered an insight relating to entitlements that supported one of the fundamental themes of this book. In January 2009, she said, "Fixing Social Security would be a confidence-building achievement." It would represent the beginnings of a paradigm shift. The Brookings economist's instinct here is bolstered by the fact that polls showed nine out of ten of President Obama's voters in 2012 were worried about the solvency of Social Security and Medicare, according to a survey that year by Third Way, a group that favors entitlement reform. Many are still worried, despite today's new rising tide of denial.

In the United States, many millennials, particularly those in the high-tech world, have fallen victim to the "learned helplessness" syndrome on the issues of debt and entitlements. They are not motivated by issues related to Social Security and Medicare because they believe these systems will not be solvent when they'll need them. They are young and don't think ahead about issues their parents and grandparents fixate on. For them, the entitlement programs are abstractions. Many millennials are motivated by the thought that there will eventually be more trusted private versions of the entitlement programs in the future.

Don't bet on it. Such thinking reflects naïveté at its worst. For most of their lives, the millennials will have no choice but to support those Social Security, Medicare, and Medicaid entitlement programs upon which their parents and grandparents are so fixated. The load will be extraordinary. In short, unless they wake up as a political force, the Baby Boomers will keep outvoting the millennials during every election. The great Washington denial is that there is a tradeoff between continuously rising payments to retiring baby boomers and the goal of bolstering the millennials with the tools (education, competitive fiscal policies, etc.) needed to be able to build a robust enough economy to support those retirees.

Don't get me wrong. When all is said and done, America's projected financial shortfall is not the result of ordinary people in America living large. For starters, Club Big—big government, big business, and big finance—is inhibiting the economy from achieving its full potential in output. Under Corporate Capitalism, tax revenues are not nearly as high as they could be with a more robust Main Street capitalist economy.

But an even larger factor, again, is the state of unfunded entitlement obligations for programs such as Social Security and Medicare. America's "debt" problem is driven largely, but not exclusively, by rising healthcare costs. True, things like waste in the Pentagon budget are troubling. But when someone mentions "public debt," think about the popular programs Social Security and Medicare.

At the heart of America's long-term funding problem is one thing above all: medical corporate welfare. For starters, corporate monopolies to maintain high healthcare costs in medical insurance, hospitalization, and pharmaceuticals combined have created a cost explosion as healthcare costs, especially for Medicare, are turbocharged by the aging demography of baby-boomer retirement. In the last several years of the Obama Administration, some spending projections for healthcare have come down as the U.S. economy has slowed. But the long-term healthcare cost picture is sobering. It is also confusing. Why does an MRI scan cost $400 in some parts of the United States and $1,500 in others?

Fighting corporate welfare in healthcare is no easy matter. After watching the outpouring of policy cronyism in response to the 2008 financial crisis, it is easy to see why average folks are reluctant to sacrifice entitlements to achieve long-term solvency for the programs. The financiers, the military, the medical cronies, Congress, and the White House express no real concern for the ballooning debt. Neither do the national media, nor most of the 2016 presidential candidates, led by Donald Trump, Bernie Sanders, and Hillary Clinton.

Yet the facts are stunning. In 1950, 16 workers (by paying their payroll taxes) supported every retiree. By 2030, two workers will be forced to support each recipient, including the masses of baby boomers who have entered retirement. Today a 25-year-old worker is slated to receive a monthly benefit 50 percent greater (adjusted for inflation) when he or she retires than the amount received by a person retiring today. How can a shrinking labor force pay for this jump in benefits? Answer: It can't. This is a recipe for the bankruptcy of our children's future.

America is at risk of a perfect storm hitting. The baby boomers are retiring, and they're living a lot longer. Unless there are reforms to the entitlement system, America's young people will be the losers. But there is not a lot of room for optimism. Why should a person on Social Security agree to even modest sacrifice to save the system? Since the financial crisis and collapse in interest rates, the return on their retirement savings has been minimal even as the winning lottery ticket went to Wall Street.

And, from the standpoint of demographics, not all Americans are created equal. A white college-educated female is expected to live well into her 80s. A high school–educated black male? Only into his late 60s. So adjusting the Social Security retirement age because people are living longer is not without complication. And let's also not forget that medical cronyism—the medical-industrial complex—is supported by one of Washington's most powerful lobbies. Any hope of reform would have to be part of a larger package of stimulus reforms—a grand bargain between Republicans and Democrats as part of a greater vision of national economic revival.

Recognizing that reform is complicated and politically difficult does not make America's financing problem go away. America's future is at serious risk. Notice that an even worse demographic situation is unfolding in Japan, Europe, and China. Most of the world is flirting with a demographic challenge tied to some form of an entitlement funding shortfall. In 1950, 8 percent of the world's population was classified as 60 or older. Today that number is 12 percent. By 2050, almost a quarter of the world's population will be older than 60. Why? In 1950, the average female gave birth to five children, according to World Bank data. Today that number is 2.5.

Investor Stan Druckenmiller offers a unique take on the U.S. demographic situation: "If you go back to 1965, the senior poverty rate in America was 30 percent. Now it's 9 percent. That's a great achievement. The problem is if you go back to 1965, the child poverty rate was 21 percent. Now it's 25 percent. So, all the gains made in terms of poverty the last 40 years have accrued to the elderly. If you look at the average per-capita income, America is spending 56 percent of every worker's dollar on the elderly, and only 7 percent on children."

The answer is not to "simply let the billionaires pay to fix the system," the approach favored by the Democratic-socialist U.S. presidential candidate Bernie Sanders. That analysis is a heartless deception. If billionaires in America were taxed at a 100 percent tax rate, the resulting revenue would barely be enough to solve America's monstrous entitlement short-fall funding problem. The combined worth of America's 540 billionaires is $2.4 trillion. The annual cost of Social Security: $888 billion. A policy of total confiscation, would, therefore, pay for Social Security for only about three years. And such a policy would almost certainly produce a billionaire stampede offshore.

Notice the emerging theme developing: a new culture of selfishness toward future generations. This trend may be one reason American youth today are more hunkered down, insecure, and risk-averse. They know Washington policymakers have put their fiscal future at risk. We are witnessing a collapse in their faith in American possibilities.

Our kids aren't stupid. They know the politicians are avoiding the debt issue. They also recognize the hypocrisy surrounding it. When George W. Bush was in power, the Democrats pointed to the dreaded fiscal cliff, where the debt leads to a financial crisis. The GOP remained silent. When Barack Obama came into power, just the reverse took place. It's all a political game, and it's not surprising that Americans under age 35 are deeply troubled about their future and highly skeptical toward Washington. They should be.

History shows that large economies like the United States have three options when dealing with a massive debt threat.

> OPTION ONE: Weaken your currency and inflate. Not a good idea. True, the value of the debt is shrunk over time, but sadly so is the value of the purchasing power of the incomes and savings of working families. Inflation kills the livelihoods of most people. Yet countries all over the world are attracted to this approach. Inflation mostly helps the rich because it causes the nominal value of their massive real estate holdings to rise. But many countries would love to inflate their way out of their debt problems anyway.

> OPTION TWO: Default like a Third World banana republic. Also not a good idea. You are denied future access to the credit markets. Your country cannot get a new loan for a long time. You

have to balance your budget now, with spending cuts and tax increases that could kill your economy. Life for working families becomes miserable. The economy stagnates with little chance for the next generation to do better. The default option is not really available in the United States. Because its debt is denominated in U.S. dollars, the Federal Reserve, in lieu of default, will always opt to print more dollars.

OPTION THREE: Encourage new innovation with the goal of keeping growth rates above the level of interest rates while initiating reforms to achieve fiscal discipline. The enhanced innovation approach is what the British did in the early part of the nineteenth century after their massive spending during the Napoleonic wars produced a mountain of debt. Argues economic historian Niall Ferguson: "The British produced a successful noninflationary debt deleveraging along with a revolution in bottom-up innovation. This approach is the best choice for a country trying to solve a debt problem."

Encouraging innovation—empowering Main Street Capitalism—not only helps economies achieve robust growth but enables debt-ridden economies to transition from a period of low interest rates, in which future economic activity has been pulled back into the present, without the destructive bursting of asset bubbles. The more innovation breakthroughs generate real economic growth, the less the chance financial markets perceive asset prices as artificial, and the less the chance of financial panic as a result of debt.

But let's be honest: A lot of the old rules on debt in the short run no longer seem to be working. U.S. debt projections are enormous, yet inflation and interest rates remain low. The same is true for the rest of the world. How could this be, and how do central banks fit in? Wasn't it the rule that debt has a "crowding-out" effect on capital markets that quickly leads to both inflation and higher interest rates?

The essential point is this: Private and government debt interact. One reason the explosion in the size of government's debt projections has not yet produced dramatically higher interest rates is that the greater debt has been accompanied by a slowdown in private borrowing as people's expectations of the future have soured.

In fact, debt brings the risk of deflation, or disinflation, because it commits more income now and in the future to pay for past consumption. As Ruchir Sharma of Morgan Stanley Investment Management calculates, "Rapid debt increases make it virtually impossible to avoid a slowdown. Since 1960, nations that indulged the 30 biggest credit binges all saw credit rise as a share of GDP by at least 40 percentage points over five years. Of those 30 cases, 70 percent ended in crisis." All those economies stumbled, plummeting from an average high of 5 percent GDP growth to a low of 1.5 percent.

And here's the important question: Did economic growth slow because the fear of rising debt inhibited economic ambition? Certainly, the financing of entrepreneurial startups is not related to the level of a nation's debt. The initial startup capital comes from personal savings and from borrowing from family and friends. But the larger question is whether people, affluent ones in particular, hold back on their spending and job-creating investment decisions in anticipation of future tax increases as a consequence of soaring debt. Can a nation's public and private debt, if it grows large enough, inhibit small business confidence? Or is there a difference in the public's attitude toward its private or personal debt and its view of the nation's public debt? Does fear of public debt become like a heavy destabilizing mountain backpack that makes the economic climb more challenging simply because, when all is said and done, people know in their gut the debt has to be repaid? Or is today's extraordinary level of public debt irrelevant to people's expectations about the future? Because interest rates are near zero percent, the monthly cost to service the massive debt is minimal.

One thing appears certain: The evidence shows that the level of an economy's *private* debt can influence human behavior. Just after the financial crisis, for example, the U.S. economy responded slowly to President George W. Bush's and President Barack Obama's combined trillion-dollar emergency fiscal stimulus package precisely because of debt. That's right. The economy was caught in a private debt–deleveraging trap. To the surprise of many experts, average folk became fearful of the future. Despite the attractiveness of the fiscal stimulus, families began to personally deleverage. In response to the financial crisis, they rapidly paid off their personal debt. Household debt liabilities were 100 percent of GDP before the 2008 crisis, according to the Federal Reserve. By the end of 2013? About 80 percent of GDP. At the same time, of course, banks also deleveraged.

In Europe, it was not households but mostly corporations that engaged in deleveraging in response to the financial crisis and rising debt. In lieu of lending, corporations improved the health of their balance sheets (a process Japanese firms have engaged in for two decades to the detriment of the economy's performance). Corporations paid down debt. Again, as a public policy issue, debt is hardly irrelevant. At minimum, private debt appears to matter a lot. Public debt may have an influence as well.

Since the financial crisis and collapse in global trade, China has experienced a borrowing and spending explosion. Its total debt has reached the level of 237 percent of GDP, according to the *Financial Times*. In 2007, its total debt was less than 150 percent of GDP. China, debt-wise, is now at risk of becoming another Japan. Whether coincidental or not, during the same period that China's debt exploded, its GDP growth rate was cut by more than half. China's cost simply to service its private debt amounts to more than 20 percent of GDP as of 2015, according to the Bank for International Settlements. And that percentage keeps rising. In 2009, the cost to service China's private debt was 13 percent of GDP. So new debt is being used in large part to make payments on old debt.

Around the world, corporations and average working families appear to be factoring debt into their behavior patterns. Why? Because they understand that someday someone, probably they themselves, will have to repay the debt. It stands to reason that the level of *public* debt is hardly irrelevant. Robert Johnson, the head of the Institute for New Economic Thinking, is hardly a right-wing economist. Yet he put America's public and private debt worry in personal terms in the form of a rhetorical question said with great frustration: "How will our kids ever unwind this stuff?"

Whether today's monstrous public debt becomes economically risky depends on the certainty of future interest rates. In a perverse sense, today's "new normal" of mediocre 1–2 percent GDP growth has been the central bankers' best friend because, again, the cost of servicing America's rising public debt has remained low. Harvard economist Richard Cooper warns, however, that if "global interest rates really start to rise, once the world economy fully recovers, the United States and Europe will be highly vulnerable." That's because both have huge amounts of public debt with short-term maturities. As these short-term bonds mature, new bonds must be issued but at much higher interest rates. The servicing cost of America's public debt, therefore, could skyrocket overnight. It would be like your bank calling twice a week to say your home mortgage interest rate is going up. As each call comes in, you suddenly feel economically less secure. You sense your economic future is slipping away. Whoops! The mortgage company just called again with the latest mortgage payment hike.

Some experts say the level of public debt doesn't matter because central banks can keep buying the government debt forever (a practice that could eventually lead to credit rationing, which happened during and just after World War II). Some say the debt will not matter in our lifetimes, so let the good times roll. Those who make this argument generally hold the view that secular stagnation's mediocre growth is here to stay in part because Washington is in endless policy paralysis.

Don't get me wrong. In response to today's mountain of public debt, nobody wants an abrupt move to austerity policies. In today's underperforming growth climate, austerity would be economically suicidal. Massive spending cuts and/or tax hikes would only weaken the economy, creating more debt. In places like Greece, austerity policies to reduce debt actually produced greater debt. At the beginning of the Greek financial crisis, that country's debt-to-GDP ratio was 126 percent, according to Eurostat which compiles European economic data. After a series of forced austerity policies, that ratio jumped to 180 percent. The economy fell into a depression. In this case, the vast majority of economists, led by Paul Krugman, were at the forefront in warning not only of the heartache but the economic futility of an economic policy based exclusively on austerity. In this case, the economists got it right.

But what is interesting are the emerging battle lines in this debate. For the neo-Keynesians, slow growth causes high debt. For the neoclassical economic crowd, high debt causes slow growth. How about this for a conclusion? It is possible both schools are correct. Therefore, in this age of economic uncertainty, how about a common-sense compromise, a kind of hedge-your-bets approach to America's massive funding gap projections? Such an approach must take into account both the views of the experts who believe the economy is underperforming because of inadequate demand, as well as the views of those who believe the negative psychology produced by the debt projection monster is impeding the economy's performance.

First, we need to reform entitlements, but with enacted changes affecting only those retiring a decade from now and later. Reform should include means testing. Why are Warren Buffett, George Soros, and other billionaires receiving checks from the Social Security Administration? That should end. And cost-of-living formulas should accurately reflect rising costs. Essentially, adopt the Alice Rivlin balanced approach.

Second, using today's cheap credit (see below for my proposal to have U.S. corporations repatriating capital via some form of temporary tax holiday agree to purchase set amounts of new 1 percent infrastructure bonds), increase federal spending for essential, nonpoliticized infrastructure projects such as modernizing airports, schools, bridges, and water treatment plants, which have to be improved anyway. In other words, fashion a bipartisan grand bargain to bend the long-term entitlement spending debt curve downward and to save the entitlement systems without inflicting austerity on a struggling economy. Send a bipartisan message to global financial markets that the United States, for once, is serious about confronting its public financing problem and rebuilding its crumbling infrastructure. Make clear to our children and grandchildren that they really have a future. Change the American people's expectations.

But here's the thing. Under any grand bargain, infrastructure spending must be controlled by a nonpolitical commission of distinguished decision makers, the kind of successful model that was used in the 1990s for the politically sensitive task of closing U.S. military bases. No Republican spending on bridges to nowhere. No Democratic alternative energy deals to political fundraisers. Stated bluntly, when it comes to handling money, Washington politicians can't be trusted. The result is always too much leakage.

Since the 2008 crisis, the big emerging markets led by China, Russia, and Brazil all spent trillions of dollars on hasty, poorly thought out, politicized infrastructure projects. What was the result? It now takes more debt to achieve the same level of economic expansion. The number of units of investment necessary to facilitate a given level of GDP has jumped. In this proposed grand compromise, the United States cannot make the same mistake.

But there's a second common-sense compromise aimed directly at the medical cartel of corporate and legal welfare, which accounts for a significant part of America's long-term funding problem. Drug companies are a major source of Republican campaign financing. Trial lawyers are a big source of Democratic campaign money. Make drug prices competitive under Medicare (these prices currently are set by the drug companies).

More than 200,000 patients are killed each year because of medical errors. But is the legal system the best way to reduce this tragic number? What about better hospital management and other reforms? The legal and medical fields are in the midst of an endless debate over whether the cost of medical malpractice insurance is causing doctors to either retire early or to scale back their practices. Some experts point to other reasons, including excess paperwork tied to reimbursement rates, for why doctors in frustration are pulling out. Doctors themselves, however, never fail to mention the high cost of insurance. And here's the essential point: America's doctors are aging. One in three is over 50 years of age, according to a 2013 Deloitte survey of over 200,000 physicians. One in four is over 60. While Washington's think tank experts engage in their endless debate over the degree to which malpractice lawsuits are wreaking havoc among the medical profession, America's pool of top medical doctors is, if just for demographic reasons, quickly moving off the scene. It is time to give our doctors the benefit of the doubt with some form of tort reform.

No doubt, all these reforms will meet a fierce wall of resistance from the forces of the status quo. The only hope of success is to frame the debate as a kind of crusade to raise the level of the economy's performance. Everyone gives up something, but the entire economy wins. As a result, our children and grandchildren have a healthy economic future.

I know. This all sounds like a pipedream in a world where Washington policymakers never accomplishes anything. But bear with me for a moment. There is a history of nations pivoting to new policies. In 2012, for example, at a conference in Berlin I met a man named Paul Martin. He told me a compelling story about Canada's fiscal situation that relates directly to the economic predicament of the United States. A member of Canada's Liberal Party, Martin was prime minister from 2003 to 2006. Several years before he became prime minister, Canada, under his predecessor, also a Liberal, had become a fiscal disaster. Its deficits and debt were by far the worst of the major industrialized countries. Its level of foreign debt was the highest in the developed world. The International Monetary Fund dubbed Canada all but bankrupt. Canada was a fiscal basket case. Martin explained how his country began to change:

> Four years later, our debt-to-GDP ratio was dropping like a stone. Canada's deficit was no more. The vicious circle turned virtuous and the positive payback for the real economy was not long in coming.
>
> So how did we succeed? We made debt and deficits a national priority. I traveled the country and in hundreds of town meetings stressed this message: Deficit and debt reduction must be a national priority. For the effort to gain public support there could be no winners while most people were losing.
>
> Sick economies can be nursed back to health. It happened to us. It can happen to the United States.

Canada might have rebounded economically even more had its leadership also tried to make its economy more a hothouse of cutting-edge innovation and center of entrepreneurial risk-taking. But the message is still clear: A nation with massive debt was able to achieve fiscal sanity. What was required was that a leader travel the country holding town meetings explaining the importance of compromise. Saving America's entitlement system is not a trivial matter. Half of U.S. households receive benefits from Social Security, Medicare, Medicaid, or some other federal or state government program. The greatest threat to these programs is that policymakers do nothing, continuing for political reasons to look away.

People are desperate for change. They are angry, and the political establishment in Washington should think long and hard before getting in the way of reform. Out of anger and desperation springs opportunity. This is the moment to strike the deal.

Don't underestimate the potential paradigm shift toward renewed confidence if Washington begins to tackle the entitlement shortfall in exchange for a nonpolitical, no-nonsense plan to rebuild America's crumbling infrastructure. A grand bargain along with provisions that deal directly with corporate welfare in the form of medical and legal cronyism would send a powerful message that Washington policymakers have finally broken the logjam of policy stalemate. Be assured, in the financial world, this would be the Main Event. Financial markets would soar. The world would sit up in astonishment.

The secret to success is to present the grand compromise to Congress as a package with a strict up-and-down vote, with no amendments, backed by a national crusade, not unlike the methods used by the bipartisan Social Security commission in 1982. The recommended reforms were voted on without changes or amendments allowed. The vote was between two options: saving Social Security or doing nothing.

Debt matters, so it is time to have the debate. Today's global public and private debt jumped to over $180 trillion by 2015, and now is even higher. It is an amount almost beyond comprehension. This amount represents an astounding 286 percent of GDP. The world is a circus undergoing the ultimate debt high-wire act on a frayed wire. The world may survive this experience, but there are no certainties about anything. Debt reduction is tricky. It is easy to talk about deleveraging, but much more difficult to achieve deleveraging without a dangerous decline in savings that is detrimental to the economy.

Experts in other countries say little about debt. Yet half of China's current debt, linked to an overheated real estate market and to a dubious shadow banking system, may now be all but unserviceable. Several years ago, China's much smaller borrowing could still be financed by domestic savings. Not anymore. And the danger in China is not default on that debt, but a kind of quietly disguised series of defaults, particularly on dollar-denominated debt. A tradition exists in China in which debt holders simply receive letters stating that debt payments have been suspended. Period. No explanation. No official default. No transparency. In less than a decade, China has quadrupled its total debt, according to the McKinsey Global Institute. More than half of new debt issued is intended for the purpose of rolling over existing debt, estimates the Hong Kong–based financial research firm PRC Macro Advisors. China's debt is a potential global disaster in the making.

Yet many partisans still insist the issue of debt is irrelevant. The world, they are essentially saying, can forever eat the equivalent of mountains of chocolate cake, cotton candy, and pizza five times a day, every day, and never gain weight. There really is a free lunch, a calorie-free affair. The central bankers, if need be, can buy all the debt—all of it—for the next thousand years with no downside and no unintended consequences. "Don't worry, be happy," they say. Maybe so. But wasn't this the same kind of blind thinking that assured us back in 2007, just before the great financial crisis, that housing prices would never go down? The ultimate danger is that the entire world, including the United States, becomes like a giant Japan—a sluggish, risk-averse, debt-ridden economy of mediocre growth with low unemployment rates because most people, holding low expectations toward the future, have given up the job search.

If you think this discussion is too tough on Japan, consider these facts: To stabilize the Japanese stock market, the Bank of Japan, the central bank, has been forced to buy stocks. In the case of many Japanese corporations, the Bank of Japan is one of their top five shareholders. But stocks are not the only things the central bank has been purchasing. It has also been aggressively buying government bonds. The Bank of Japan is purchasing more ten-year government debt (called JGBs) than the Ministry of Finance is issuing (they thus are also buying these bonds from the private sector). All of which raises the question of whether the Japanese financial market is even a market anymore.

Could the Japanese stock market seriously stumble? Again, consider the statistics. The Tokyo stock market is valued (its market capitalization) at roughly $5 trillion. Foreign investors own roughly $1.5 trillion of the market (an averaging of the private estimates of several financial firms). Japanese state pension funds hold roughly $400 billion, according to the Japan Exchange Group. Let's assume foreign investors become nervous about the Japanese stock market and the nation's massive debt. They pull, say, 20 percent of their investment funds out of the market ($300 billion). Japan would have a serious problem. That's because the Bank of Japan, even when it is being most aggressive, typically purchases only $50–$60 trillion a year in Japanese equities (the state pension funds are already near the legal limits for their equity purchases). The message here: The central bank can prop up the financial system and the economy's massive debt for a while, but there is no guarantee it can do it forever. When analysts commenting on debt say the entire world financial system could become like Japan's financial system, they are not offering up a compliment.

Geoffrey Canada, the president of the Harlem Children's Zone in New York, puts America's debt problem in human terms. Canada is a pioneer in finding new ways to educate poor, underprivileged, inner-city youth. Our family financially supports his groundbreaking efforts at his charter school in Harlem. Canada is an unlikely voice in the debt debate. Politically, he is a liberal Democrat. Yet he believes fixing the U.S. entitlements system is the only way the young will have a chance:

> I'm in my 60s. The current spending on my generation, if it continues, will erase any chance the kids at my school will have the safety net of social, educational and healthcare services they will need. America is eating the seed corn of the next generation.
>
> But I'm telling kids in Harlem that if they work hard, stay in school, when they become adults around the year 2030 they'll have a job. They'll have a secure future with Social Security and Medicare. But those important entitlement systems will have run out of money. And the way things are going, there won't be many jobs either.

For the United States, common sense suggests the debt issue is likely to be a serious long-term obstacle to full-fledged prosperity. In a global market, capital flows are extraordinarily difficult to predict, particularly with the global exchange rate system increasingly politicized and manipulated. In one decade, capital inflows can be a pleasant constant helping keep a nation's interest rates low. Yet in another decade, capital flight can become a terrifying threat, putting upward pressure on interest rates. That is why it is time for common-sense fiscal reforms. America needs a national campaign to educate average working families on both the risks of excessive debt and the bottom-up aspects of innovative growth. In today's dangerous global economy, in which the dollar's reserve currency role is under global review at a time of declining growth and trade and rising exchange rate protectionism, the wise choice is for America to quickly get its financial house in order. The United States needs to be the fiscally sound exception to a potential emerging world of financial chaos and, in some cases, insolvency.

In some quiet policy corners, some experts are arguing that it is probably too late. The world's financial situation is beyond repair. The U.S. economy, indeed the entire world economy, is trapped. The political risk of a debt and central bank liquidity collapse are too severe. In the next global downturn, they whisper, the United States has no choice but to close its borders, default on its debt, print money, and inject new spending into the economy. A government-controlled Corporate Capitalism on steroids of top-down control and of mediocre long-term economic growth cannot be avoided.

Yet America does not have to make that blind jump into the unknown. With a grand bargain, the United States can begin to create a new paradigm that changes the expectations of investors, innovators, and consumers alike. But another decade of delay in addressing the financing shortfall is not only risky but unfair to those young people at the bottom rungs of the economic ladder being told the cruel joke that the future is theirs. If the status quo persists, it's not.

The world's policymakers have made the greatest wager. If the current growth trend in debt holds up, the world's young people will have no future. What they'll have, instead, is a world of growth far below potential with no one in charge and where terrifying things they thought could never happen will happen. The question is, what else do we need to do to create a paradigm shift for growth? As the next chapter shows, America needs to resume its global leadership role not as the world's police officer but as its symbol of a core set of values that provide stability under a new global economic and financial architecture.

SIX

It's Nobody's Century
(or Maybe Everybody's)

Washington, D.C., is a strange land of unpredictable, sometimes bizarre occurrences. In the summer of 2014, I experienced such an occurrence. I was invited to a luncheon to meet the Chinese ambassador to the United States. The handpicked guest list for the gathering included about two dozen think tank academics and former diplomats. The event seemed routine but was not what I had expected. It actually proved troubling and reminded me how much U.S. working families are vulnerable to global developments.

The luncheon's guest of honor, Ambassador Cui Tiankai, a smart and amiable Chinese diplomat who had earlier served in the sensitive position of China's ambassador to Japan, began with some general remarks, which were followed by a question-and-answer session.

The U.S. foreign policy specialists and think tank scholars fired away. They focused their questions on China's militaristic behavior in the South China Sea in dealing with territorial disputes with its neighbors. China is making every conceivable military move, short of direct confrontation, to put America at a severe disadvantage, the U.S. strategic experts charged.

As if playing a friendly verbal game of ping-pong, the ambassador easily swatted back the various accusations. Defending China's aggressive behavior in the region had become routine. His attitude was smug but friendly.

When the luncheon was almost over, I intervened. I commented that no one was connecting China's militaristic behavior to its weakening economy and challenged financial system: "The world is in a period of deglobalization that is hardly to China's advantage," I said. "Global trade, the movement of capital across borders, and economic growth are all in decline. As a result, China's economy is growing at a slower rate even as economic expectations among Chinese middle-class families are still very high. Your country has already picked the international system's low-hanging fruit. Your economy's rise was powered by exports to a highly leveraged, fast-growing world economy that no longer exists."

The ambassador gazed at me attentively. I continued: "China has been forced to pivot from a predominantly export-led to an investment-led economy and now to a consumption-led economic model. But with your aging demographic, isn't that transition now problematic?"

A little background: I have always been skeptical of the China-will-economically-run-the-world theory. Simply because of its size, China will always be a major global economic player. But as for taking over the world? That's what the experts said the Russians would do in the early 1970s, Japan in the late 1980s, and Europe (under a common currency) in the early 1990s. It's an easy bet. If the conventional wisdom says some new nation will soon run the world, wager the opposite.

I ended my questions with this observation: "The global financial markets worry that China's massive infrastructure and real estate over-investments have been financed by its unregulated shadow banks with the help of unsustainable low interest rate global capital that's now drying up." I explained that global investors are backing off.

Instantly, as if a switch had been flipped, there was tension in the air. The ambassador's aides attending the lunch, staring down, were suddenly nervously, and ferociously, scribbling notes. I wondered if my comments were somehow culturally offensive.

I hesitated, but then continued: "Has China, Mr. Ambassador, become aggressive with its neighbors as a diversion to stoke up nationalistic sentiments back home? Is your financial system in trouble? With slower domestic growth, perhaps slower than your official statistics suggest, your debt is expanding rapidly."

I had planned to add that China is in the grips of a major environmental crisis with an acute water shortage in the north of the country. Corruption is rife. Birthrates are falling, and there is a rising lack of domestic trust in Chinese institutions. Parts of the Chinese government seem surprisingly tolerant of domestic cyber-warfare assaults against U.S. and Western European targets, despite China's still heavy dependence on export markets from that part of the world.

But by then, the ambassador's demeanor had completely changed. No more Mr. Nice Guy, smiling while swatting away ping-pong balls. The official's gaze morphed into a steely-eyed, almost mean look in my direction. It was the kind of deadly look boxers give to each other when they meet for a weigh-in the day before a major title event. I was hardly yelling "fire" in a crowded theater, I thought. This was a small private group. We were invited to ask questions. What happens in China could affect the entire world. China is one of the largest holders of U.S. debt, with four of the world's five largest banks and the world's second-largest stock market. Why wouldn't we ask tough questions?

But I was struck by the intensity of the ambassador's glare. He responded sarcastically, chiding me for the temerity of offering such commentary. I countered: "But I'm in the business of asking—" He intervened dismissively, suggesting some vague notion that China is in favor of capital and trade flows. But his steely gaze continued. It was the kind of look that seemed to say, "In my country, you wouldn't get away with dealing with such sensitive issues in such a public and cavalier way."

As I was leaving the luncheon, one of the other guests grabbed me by the arm. He said, "I learned one new thing today about China, and it didn't come from the ambassador. What was intriguing was the intensity of the reaction to your questions. The non-answers." Of course, a lot of disappointing economic and financial news about China is now well known. Back then it wasn't.

The Chinese economy should be a concern for the new U.S. administration. China's forever-expanding export machine, which stokes excess supply, has helped throw a disinflationary wet blanket over the entire world economy. That is why, in the 2016 presidential campaign, Donald Trump's and Bernie Sanders's attacks against China resonated more than expected. Chinese policies have become a major threat to average working American families. There is a desperation to a lot of China's most recent activities. For example, Chinese policymakers set up a complicated network of new regulatory requirements for foreign technology companies that the U.S. Chamber of Commerce describes as nothing less than "a blueprint for technology theft on a scale the world has never before seen." Today China is on a global buying spree. But is that a sign of weakness, a loss of confidence in the opportunities for high-growth investment at home?

If so, that was not always the case. At the beginning of the twenty-first century, China was the new miracle economy, the world's welcomed new economic locomotive. Export-dependent China was to be the world's factory, while the United States was to assume the role as the world's permanent consumer of last resort. The two economies would run the world.

After the 2008 financial crisis and collapse in global trade and cross-border capital flows, China's economy was forced to pivot. China engaged in an investment bonanza the size of which the world had never seen. China built urban infrastructure, business complexes, and apartment high-rises equivalent in size to more than 320 Manhattans, according to the *Wall Street Journal*. During a three-year span, from 2011 to 2013, China poured more concrete than the United States poured throughout the entire twentieth century, according to the *Washington Post*. Yet many of these office and residential buildings still sit empty even as a lot of China's newly acquired debt could become unsustainable. With the global economy slowing, China is still stockpiling a mountain of commodities regardless of global demand. Yu Yongding, a former senior Chinese central banker, wrote in *China Daily* that this extraordinary but unsustainable investment-led growth "has been achieved at an extremely high cost. Only future generations will know the true price."

In recent years, in response to the disappointing results of that investment-led growth, the Chinese leadership attempted to pump up the stock market, sometimes through outright stock market purchases by the central bank. The market soared, then plummeted, then rose, and then dropped again. But the "start-stop" strategy never made sense. Fewer than 7 percent of Chinese families own stocks. How could the average Chinese benefit? The beneficiaries of this stock market price-fixing operation turned out to be big state-run companies and international investors. Sound familiar?

To avoid a banking crisis, China's central bank is now being forced to maintain a huge spread between the banks' deposit interest rate and the lending interest rate. Keeping the deposit rate artificially low helps the inefficient state-run banks enormously, but at the cost of financial suffocation for China's average savers, who earn even less from their modest savings accounts. Again, sound familiar?

The latest point in the Chinese narrative presumes that the economy will somehow pivot again to becoming the world's consumption behemoth, accompanied by a new, globally competitive services sector. China will replace the West as the leader of a pan-Asian center of economic dynamism.

Whether this transition to consumption can be driven by a society that is rapidly aging seems hardly certain (as people age, they generally consume less and save more). In per-capita household consumption, China ranks 106th globally, better than Algeria but behind Swaziland.

To be sure, some parts of China's private economy are vibrant. Global venture capitalists hardly ignore China's tech sector in their investment decisions. China's ultimate uncertainty concerns the potential for a breakout of nasty political and social strife—and its inability to come to terms with its stifling state-run corporate behemoths that are all but on life support systems.

China's elites are vying for control of the nation's destiny via an internal fight over the culture of corruption that afflicts their country, what Chinese analysts themselves describe as "the unholy alliance" between big business and government. The fear is that China will experience a coming period of power struggles among families and interest groups from disparate regions and from different segments of the nation's economic and social structure.

With the world economy having slowed, China must reduce by half its enormous excess supply capacity, which was produced in recent years to a significant extent with borrowed money. (China's total steel capacity, for example, exceeds by fivefold the steel capacity of the United States and Japan combined.) The question is whether China will have the adequate cash flow necessary to service its massive newly acquired debt during that adjustment period. All of this will have to happen at a time when the vast majority of China's large corporations have speculated heavily in the domestic real estate market using cash reserves or massive borrowing from the banking (or shadow banking) system. The entire financial system is based on a one-way bet that the price of real estate never declines. Again, sound familiar?

The temptation will be to have the Chinese central bank dramatically increase its monetary stimulus to drive down the value of the yuan. Yet the more the yuan weakens, the tougher it is for Chinese companies to pay off their debt, a significant amount of which is denominated in dollars. The fear of a Chinese currency collapse explains why the most reputable, non-state-run Chinese companies are now paying off their dollar-denominated debt as fast as possible. They can sense that political pressures are building for a much weaker currency to try to spur exports, regardless of the opposing views of senior Chinese central bank officials that such a policy direction could risk a global currency war.

Until now, in its dealings with its industrialized-world competitors, China has often been given the benefit of the doubt. Everyone wanted to curry favor with the world's new economic giant as it picked the global economy's low-hanging fruit. But the international mood is changing. One reason is that China has failed to meet an increasing number of the commitments it made for its membership in the World Trade Organization (WTO).

China's major manipulation of WTO rules has damaged the global trading system. Lately, for example, Chinese authorities have been ramping up their mercantilist weapons aimed at the rest of the world's technology centers. As Adams Nager of the Information Technology and Innovation Foundation argues, China is now deploying "the world's largest export subsidies, even on a per capita basis, which distorts international trade in many industries, including steel, wind, turbines, solar cells, glass, paper, and auto parts. The subsidies contribute substantially to Chinese trade surpluses and to global overcapacity in these sectors." This abusive policy cannot continue.

China engages in such abusive policies because it has an innovation problem. Multifactor productivity, a broad measurement of an economy's innovative and technological prowess, is dropping fast. Since 2010, innovation has represented just 30 percent of China's GDP growth, compared to 40–48 percent for the previous two decades, according to the McKinsey Global Institute.

Given China's overall economic and financial situation, it is popular in many Western circles, therefore, to suggest that China is vulnerable to a major financial crisis, a so-called hard landing that could roil global financial markets. Maybe. But my hunch is that such a China crash scenario is unlikely. Instead, China's ultimate risk is that it stumbles down the road to becoming another Japan. With its extraordinarily high debt and crushing debt service costs, China risks slowly finding itself, like Japan, muddling through. Because of political pressure, market prices will not be allowed to clear—that is, to reflect their true value. States the British journalist Ambrose Evans-Pritchard: "The Communist Party's state-owned banking system will not allow a financial collapse. The trauma will manifest itself 'a la japonnaise.' It will be a slow loss of dynamism, a medscape of companies kept on life support."

As I was leaving that Washington luncheon with the Chinese ambassador, I was struck by how little Washington policymakers think about global financial risk. It also dawned on me how much the U.S. economy is being stymied because of a terrifying world. Why are America's risk-takers holding back? Could it be that they clearly see the world has become an uncertain place in which to do business? Global corruption is rampant, and is becoming increasingly sophisticated. Even the Society for Worldwide Interbank Financial Telecommunication (SWIFT) system, the supposedly ultra-secure and highly respected global bank messaging system, was attacked by a sophisticated band of hackers. In one case, hapless New York Federal Reserve officials were tricked into sending $81 million to an international hacking syndicate through an elaborate sneak attack going through Bangladesh and some Philippine casinos.

Since the 1989 fall of the Berlin Wall, Americans have been living a foreign policy illusion about the stability of the world. Globalization of finance and trade was supposed to rid the world of serious conflict. Instead, potential tectonic shifts in the global power landscape are everywhere. The United States has seven formal defense alliances, with NATO the most prominent. The others are with Japan, the Philippines, Australia, South Korea, Southeast Asia, and the Americas. As analyst Criton

Zoakos observes, "Most of these treaties appear to be in the cross-hairs of Chinese and Russian long-term plans to achieve regional hegemony." And that's assuming that China and Russia don't implode politically from within. American investors are right to be scared.

The world has returned to a highly volatile period (resembling the late nineteenth century) that contributes to acute economic and financial uncertainty. It is a new Wild West of disorder, unpredictability, and rising nationalism. Countries want to remake the global map, either returning to borders in place before the era of colonialism or, in the case of Russia, before the 1991 collapse of the Soviet Union. The so-called world order of the last three-quarters of a century, first defined by the ideology of the Cold War and then by a common devotion to the stability of globalized markets, is fading. In some cases, anarchy reigns. In others, such as in North Korea, leadership insanity is the order of the day.

Uncertainty is everywhere. A new nationalism is driving economic considerations. And here's the most threatening development: Since the 2008 financial crisis and economic slowdown, the emerging market economies led by China have overproduced, overinvested, and under-consumed. They have produced what economic analyst Michael Power calls a "supply tsunami" that is threatening to destabilize prices throughout the entire world economy and make the world's central bankers' jobs of maintaining global price stability nearly impossible.

Today's debt-ridden Eurozone is still a picture of enormous uncertainty, made more so by the June 2016 Brexit vote. Eurozone banks, suffering from today's negative interest rates that have devastated earnings, are also still vulnerable to a collapse in emerging market economies where the European banks have been major creditors. Even Germany's banks have been dangerously weakened by the profit-killing effect of the European Central Bank's negative interest rate policy and its banks' exposure to faltering emerging market economies. Europe's increasing refugee population is another wild card. A prominent European official, when asked in May 2016 about the nature of Europe's refugee problem, told me over breakfast: "To use an American analogy, we are only in the second or third inning of our problem. All of Africa will soon be a concern."

American working families and potential innovators have good reason to feel anxious about the rest of the world. It has been roughly

100 years since the start of World War I. That major catastrophe was sparked by a collection of seemingly unconnected and disparate policy events, some tied to economic and energy issues. Government leaders then lacked the strategic vision to determine whether these events were interrelated.

Is the world flirting with a repeat of a 1914 scenario? It's too early to tell. The world today benefits from far more advanced communications technologies than back then. Today's economies also involve technologies that are shared. So war would clearly be seen as having a negative worldwide economic effect. Back in 1914, the public had no idea of the brutal effects a new military technology would unleash. Today the crisis points of a potential world war seem ambiguous. Are they isolated crisis points? Or are they interlinked at a time when global trade growth has halved and liquidity is shrinking, with potentially extraordinary economic and geopolitical repercussions capable of generating events of financial uncertainty? It is difficult to tell.

The world wasn't supposed to be this way. This was to be a time of global cooperation and unprecedented prosperity. Sadly, the opposite scenario is setting in. In their primary campaigns, both Donald Trump and Bernie Sanders stuck a dagger into the heart of the very bipartisan, internationalist economic thinking that has dominated Washington, D.C., for the last quarter century. Both touched an acutely sensitive nerve in the American public's consciousness. Both targeted the so-called Washington Consensus—that is, the global understanding established in 1989 to form a "new world economic order." Nations would agree to free up global capital and trade flows, to liberalize market access, to encourage greater domestic competition, to reduce public debt, and to bolster the rule of law, including the protection of property rights.

At the heart of the Washington Consensus was the creation in 1994 of the North American Free Trade Agreement (NAFTA) among the United States, Canada, and Mexico; the founding in 1995 of the World Trade Organization; and China's entry into that organization in 2001. If all the world's major economic powers followed the script, one thing was certain: A new era of amazing prosperity was theirs for the taking.

Both candidates—Sanders and Trump—offered essentially the same response to the internationalist agenda. They said: That's all well and good except for one problem. While the United States plays by the rules, many of its trading partners don't. They "raise obstacles, invoke exemptions, plead special hardship and, when all else fails, cheat and steal (especially intellectual property and trade secrets)," as analyst Criton Zoakos succinctly put it.

As a result, both candidates argued, the world economy has grown out of balance. U.S. current account and trade deficits have soared. Other nations poured their burgeoning surpluses (the surplus savings piled up as a result of the world's new lack of balance) into U.S. financial markets. This flood distorted the U.S. economy in favor of Wall Street and to the detriment of Main Street and set the conditions that led to the 2008 financial crisis. Most Americans knew exactly what was happening. Working-class incomes were flatlining. The American Dream was slipping away. Yet Washington policymakers hadn't a clue.

Both candidates, again, rode a full-blown populist wave of anger that is probably not going to dissipate any time soon. Their message: No more lectures from the ivory tower about free trade. Renegotiate the trade and investment deals. Stop the currency manipulation. Force other nations, led by China, to kill their non-tariff barriers. And stop the cyber war and rampant intellectual property theft. Now! Needless to say, our new president faces a major challenge in resolving these tensions. It is not clear, however, that even if the Chinese were cut off from the international markets through a series of tariffs (taxes and fees) that America's trade deficit would dramatically shrink. As analyst Richard Katz wrote in the Summer 2016 issue of *The International Economy* magazine: "While computers are the largest single item in China's exports to the United States, 99 percent of those exports are made by foreign-owned firms who choose to locate the final assembly stage in China rather than elsewhere. If not China, then some other emerging market economy will complete the final assembly stage."

The lives of average American working families have become intertwined with the uncertainties of this global trade and financial system. International investors have purchased U.S. financial assets equal to an incredible 20 percent of global GDP. All well and good. But does anybody really know what these extraordinary cross-border capital flows, and their influence on the U.S. dollar, mean for the long-term economic welfare of average American families? Most Americans have become pawns in the global financial system. And although the globalization of goods, services, and capital may be receding some, the globalization of information is expanding exponentially. What this trend means for the future of the U.S. economy and for the American people's security is still not certain.

Having grown up in Baltimore, I think how removed folks living today in my old neighborhood are from the stark realities of today's often terrifying global financial system. Average working families are struggling to survive, to stretch a dollar, to get their kids or grandkids through school or to pay for retirement. Yet they are unaware of the global financial forces of awesome power that, at a moment's notice, could crush them economically like a bug.

Many of these folks have known economic heartache. They had parents who worked at Sparrows Point, the Bethlehem Steel plant down the road. In the 1970s and 1980s, a lot of their parents were laid off when the plant all but closed down as a result of foreign competition. The father of one of my best friends always seemed in and out of work at the steel plant. Now the kids of these folks, who are adults with their own kids and grandkids, are the potential victims of the twists and turns of a new global financial system with the U.S. dollar as the central focus.

The American Greenback bears the burden as the world's reserve currency, the currency of choice for international transactions. Like it or not, the world economy is heavily influenced by the dollar's strength or weakness. The Wall Street Journal Index measures the dollar's strength against a basket of 16 currencies. In January 2016, that index showed the dollar had reached its highest level since just after the turn of the century.

The dollar plays a unique role in the world economy. Most nations would prefer an exceptionally weak currency relative to the dollar and to the currencies of their major trading partners. That's because with a weak currency, the price of a nation's exports of goods and services becomes cheaper compared to the domestic alternatives of other economies. With a weak currency, a nation's tourism increases. International investors often pour capital into the weak-currency nation, seeking to buy things like companies and real estate on the cheap. Theoretically, the country with a weakening currency experiences a rise in prices. When import costs rise, so do the prices of domestic goods. The downside is that the world commodity prices (including the price of oil) are measured in dollars. If a nation's currency weakens against the dollar, the domestic prices of essentials like food, gasoline, and clothing rise.

The country with the stronger currency enjoys some benefits, including cheaper tourist travel abroad for its citizens. The stronger currency is also an effective check against inflation. That's because cheaper import costs discourage domestic companies offering the same or similar goods and services from raising prices. But the downside is that when a currency becomes too strong, two things may happen: (1) the strong-currency country's exports decline because of their new lack of price competitiveness; and (2) domestic corporations move plants offshore where, because of a cheaper currency and lower labor costs, the price of doing business is a lot more attractive. The strengthening currency often becomes the tipping point in the decision to move offshore.

There are a lot of nuances and exceptions to the rules of the international currency system. Many nations with aging populations know that consumption will never be a major economic engine for prosperity (again, as people age, folks tend to save more and consume less). So policymakers use monetary policy to weaken their currency as a means of bolstering an alternate economic engine—exports. Some nations have a strong currency simply because they have an impressive economy (relative to other economies) that attracts global investment into that currency. The U.S. dollar has in recent years been in such a position. But what is happening in the world today is unique: Nations are scrambling to manipulate their currencies against the dollar and the currencies of their major trading partners (again through central bank policies) to try to gain trade advantage. A worldwide desperation has brought the world to the edge of an outright currency war. Like it or not, the U.S. dollar, as the world's reserve or premier currency, is at the center of this battle. And it is unclear whether the dollar's unique role is good for the people living in my old Baltimore neighborhood.

The credibility of a currency depends on its ability to be fully integrated into trade and capital markets in such a way that the currency becomes "the symbol of freedom and opportunity," as Lorenzo Codogno, former director general of the Italian treasury department, put it. So it is quite understandable why, given the increasing lack of transparency around the world, the U.S. dollar, and not the European, Japanese, and Chinese currencies, continues to be trusted globally. That has been the case despite America's reckless fiscal and monetary policies and domestic political stalemate. The credibility of a currency is all about *relative* perceived freedom and opportunity. And the U.S. economy is still perceived as being protected by the rule of law and as being relatively free. For now, the world has no other choice.

What my former Baltimore neighbors should know, however, is the surprising degree to which many of the world's central banks, led by China, regularly game this system for short-term trade advantage at the U.S. economy's expense. Again, foreign central banks expand their balance sheets in an effort to keep their currencies relatively weak, to increase or maintain the price competitiveness of their country's exports. That is one reason America's "new normal" economic growth rate is so low. Jared Bernstein, former chief economist to Vice President Joe Biden, argues that the dollar's reserve currency status has made the dollar too strong. The cost: about 6 million American jobs. He wants the system changed.

But would the alternative, a multipolar currency system, be worse? Talk about a world of global financial uncertainty, mistrust, and international financial dysfunction! Do we really want a global currency system tied in part to a Chinese or Russian bureaucracy full of officials who are masters at avoiding financial transparency and who regularly look the other way as domestic hackers (thieves) target Western technological interests? A world without a credible currency anchor, and without transparency and a core set of values, could foster conditions ripe for enormous global financial volatility, if not outright corruption and anarchy.

That's why the world desperately needs a transparent exchange rate policy. It is time to lay the groundwork for an international currency agreement, a Plaza Accord II (the first Plaza Accord was the global currency agreement achieved in 1985, signed at New York's Plaza Hotel) that is committed to some sense of international currency understanding and order. The industrialized world still has the requisite political and economic leverage to establish more order in the global foreign exchange system. Delay much longer and it will be too late. Do nothing, and most

Americans will be even more economically vulnerable in the future to massive foreign-exchange manipulation.

Today the White House lobbies for free-trade agreements with both the Pacific and Euro-region countries. With a level playing field, the economic benefits of free trade are enormous. But such agreements make no sense if currency valuations can be easily manipulated through the back door. In trade, countries can't suddenly be allowed to do the currency equivalent of declaring that a foot is 12 inches for every other nation but them. For them, a foot is suddenly 15 inches. Neither do trade agreements make sense in a world where countries can argue that they technically and legally follow the rules of trade, but then manipulate domestic conditions to frustrate foreign competition. The 2016 U.S. presidential election showed that many average Americans feel they've been played the sucker for trade policies that serve not them but big corporate interests and Wall Street.

Nothing about the foreign exchange rate system, however, is simple. Abrupt currency depreciation as a means of achieving higher rates of growth doesn't always work. For example, the Bank of Japan's attempt to weaken the yen, as part of Prime Minister Shinzo Abe's economic plan, did little to revitalize a Japanese economy in the stranglehold of Corporate Capitalism on steroids. I suspect we will see the same disappointing outcome if China further weakens its currency without reforming its economic and financial systems. Between 2004 and 2014, the U.S. dollar weakened against the Chinese yuan by 25 percent. Yet America's trade deficit with China went through the roof, from $162 billion to $343 billion.

But here's the greatest fear: If the currency devaluation medicine is not working, policy officials worldwide will be tempted simply to up the dosage. And that's how trade wars start, when nations impose tariffs (taxes and fees) on each other's imports, as they did in the 1930s. Central banks have created so much liquidity to reduce their interest rates and weaken their currencies, but they have failed to plan their exit from a world of low interest rates. That may end up being the world's greatest problem of all.

Notice an important nuance here, which may signal significant problems ahead. There is one other reason why the future of the global economy is so uncertain. The world's export-dependent economies, led by Europe, Japan, China, and other emerging markets, account for roughly 75 percent of global GDP. To achieve the competitive exchange rates necessary to keep their exports robust, these economies have increasingly lost control over their domestic monetary policies. That's right. Their exchange rate policies (the value of their currencies) are no longer determined to a large degree by their own trade and capital flow imbalances, as was the case in the past, but increasingly by the anticipation of interest rate changes in their country relative to U.S. interest rates. Put another way, the Federal Reserve is now king of global interest rates and currency strengths. For all practical purposes, the Federal Reserve is the world's central bank.

But having the Fed as the world's central bank could become a problem. Large parts of the world already resent the global dominance of the U.S. dollar and the Federal Reserve. With the world as much as $20 trillion in dollar-denominated debt (half held by emerging markets such as China), foreign governments know that if the dollar rises further, the cost of that debt, and the price of risk, will jump throughout the world. So will the cost to the rest of the world of commodities—including oil—which are denominated in dollars. The great irony is that the strong dollar is hated for the reasons just stated, but a weak dollar is hated just as much. That might make foreign products and services exported to the United States more expensive relative to comparable U.S. domestic products, putting those nations at a trade disadvantage.

So the U.S. dollar, whether strong or weak, is the great global headache. Large parts of the world, including Russia, China, India, and parts of the European Union, are already working feverishly to try to undermine the dollar as the world's reserve currency. An effort to move trade financing away from the dollar has already begun. Russia's Vladimir Putin has been conducting a one-man campaign to challenge the status of the dollar. He is playing to a particularly receptive European and Chinese audience.

Putin's message is that there needs to be a substitute for the dollar, particularly because Washington's "abusive policies" are hurting the global economy. Does that sound like a line from some farfetched James Bond movie script with Vladimir Putin playing the role of chief villain, the new Dr. No? But in August 2014, the European Central Bank produced a report that essentially agreed with Putin. The report pointed out all the drawbacks to the world of the dollar's reserve currency role.

The Austrian central bank went one step further, bluntly arguing that the dollar's dominance is so damaging to the world economy that it overwhelms any good done by the American economy's contribution to global supply and demand. Translation: A growing part of the world wants a de-dollarized, more easily manipulated international financial system of less transparency (i.e., more secrets). Talk about a coming world of financial uncertainty, mistrust, mercantilism, and international financial dysfunction. A world without a transparent currency anchor in an era of unprecedented global debt is a recipe for financial chaos and reckless retaliation.

As a result, it is hardly surprising that many in the international system are desperately seeking an alternative currency. First there was Bitcoin, the pioneer in the alternative currency world. Bitcoin's key feature is that it involves no central authority. There are now hundreds of other virtual currencies under development throughout the world because of fear of the lack not just of global financial transparency but also of trust in a post-dollar world.

The world's economic report card is sobering. The total debt (government, corporate, and household) of the world's major centers of economic power—the United States, China, Japan, and the European Union—has soared to breathtaking levels. What's the significance of so much debt? Again, nobody knows. Not long ago, many experts were certain that the downside was a rising tide of global inflation. Instead, many economies, such as Europe, Japan, and now China, are experiencing just the opposite—disinflationary or even outright deflationary pressure. Prices have faced downward pressure accompanied by an epidemic of economic malaise. Both consumers and producers are holding back. And here's a really troubling development: As a stimulus, China's massive new debt appears already to be losing its punch. In the six years before the financial crisis, each yuan of new credit in China produced five yuan of economic output, reports *The Economist* magazine. In the six years after the crisis, each yuan of new credit has been responsible for only three yuan of new output.

In the world economy, it is increasingly the case that as debt grows, growth slows. If an actual broad-based global deflation rears its ugly head, the real cost of servicing that more than $180 trillion in global debt will skyrocket.

The United States should be quietly laying the groundwork for an international debt conference. Given the threat of rolling defaults, or disguised defaults, of the world's dollar-denominated debt alone, contingency plans are essential in preventing a full-blown global debt crisis. The debt must be addressed in the context of the formal relationship of the world's currencies as defined by a new accord, Plaza II.

And one more thing: Until now, the discussion has centered on the U.S. dollar's relationship to other currencies. But what about the dollar's relationship to its own purchasing power? There the story is striking, and the investor Warren Buffett tells it well: "The dollar dropped a staggering 86 percent in value between 1965, the year I joined my firm Berkshire Hathaway, and 2012. . . . It takes $7 today to buy what one dollar did at that time." All of which raises the question: Is paper money in today's economy what Buffett calls "a fool's game?"

The entire global economy faces serious headwinds in the decades ahead. Relatively speaking, the last half of the twentieth century produced the golden years, a marvelous period of economic expansion and global order. Average per-capita income tripled as the global economy expanded in size by 400 percent. That was then. Today, on paper, the economic future looks worrisome. Longer life expectancy and slower population growth have become the enemies of global long-term growth. From 1964 to 2000, productivity and employment both grew at brisk rates. The output of an average employee soared. By contrast, global employment in the first half of the twenty-first century is expected to grow at a tiny fraction of those rates, argues the McKinsey Global Institute. It will, that is, unless the world somehow quickly transitions to a more entrepreneurial, high-growth form of empowering Main Street Capitalism.

Do you think you know what is happening in the global financial system? Consider this: London has long been the headquarters and intermediary of global finance. Yet, in 2014, when London was still the supposed headquarters of global finance, more people passed through the Dubai airport than through London's Heathrow. A tectonic shift in financial and energy power was underway. The old centers of industrialized-world financial intermediation and power were increasingly being bypassed. Now, the June 2016 decision (Brexit) by the United Kingdom to leave the European Union will weaken London's and probably the West's global financial position further.

Although the old form of globalization may be fading, the globalization of information is not. The size of the world's cross-border bandwidth has grown 45 times larger than it was as late as 2005, according to the McKinsey Global Institute. Digital flows of information are expected to increase by an additional nine times over the next five years. These flows could have a larger effect on global growth than the traditional trade in goods. The implications for the future are beyond our current ability to comprehend and predict.

For the United States, the newest uncertainty from that globalization of cross-border bandwidth relates to whether America is prepared for foreign cyber attacks across multiple networks. Paul Stockton, the Assistant Secretary of Defense for Homeland Defense and Americas' Security Affairs during the Obama Administration, argues that America is particularly vulnerable "if a cyber-adversary takes down our power grid, our electric utility companies." Both telecommunications and financial transactions and other essential services would be compromised. The electric grid, the financial sector, and the telecommunications industry depend on each other. Warns Stockton: At this time, the government's response plans would likely fail in the event of a strike on all three. Better planning and coordination are desperately needed.

Since the 2008 financial crisis, the size of the central bank liquidity supplied to the world has been extraordinary. Yet ironically, and as amazing as it sounds, total global liquidity has been shrinking despite the central banks' best efforts. How can that be? For starters, measuring it can be tricky. One minute the liquidity of global financial markets can appear to be abundant. Financial markets look like a well-run engine, with pistons dripping with motor oil. But the next minute, the liquidity dries up. Almost overnight, the engine's pistons seize up. The engine sputters. And what is the reason for this? When all is said and done, liquidity is confidence. Liquidity dries up because economic decision makers lose confidence. Less confident, they become risk-averse and turn inward. They hold back. They become "chicken."

The next crisis of confidence for global liquidity could come over interest rates and the uncertainty of price levels as a result of not only (1) excess supply capacity in emerging markets but also (2) huge advancements in information technology that affect the marginal pricing of goods and services and create confusion about profit projections. The world's interest rates are at, or near, their lowest levels in history. If the world's central banks eventually succeed in raising interest rates back to their normal, historical levels, will another systemic liquidity crisis develop with ugly unintended consequences? Will the central bankers even be able to raise those mid- and long-term market rates if they try? Nobody knows. The developing world, led by China, has been exporting disinflationary pressure to the rest of the world at an aggressive pace. Who knows when or how this pressure will subside, given the timidity of the industrialized world's leadership?

Larry Summers, former adviser to both Presidents Clinton and Obama, argues that economies at risk of recession historically have required at least 300 basis points (3 percentage points) of short-term interest rate reduction to avoid a recession. U.S. interest rates today are nowhere near that level. Summers makes the important point that it is highly unlikely that the Federal Reserve will be able to lift interest rates back above the 3 percent level any time soon. Translation: In the event of a U.S. or global recession and/or financial crisis, the Federal Reserve might not be able to come to the rescue as it has done in the past. Currently, real interest rates are negative, but in every recession in recent memory, real interest rates were positive. The world financial system is sailing in uncharted waters.

Given all this international uncertainty, it is hardly surprising that average working families have sunk down into the psychological quicksand of economic malaise. People can sense that around the world, no one's in charge. In the United States, no global chess master has stepped forward with a game plan to protect America's interests. The world faces a nexus of troubling factors that includes the following: unprecedented

debt, record low interest rates, excess supply capacity, unstable commodity prices, exploding central bank balance sheets, declining growth,
a potentially rising U.S. dollar with a mountain of dollar-denominated
debt held throughout the world, rising cyber technological and financial
theft, a Middle East forever in the process of imploding, and worldwide
asset prices that may or may not reflect true value because monetary policymakers have had their thumbs pressing down on the scale. Polls consistently show people believe that their children's future is in jeopardy.
Average folk are worried. The global economic engine is sputtering in a
world with no one in control. People worldwide are in despair because
the international economic experts seem not to know the end game to
this troubling picture.

The question is whether the U.S. economy can decouple from this
madness. Can Washington policymakers under a new president come
together behind a bipartisan game plan of common-sense, high-octane
growth solutions? Can America be the exception with an explosion in
innovative daring? In our lifetimes, America has always been the global
economic leader. Dreaming big has forever been in the American DNA.
Only now there are troubling signs. Thirty-five years ago, new startup
companies a year old or less accounted for 15 percent of U.S. companies,
according to the Brookings Institution. Now, in today's "new normal"
economy of modest growth, that figure has been halved. If Main Street
Capitalism continues on the decline, America is in trouble. A nasty financial contagion (what financial traders call a "negative risk premium") will
continue to spread.

Some analysts theorize that if the global economic, financial, and
geopolitical environment becomes too threatening and corrupt, the
United States has the ability to fall back into near autarky (economic
self-sufficiency). As Ambrose Evans-Pritchard of London's *Daily Telegraph* argues, the United States can "retool its industries behind tariff
walls, as Britain did in the 1930s under Imperial Preference. In such circumstances, China would collapse. Statues of Mao would be toppled by
street riots."

The winner in this currency duel would be the country that first
experiences a serious breakout in inflation. But the collateral damage to

middle-class families from such a fight would be immense. There would be no winner.

To be sure, the U.S. economy has improved since the financial crisis and post-crisis recession period. But the larger global economic picture still looks ominous. And it is not clear that, without a return to a period of really robust economic growth, the United States can continue to insulate itself from the world's problems. It may be able to *economically* decouple to some degree. But it is not certain if the U.S. economy can *financially* decouple from today's troubled world. Nor can the United States easily decouple from a world of terrifying geopolitics and rising homegrown terrorism where you can't take your kids or grandkids to a movie theater without thinking, in the back of your mind, this might be the day your world comes to an end.

Therefore, growth is everything, but not simply so Americans can have a better life back home. High growth rates are essential to protecting the United States from a dangerous economic and financial world. In foreign policy, weakness is provocative. Economic weakness is too.

The one thing we know for certain in this frightening world is that America has a much better chance of protecting itself from the global chaos with a 3.2 percent long-term GDP growth rate than with a 1.4 percent growth rate. Unleashing an empowering Main Street Capitalism is the answer, but it is unclear whether the political will and imagination exist to reject a policy consensus in the capital that seems to worship large institutions, public and private, and where the entrepreneurial small business startup sector is seen at best almost as an afterthought and at worst as a disruptive nuisance.

As I left that Washington, D.C., luncheon with the Chinese ambassador, I began thinking about how the conventional wisdom about the world's future may be all wrong. In the conventional view, two superpowers, the United States and China, two wary competitors, will try to reach some accommodation as both attempt to run the world. After the luncheon and subsequent events occurring in Asia, I began to wonder instead whether China will be in a position to lead the world in anything.

For years the experts said China would quickly surpass the United States. They said that the American Century was over. They said that the world's new economic dynamism will move eastward. But the experts were wrong. With a world economy mired in debt and excess capacity, this will likely not be the Pacific Century and probably not the American Century either. The way things are going, it will be nobody's century. But the fact is that, with better policies and more compelling global leadership that encourages a bottom-up revolution in spirit and attitude, this could be Everybody's Century.

SEVEN

Americans Are Fighters

There was once a king who met the inventor of the game of chess. Impressed by this new game, the king rewarded the inventor with anything he wanted. Without hesitation, the humble inventor asked for merely one grain of rice for the first square on the chessboard. The only stipulation: for each subsequent square, the number of grains was to be doubled.

It seemed like a modest request: one grain for the first square, two for the second square, four for the third, eight for the fourth, and so forth. It wasn't. For the final square alone, square number 64, the king was required to provide the inventor with 9,233,372,036,854,775,808 grains of rice. The total number of grains of rice due for the entire chessboard: 18,446,744,073,709,551,615. That would equal 390 times the world's annual production of rice in 2012. The king went broke.

This is the exponential function. It means that change can come—for good or bad—in ever-larger sizes and at an ever-faster pace. Problems such as slow GDP growth, social unrest, underperforming educational systems, and runaway debt can build. At first the difficulties seem benign. Then they seem manageable, or at least easy to ignore. Then, they suddenly begin to spin out of control. Change keeps forever expanding, sometimes to the point at which we lose control over our destiny.

History shows the race to the bottom can be quick. It is easy to assume that civilizations never change. Yet civilizations change all the time, usually along a boom-bust cycle of about 200 to 250 years. That, incidentally, is about the time span the United States has formally existed.

But so, too, can the move to prosperity on the upside unfold at an ever-expanding pace. With the outbreak of the Industrial Revolution, something extraordinary happened: The size of the world economy tripled between 1820 and 1900. The economy grew more than 50 times faster than during the previous agricultural period. Today's cyber revolution could lead to a similar exponential expansion in prosperity.

Peter Thiel offers this useful reminder: "Every culture has a myth of decline from some golden age, and almost all peoples throughout history have been pessimists." And they have been wrong. Somehow each generation's inventors and visionaries plowed ahead anyway. Economically, things looked gloomy. The future dark. But innovation saved the day. Read that: People saved the day.

America is in a unique position to reinvent itself as a broad-based innovative powerhouse far beyond the tech sector. It all comes down to attitude. "German, Japanese, and French workers . . . don't storm out of their places of employment to start new companies, confident that sometime in the foreseeable future they will create something bigger, better, and more valuable than the company that employed them," argued the late Joel Kurtzman in his 2014 book, *Unleashing the Second American Century*. "Except for a very small handful of people, researchers in other countries don't mortgage their homes, max out their credit cards, and beg money from their friends to form companies dedicated to commercializing their ideas." The rise of America out of a global sea of malaise, as an exception to the rule, is hardly out of the question. The good news is that America's economic future is not baked in the cake.

Yet there is something troubling about the current direction of American society. In 2012, at Harvard, on an exam about the workings of the U.S. Congress, half the students cheated. Most of these elite, educationally privileged cheaters said they felt they had no choice. They were desperate, they said, because they knew so many others were cheating. In a class at Dartmouth, 24 percent of the class was found cheating. And the ironic subject of the class? Ethics. A similar situation occurred at the Malmstrom Air Force Base, Montana, on monthly tests. All of which begs the question: Have the American people not only lost their confidence but become so discouraged that they are losing their collective soul?

OK, I know. People always bemoan society's loss of values compared to the "good old days." The 1950s did produce the game show scandals, and the 1970s gave us Watergate. But there is something uniquely troubling about today's collapse in values. It is not clear we even know who we are as Americans anymore. We don't stick together. Something is terribly wrong when the people running the Veterans Administration openly tolerate a conspiracy of widespread indifference that has led to the deaths of some of those who have protected us from harm. Yet the system is slow to improve. America has entered a new era of lost identity. The United States is at risk of not only succumbing to a state of internal division but of becoming a country without a core.

This talk of values may sound corny. But there is a real question whether a discouraged America is up to the challenges of the twenty-first century. Do we collectively have the character to achieve big-time success? Can we reach down within ourselves and reignite that can-do optimism and boundless joy, the sense of collective national purpose that once defined our nation? As Yale's Jeffrey Garten suggests, leadership requires "the ability to come to grips with values and ethics." You have to "balance technological progress with a sense of humanity."

As a society, America needs to undergo a transformation, with all citizens bonding together behind a common purpose, a set of values, and a commitment to fair treatment for all. Unless, in the process of that transformation, Americans regain their sense of optimism, purpose, and national spirit, a dynamic culture of Main Street Capitalism will remain elusive. America will remain in retreat, its people mired in malaise and on the verge of giving up.

Think this is all an exaggeration? There are growing signs that many Americans are already giving up. The new president of the United States faces a huge task of persuasion—of convincing Americans to believe in themselves and their country. For years, the most popular course at Harvard was not a course on how to start a business, or on effective regulation, or on the secret to high levels of economic growth, or on how to be a leader. It was a psychology course on happiness. Students for years were being taught how to run away from ever-present bad news.

There is, of course, nothing wrong with the goal of happiness. What could be better than the boundless joy of discovering new things and achieving major breakthroughs? And, to be sure, Harvard students are inundated with offers from the tech sector. They're being told to follow former Harvard undergrad Mark Zuckerberg's Facebook lead. Drop out, start a business, or even start a business while still in school. But as an insurance policy, they are offered a course on successfully being happy.

The Internet may play a role in today's narcissistic detachment. Young people in particular have become absorbed so completely in the separate world of social media that many are losing their autonomy and sense of self. Significant parts of the millennial generation have decamped to a separate world where, unless they continually face short-term stimulus on a regular basis, a feeling of hopelessness sets in. They tune out any concern for the longer view of things.

Sherry Turkle of the Massachusetts Institute of Technology asks: "Are we moving to a culture where kids are incapable of conversation particularly when things are complicated? They Tweet, feel great, but actually having conversation with other people is not happening."

This trend is bad news for the process of governance. Governing entails compromise, which requires empathy. Empathy entails being part of a community (i.e., as Turkle says, talking to, and not merely texting, other people). But this communal sense that we are all in the same boat has faded.

In the United States, a large reason for grassroots disillusionment is that both political parties have ignored human capital. Both have worshiped at the shrine of Corporate Capitalism and its foot soldiers in the legal profession.

They deny this, but look at their campaign finance filings with the Federal Election Commission. In different ways and from different sources, both parties have been compromised.

For decades, both have fixated on the needs of physical and financial capital while doing too little to nurture human capital. Machines and credit have consistently won out over people. Companies have an extraordinarily rapid ability to expense capital for tax purposes. At the same time, not enough is being done to modernize the labor force. Or, to be more precise, to encourage the labor force to modernize itself. The U.S. workforce desperately needs to upgrade its information technology and Internet–related skills. One idea adopted by Britain is to provide federal grants so community colleges can offer adults free training in the use of these technologies on evenings and weekends. An even greater, more intense effort must be directed at the task of empowering human capital. The rise of online training by firms such as Udacity and the new, quickly expanding computer coding boot camps are a good start.

Corporate profits as a percentage share of the U.S. economy have increased. At the same time, wages as a share of the economy have dropped, although benefits and access to cheap credit for things such as car loans have increased substantially. The wage share of the economy for average working families is still disappointing, despite government benefits. Washington's political establishment should be concerned. True, as Mark Perry of the American Enterprise Institute notes, some of this income stagnation results from demographics—"the increase in the share of U.S. households with no earners, which is largely driven by the aging U.S. population and the increasing number of retired workers, and to a lesser extent by the increasing number and share of disabled workers [and also the] decline in the share of U.S. households with two or more earners since 1999." But demographics explains only part of the problem.

To partly confront the wage stagnation problem, the minimum wage should be raised. But notice how this issue is politically abused by both political parties. Some Republicans act as if even a modest minimum wage hike is an abominable poison pill that would kill the economy. Certainly a doubling of the minimum wage would increase joblessness. But a modest hike would be consistent with hikes going back to the late 1960s. In my first job in high school, I was initially paid the hourly minimum wage of only $1.00. But it was quickly raised to $1.30 an hour and then to $1.45 an hour. The economy didn't collapse. In a growing economy, a gradual rise in the minimum wage is to be expected.

By the same token, some Democrats act as if a minimum wage hike is the magic pill to reverse the flattening of workers' wages since the turn of the century. That assertion is a heartless deception. Fixing the stagnant wage problem is a lot more complicated. The essential requirement is more robust GDP growth rates driven by more business startups and an explosion in the commercial application of new innovation and increased productivity. The key requirement is a return to Main Street Capitalism.

The genius of the American experiment, the American Dream, has been the economy's amazing ability to produce social mobility. Thirty years ago, a person born into the bottom 25 percent of the income distribution ladder had a 25 percent chance of ending up in the top 25 percent. That is my life's story. I did. Today if you start out in the bottom 25 percent, you have only a 5 percent chance of arriving at the top. This is what happens in a 1–2 percent growth economy, and it is devastating for America's future. A lot of competitive talent, perhaps the next Henry Ford, Steve Jobs, Marie Curie, or Nancy Bray, is being denied access to the top.

A fully employed workforce enjoying rising wages requires a high rate of job mobility. In 1950, one in five Americans moved to begin a new job in a given year. Now it's around one in eight. Many Americans simply lack the self-confidence, faith in the future, and resources to search for jobs in a new city. How do we fix this situation?

Stanford economist Raj Chetty conducted a study that discovered the geographic differences in the opportunity for economic mobility. The economic environment of Salt Lake City, for example, provides a significantly higher level of opportunity to reach higher rungs on the economic ladder than, say, the economy in Atlanta. One solution: Help disadvantaged Americans, perhaps with financial vouchers, to move to areas with greater opportunity.

Washington policymakers must attack the problems of both social and job mobility with a fierce determination. Three decades ago, nearly half of Americans identified themselves as members of the middle class. Not anymore. Now half instead identify themselves as working class, according to the University of Chicago's General Social Survey.

The ultimate solution to middle- and lower-middle-class collapse comes down to three words: higher economic growth. Begin with America's inefficient tax system. Today's tax code is a metaphor for an economy without a level playing field where only those with connections truly prosper. Today's U.S. tax code is five times larger and ten times more complicated than it was *after* the code was simplified in 1986. The tax system breeds economic inefficiency. The special-interest tax lobbyists have run rampant, cutting their special deals. It is time for another bipartisan tax reform plan, this time for the twenty-first century.

I worked some on the 1986 tax reform effort. What was amazing was the level of bipartisan trust that brought about legislative success. Democratic Senator Bill Bradley (NJ) and Representatives Dick Gephardt (MO) and Dan Rostenkowski (IL) joined Republican Senators Robert Packwood (OR) and Robert Kasten (WI), Representative Jack Kemp (NY), and Reagan Treasury Secretary James Baker (his predecessor, Don Regan, had moved to the White House to serve as Ronald Reagan's chief of staff) in fashioning a compromise reform plan. One achievement of that legislative success is that it produced a paradigm shift. Bipartisan economic policy compromise contributed to a public perception of fairness and certainty in taxation. The message: The corrosive power of the special interests is on the run, attacked jointly by both political parties.

Second to France, America has the highest marginal statutory corporate tax rate in the world. Here's an example of how corporations maneuver under the current U.S. tax code to avoid paying that rate. Burger King, a U.S. company based in Miami and owned by a Brazilian private equity firm (with the help of Warren Buffett's financing), purchased a Canadian company, Tim Horton's, in 2014. Burger King would then be taxed at Canada's lower tax rates even though its headquarters would, for all practical purposes, remain in Miami.

Sounds absurd, which is why it is time to end this practice of corporate tax inversion in which corporations move offshore to avoid taxation. Corporate tax reform, including a lower, globally competitive tax rate and dramatic elimination of loopholes, would bring U.S. firms and jobs back home. Not all tax deductions are loopholes (example: deductions for interest and depreciation). But the only acceptable deductions should be those that allow for the accurate measurement of income. One idea is that in exchange for the U.S. corporate sector repatriating its nearly $2.5 trillion in offshore capital via some form of one-time tax holiday (putting that money to work creating employment opportunities in the United States), corporations would agree to purchase a specific amount of special bonds paying 1 percent interest. And the purpose of the bonds? To repair America's crumbling infrastructure.

This discussion by no means is intended to offer a comprehensive tax reform plan. It is more an effort at policy brainstorming. For example, why not adopt a bolder corporate tax reform approach? Eliminate the

U.S. corporate tax entirely. This is a tax that the corporate lobbyists regularly game anyway. After deductions, loopholes, and special concessions, very few U.S. corporations pay the top tax rate. In past years, General Electric has paid no corporate income tax at all.

Instead of a separate corporate tax rate, all business income and capital gains should be taxed at the same rate as individuals. The long-term capital gains' holding period would be long but no longer unlimited (in other words, after a specified number of years, the gains or losses on those investments would have to be marked to market—declared for tax purposes). Making all top tax rates—corporate, individual, and capital gains—the same would even out the tax burden between the billionaire stock market coupon clippers, trust-fund kids, and private equity firms that, under the current system, all have the benefit of paying the lower capital gains rate on paper financial gains. By contrast, young, small, and mid-sized enterprises that produce goods and services—and jobs—pay a much higher rate. Under this kind of tax reform, all sectors of the economy should face a lower tax rate offset by added revenues as a result of the closing of loopholes.

When I arrived on Capitol Hill in the mid-1970s, in economic circles everybody in both political parties talked about the high cost of capital that was making the U.S. economy globally uncompetitive. We were successful beyond our wildest dreams in fixing that problem. But the challenge today is not the high cost of capital. The United States, indeed the world, is awash in low-cost capital. The problem today is the disillusionment of human capital and the decline of the entrepreneurial risk-taking sector's confidence in future possibilities. That is why individual tax reform alone is not the answer. The abused corporate tax system should be eliminated with corporations and stock market investors paying their taxes at the same top (but now lower) rate of a more simplified individual tax code. Today's corporate tax gimmicks and loopholes should become a thing of history.

It is tough to tell average Americans that they need to become more daring and to start new business ventures given the current system of estate taxation. The estate tax exemption should be raised from its current $5.45 million level to $10 million. Those with the courage to start new firms should be able to have those firms more easily passed on to their children. But Washington must also eliminate all the tax scams used by the ultra-rich that, for them, have essentially made the estate tax optional.

But tax policy is not the only avenue to nurturing human capital. The first step in a new revolution of grassroots innovating is for average folk to invest in themselves through education. Americans with a college education have an unemployment rate half that of those with only a high school diploma. High-tech companies have thousands of high-paying unfilled jobs. Yet many in the American workforce lack the math and science skills to be able to meet the jobs' technical requirements.

Early on in President Obama's second term, Donald Trump gave a news interview in which he said of America: "The world is laughing at us. We're no longer a respected nation." Such hot rhetoric seemed excessive. "The guy's a clown," I thought to myself. Yet at precisely that moment, I received in the mail an update of a 2005 report entitled "Rising Above the Gathering Storm." The report summarized a global study that uncovered some cold, hard, and disturbing facts: America had dropped to forty-eighth in the world in the quality of its math and science education, sixth in the rankings of innovation-based competitiveness, and twenty-seventh among industrialized economies in the proportional number of university students receiving degrees in science and engineering. I thought to myself: "Maybe the world has reason to laugh." From what I can determine since that update was issued, there has been a lot of further talk from the policy world, but few positive results.

America's approach to public education is certainly confusing. From 1970 to 2005, the number of teachers per student doubled, according to a University of Washington study. Adjusted for inflation, spending per pupil doubled. Yet standardized test scores remained the same, way behind the scores of other countries. If the American people discovered some flaw that made all iPhones work inefficiently, with calls dropped ten times more than they are, there would be a national emergency. There would be frantic calls for immediate action. Not with education.

In a recent survey, three-quarters of America's twelfth graders couldn't list two costs to a nation of high joblessness, according to analysts Emily Ekins and Joy Pullmann. Half of young adults could not guess the effects of 2 percent inflation if their bank account provided only 1 percent interest. A third of today's college graduates cannot name a single right guaranteed by the First Amendment. At Texas Tech, a video of students on campus made by a political student group showed interview after interview of students unable to say for sure who won the American Civil War.

According to an April 2013 study by the U.S. Department of Education and the National Institute of Literacy, 32 million adult Americans actually can't read. That's about 10 percent of the total population. More than 21 percent of American adults read below a fifth-grade level. That unadulterated failure is catching up with us.

Not convinced? In June 2016, the National Federation of Independent Business estimated that 48 percent, or nearly half of small enterprises in America, have job openings but no qualified applicants. Yet before this educational crisis can subside, America needs a bottom-up transformation in attitude. It is hard to tell a kid to study hard and be disciplined if all he or she senses is that there is not much of a future in an economy of declining mobility.

Prior to his election in 2008, presidential candidate Barack Obama met for a private lunch in New York with about 20 top hedge fund billionaires. His remarks to the group were spellbinding. Many of the money managers attending became major financial supporters of his campaign. At one point in his remarks, the future president expressed frustration with the teachers' unions, saying they were becoming an impediment to educational reform. "I am within inches of going public on this issue of taking on the unions," candidate Obama said in anger at the private, off-the-record session. A lot of vital educational system reforms are being blocked, he insisted. There is not enough teacher accountability.

The hedge fund traders were ecstatic. But then nothing happened. Once in office, the president offered some reforms. But the promise of a really bold call to arms for educational reform—one that put a lot of the president's political capital at risk—withered away. The forces of the status quo won out at precisely the time the public school system should have been reinvented. That system needs to become more relevant to the twenty-first century, with an utter focus on the kind of critical thinking so key in the new entrepreneurial economy. Republicans complain about the need for better teacher quality—that is, about removing the incompetent bad apples. Democrats complain about inadequate teacher pay. Why not a grand bargain that resolves both complaints?

To improve the educational system, students above all need to start believing in their destiny. Reinvigorating human capital with improved educational performance entails a behavioral change. It requires a transition to a growth mindset that loves challenges and makes learning a lifetime obsession. It is the mindset that chucks today's conventional environment that flirts with victimhood and blind dependence. As Stanford University's Carol Dweck put it, it is an environment that rejects the notion that the highly successful are somehow "superheroes who were born different from us." Instead, they are just "ordinary people who made themselves extraordinary."

To achieve true educational success, ordinary kids need to begin to see themselves as potentially extraordinary and highly creative. In a coming world where 3D printing alone may lead to a new industrial revolution, the winners in an economy of continuous innovation will be the creators. It is not enough to stay one step ahead of a machine. The long-term winners will be those with a creative dimension who make themselves the indispensable change agent a machine can't replace.

That requires a continuous personal reinvention through investment in a lifetime of education. Given today's rapid technological change, there is no other choice. The conventional wisdom is that today's university math, science, and computer majors will always run the world economy. Maybe so, but perhaps not. Decades from now, most analytical functions in the workplace will be done by computers. What computers can't do, at least so far, is to think creatively. Could the future corporate CEOs and innovative titans of the world be those who in college majored in the classics? In other words, could the highly creative students come out on top? Could the chairman of General Motors someday soon be a fine arts major? Don't forget: One of the things that distinguished Steve Jobs from his competitors was his sense of aesthetics and appreciation for classic design.

America needs a giant educational rethink through the lens of how the culture is changing. How can American colleges and universities be the envy of the world, yet our K-12 public education be so weak?

Not everything about the U.S. educational system is bad. Recently a friend, a successful high-tech executive, had a high school student from

Vietnam staying in his home. One morning over breakfast, the host and his guest engaged in a conversation that was telling and reassuring. The Vietnamese student's achievement in math and science exams dwarfed that of his fellow American students. When my friend asked this student where, if he had a choice, he would prefer to live and be educated, he responded, "The United States!" My friend asked, "Why?" The response: "Your math and engineering studies are okay. Your advantage is that your system is also concerned with application. Back home, I can spit out a ton but have no idea what I'll do with any of it. We're engaged in rote memorization. You guys are always tinkering, always experimenting, always problem-solving. You have no fear of fucking up."

Americans have a history of taking risks. And, in an era of aging global demographics, students who happen to be immigrants will be a significant part of that risk-taking future. In the United States, people who are new to the country start businesses, and create jobs, at a rate more than twice as fast as those who are American-born. For these immigrants, perhaps the self-doubt hasn't yet sunk in. But there is also a realization that America is unique. In the U.S. innovative risk-taking sector, failure is expected. It is a necessary part of the economic growth dynamic.

Washington needs a comprehensive immigration plan. It should begin by including a green card with the diploma of every foreign graduate student in math, science, business, technology, and the classics. Washington currently sends those gifted individuals back home to places such as China, India, and South Korea, where they could eventually invent the next innovative breakthrough to the benefit of those countries. If ideas are now the world's most valuable commodity, the United States should be the safe haven and laboratory of stability for the Einsteins and Picassos of the world and their ideas.

By the same token, the process of immigration should not allow for the abuse of America's educational system. U.S. policymakers need to rejuvenate the community college system, making these institutions even more the center of basic technology skills training. America's community colleges are strapped for cash because state governments have dramatically cut back their financial support. To fill the gap, the schools enroll affluent foreign students, particularly the Chinese, with the promise that after a few years, and a mastery of the English language, they can transfer to four-year colleges. America's community colleges are fast becoming the finishing schools for the offspring of a rich foreign elite. That is a fool-hardy way to run a community college educational system designed as a stepping-stone for American kids. It is time Washington steps forward with assistance to reform these institutions.

It is also the time to engage in deep thinking about social decay. The president should organize a summit on the social breakdown of America, with political correctness checked at the door. It is hard to have robust growth with a workforce that's obsolete and in desperate need of main-tenance. But the challenge has transcended the mere changing of some tax laws, as important as that goal is. Transformations sometimes entail confronting the most politically sensitive behavioral problems of soci-ety, including rampant drug use, teen pregnancy, and racial discrimina-tion. The new administration needs to stop the political correctness and address the giant elephant in the room: In America today, the rate of out-of-wedlock births, while coming down some, is still way too high. One in five U.S. households are composed of women living either alone or with children. This is hardly a suggestion that marriage for these women will solve America's social decay. Better education and a more effective safety net can help all poor families, whether they are headed by women or men. Yet, like it or not, statistically those households with out-of-wedlock births have about a 40 percent chance of falling into poverty.

The ultimate question is this: In today's culture, does the American workforce even want to be modernized? Have self-doubt, discourage-ment, and pessimism set in too deep? Has America's social core deterio-rated to the point at which a vigorous recovery with dramatic grassroots innovating is even possible? Are Americans even capable of joining together behind a common purpose? My personal hunch is that they are. Americans are fighters at heart. They historically resist engagement at first, but eventually do battle no holds barred. All they need to start is smart, inspiring leadership.

Rising worldwide income inequality contributes to the general mal-aise. All over the world there is a growing gap between those who have capital and those who don't. In the United States, where consumption since the 2008 financial crisis has increasingly been the by-product of the gains from a stock market driven by central bank liquidity, it is difficult to deny the income inequality phenomenon. Most American families don't own large stock portfolios outside a retirement plan (private pensions, including middle-class pensions, comprise almost 60 percent of U.S. equity capital).

The Washington establishment lacks much imagination on the income inequality issue. Either policymakers deny the problem, or they propose political solutions that sound comforting but are based on little more than a utopian dream. Some argue, for example, for a return to a top marginal individual tax rate of 90 percent, the rate that existed for several decades during and after World War II (which almost no one paid because of tax loopholes and the extraordinarily high threshold of income necessary to reach the top tax bracket). Does anyone believe any taxpayer today would pay their taxes at that marginal rate? In other words, would your doctor, dentist, lawyer, dry cleaner, or business partner willingly work additional hours to give 90 percent of the additional income to the government? Of course not. The result would be crony capitalism on steroids. Every affluent taxpayer would come to Congress, campaign cash in hand, looking for their special tax exemption. And they'd be received on Capitol Hill with open arms by both political parties. Some taxpayers would increase their leisure time. The ultra-rich would move offshore.

In the early 1960s, when the official top marginal income tax rate on individuals was 91 percent, the average tax rate actually paid by the top tenth of 1 percent of income earners was only between 26.9 and 29.5 percent. But as strange as it sounds, that was roughly the same percentage, 23.7 to 29.5 percent, paid by the same top group during the latter Reagan years after the Tax Reform Act of 1986, when the official top marginal tax rate was roughly a third as high, 28 percent, according to a 2007 study by economists Thomas Piketty and Emmanuel Saez. Translation: Top income earners seem quite willing to give 40 percent of their income to the government. But above that rate, they look for tax shelters. And both political parties stand ready to provide them.

In 2012, French President François Hollande implemented a massive tax increase on high-income earners. Hordes of France's top business and creative talent moved offshore, often to London. Today Hollande is the least popular political figure in France because the public recognized stupidity when they saw it in action. This is not a partisan issue. Alan Blinder, the former Clinton economic adviser and vice chairman of the Federal Reserve, had it right: "The gap between top and bottom is clear. Not so clear is whether shaving the top is the best way to help the bottom."

Except for the ideologically extreme, most Americans don't demand equal income for all. Few call for the logical conclusion to a Bernie Sanders–style system where, no matter how hard you try or don't try, everyone earns the same. The talented, hard-working, politically progressive Hollywood titan Harvey Weinstein has produced films that have amassed over 200 Academy Award nominations. Should he be forced to give 90 percent of those nominations to other less successful producers? Would the upstart producer whose films have yet to collect any nominations be right to insist that all producers receive equal acclamation? The televised Academy Awards ceremony would go on for days.

As former Clinton and Obama economic adviser Larry Summers has said, "America succeeds by raising everybody up. It doesn't succeed by tearing anybody down." What Americans demand, however, is equal opportunity to achieve upward mobility. That mobility is disappearing because the economic pie is shrinking, and Washington has succumbed to a subtle but poisonous cronyism where corporate capitalist insiders get all the breaks. In the end, it all comes down to this: Higher economic growth is essential. As progressive economist Robert Shapiro notes, "Our analysis shows that our problems with incomes are neither long-term nor an after-effect of the 2008–2009 financial upheaval. Nor are they driven by economic impediments such as race, gender, ethnicity or education." They are driven to a large extent by a lack of robust, broad-based economic growth.

I believe that monetary policy solutions to deal with the 2008 financial crisis affected the distribution of income. True, the low interest rate/high liquidity policy produced lower mortgage interest rates for working- and middle-class families. Car loan financing and consumer credit became less expensive. But there is no denying that those with major stockholdings received the winning lottery ticket. The long-term implications for capitalism itself as a result of this windfall are troubling. To a significant degree, the Federal Reserve is responsible for American working-class anger and the belief that the economic system is "rigged." The Fed helped create the Bernie Sanders/Donald Trump effect.

One policy response would be a proposal that would essentially make, from here on, every American at birth a stockholding capitalist. When a child is born, set up a tax-free stock investment account with, say, an $8,000 low-interest federal government loan as seed capital to be paid back in 60 years, at a modest interest rate, with the interest balloon payment due at the end of the loan period. Families would choose from a list of diversified global investment options managed by top professionals. The cost to the federal government: negligible because the transaction would be a loan, not an expenditure. If the big Wall Street banks can receive extremely low interest rate loans, why not the future population of America? The British experimented with such a program. Even for poor families, every thousand dollars at birth was matched by $2,000 to $3,000 in private funds from family and friends celebrating the birth of the child.

Here's the point: An $8,000 balanced global investment account (with a series of prudent, balanced investment options) established at birth would, by age 60, rise to an amount approaching a million dollars in value. That's the miracle of compound interest. Add in the compounding effect over many decades of gifts to the child at birth, and the total could far exceed a million dollars. Over time, the child would develop a stake in the capitalist system. All of society would gradually develop skin in the game, a piece of the action. Over a lifetime, the child, as he or she grows up, should be allowed to add to that account and, perhaps, use some of the profit to pay for education.

Like the affluent, everyone should have a vehicle to invest in the financial market wave, both its ups and downs. Everyone potentially could become a millionaire. Or not. Everyone should have access to the ladder of social mobility, to be a capital owner, not just a wage earner. In a global economy in which coming digitalization could produce huge long-term productivity gains in both the industrialized world's technology sector and in emerging markets, average American families need some way to tap into that global wealth generation just as the affluent do. They just need some help getting started. Stock market investment cannot just be the domain of the highly affluent, pension funds, and other institutional investors. Let everyone have a chance to ride the financial wave in a new environment of Main Street Capitalism. If decades from now, new technologies, as some analysts expect, produce hordes of people with nothing to do, it is vital that these future generations have some means of benefiting from new wealth produced throughout global markets.

This kind of role for government is hardly unprecedented. The Homestead Act of 1862, which gave out public land grants at little or no cost, may be the most important piece of economic legislation in American history. Today, spreading capital ownership through vehicles such as community investment trusts and employee stock ownership plans could go a long way toward saving capitalism itself.

Yet when it comes to understanding this need to dramatically widen the base of capital ownership in America, too many conservative Republicans have blinders on. I know this from firsthand experience. In my 2008 book *The World Is Curved*, I introduced the British idea of giving every child an investment account and interest-free loan at birth. I also proposed to eliminate entirely the tax on the investments of low- and middle-income Americans. Some conservatives were not happy.

Years later, in January 2013, just after the Romney-Ryan ticket lost to President Obama in the 2012 presidential race, I had dinner with my friend Paul Ryan, the GOP vice presidential nominee who was back serving in Congress. It was the evening of the President's State of the Union address and, before Paul ran over to the House floor to hear the President speak, we spent several hours at the nearby Capitol Hill Club over dinner talking about politics, the economy, and the future. Toward the end of the dinner, the future Speaker of the House, with a wry smile, mentioned that after reading my book years before, some of his more conservative House colleagues grew suspicious about my suggestions of ways to expand the capital ownership base (I also called for the end of preferential tax treatment for carried interest—that is, eliminating the lucrative tax shelter used by private equity firms). "They asked me if you were some kind of closet liberal," Ryan said with a smile, clearly amused at the situation: "I told them to calm down—that you were just following in the tradition of our mentor, Jack Kemp. As a country, we must move forward but we can't afford to leave anyone behind." The conversation convinced me that the Republican Party (not to mention the political establishment in Washington in general) has no future unless it can develop policies that create an economy for everyone.

Washington's most immediate challenge is to help create the broadest possible distribution of investment. Let me set the table: The top 1 percent of U.S. income earners are flush with cash and want to invest in the future. The future is represented by the millennials, who in many cases are overloaded with student loans and lack both the courage and financing to start new firms. As a result, in America trillions of dollars of excess cash are sitting idle on the sidelines that could be deployed to create more robust economic growth and new job opportunities. The question is how to encourage a greater shift of financial resources dramatically from the 1 percenters to the millennials. Government policymakers should think creatively about this challenge.

Here's a possible approach, beginning with this observation by New York financial strategist Joseph Sprung. Every investor in the world, argues Sprung, is looking for the next Facebook. They are desperate to find the next Mark Zuckerberg—the person with the big idea who just graduated from college (or, as in Zuckerberg's case, was still in school) and could someday make it mega-big. In a unique twist on crowd funding, why not set up a system that facilitates the investment in America's future innovators in a more orderly way? Affluent investors can invest, say, up to $250,000 per person in millennials with compelling investment ideas who want to start new firms. In exchange, the investor would receive a small percentage of the millennials' income (and/or net worth) for life (the process would be monitored by some federal agency).

Most of these investments in the millennials will not pay off big. Most will be complete flops because most startups fail. Most millennials will not become the next Mark Zuckerberg. But over time, some will. And that small percentage of lifetime earnings for affluent investors makes the whole program financially worth the effort. Imagine putting up $250,000 in seed capital investment for, say, 5 percent of Mark Zuckerberg's net worth, which as of January 1, 2016, measured at more than $45 billion. The return of $2.25 billion would be mind-boggling.

The obvious criticism of this plan: The target of such investment could be unfairly restricted to graduates only of the elite schools such as Stanford, Yale, Harvard, and MIT. But that would not likely be the case. Look at the list of U.S. entrepreneurial success stories. A lot of them attended schools further down the annual ranking by *U.S. News & World Report*, such as the University of Texas at Austin (Michael Dell, who dropped out), the University of Maryland (where Google's Sergey Brin received his bachelor's degree), and the University of San Francisco (which Intel CEO Paul Otellini attended). Oracle CEO Larry Ellison spent two years at the University of Illinois at Urbana-Champaign and then did a brief stint at the University of Chicago before dropping out. The key point: To be successful, the investment net would have to be spread far and wide, paying careful attention to women who, again, are starting businesses at up to twice the rate of men. But how do investors find these talented individuals?

Gallup CEO James Clifton has developed a process to identify global entrepreneurial talent based on an evaluation of an individual candidate's strengths. Gallup's goal is to "transform the world with strengths science and strengths coaching." Just as society identifies professional athletes and musicians at an early age, and then encourages their success, Gallup is testing the feasibility of a global strengths-based organization to identify the next generation's entrepreneurial superstars.

Both of these proposals, from Sprung and Gallup, no doubt entail complications and challenges. The point here is to begin the brainstorming. In the twenty-first century, public policy discussions sadly have become less honest attempts at exploring new ideas and instead something a lot more trivial. In today's climate of hyper-politics, the overriding goal too often is to develop a narrative about a problem with a suggested, but completely unrealistic, solution that nonetheless is useful as a political weapon. French economist and government adviser Thomas Piketty, whose explosive book *Capital in the Twenty-First Century* catapulted him to fame in 2014, is the master at this political game.

To his credit, Piketty makes the effective point that if the rate of return on capital permanently stays above the economy's growth rate, income inequality will become an even worse problem for industrialized economies.

What is not clear is whether Piketty's forecast—that for the next 50 years the rates of return on capital will stay far above growth rates—is credible. Piketty is a highly accomplished professional economist, but why should we believe that his 50-year forecast is better than all the other failed one- or two-year forecasts of other economic experts that Nobel Prize–winning economist Joseph Stiglitz says are wrong 60–70 percent of the time? Venture capital investor Marc Andreessen offers a harsh assessment: "The funny thing about Piketty is that he has a lot more faith in returns on invested capital than any professional investor I've ever met. . . . He assumes it's really easy to put money in the market for 40 years or 80 years or 100 years and have it compound at these amazing rates. He never explains how that's supposed to happen." In essence, Piketty implies the world is about to experience a long-term period of explosive productivity growth but never explains how that growth will come about.

Piketty's ultimate solution is that the world should politically integrate and enact a global tax on wealth concentration, with annual taxation on stock and bond market investment and other assets. There are two words to describe this proposal: utopian fantasy.

Look at the dismal European experience with political integration so far, especially in light of the June 2016 Brexit vote. Officials have found establishing a desperately needed fiscal and banking union virtually impossible to accomplish. And remember, the Eurozone is comprised of countries with leaders fiercely determined to seek political cohesion. Why? Their countries have been at war with each other twice in the last hundred years. They desperately want political union, yet it remains as elusive as ever. Now even the Eurozone monetary union itself appears to be vulnerable. Yet in the narrative of Thomas Piketty, establishing a global political union—a United States of the World—is an easy affair. It's not.

Political leaders are attracted to the utopian narrative because they are unwilling to do the hard work of reform. Change is difficult. So too is bipartisan compromise. You make enemies. You lose popularity. It's a lot easier to spin off demagogic rhetoric. Change requires the courage to compromise, and sadly we have gotten soft. We'd love some painless, partisan magic pill to fix things, but we're not likely to find one. We've got to roll up our sleeves and get to work.

In America, our leaders have to stop the nonsense and unite the country behind a Main Street Capitalism agenda. If we are lucky, that agenda will help create a series of paradigm shifts that restore a national sense of confidence in the future. The task of economic reinvention and revival is doable. In the early 1940s, the American people faced more than economic malaise; the very future of Western civilization was at stake. America's so-called Greatest Generation went to war. But back home they rolled up their sleeves and took the reins of leadership in peacetime as well. Examine their track record after the war. The environment established was impressive. A person didn't just start a company. He or she was part of a larger national effort—a larger purpose—to achieve security through economic strength.

They made mistakes. That generation should have passed civil rights legislation a lot earlier than it did. But the nation was unified despite its differences. In most cases, the political parties worked together. Attitude mattered. Americans sensed they were exceptional because their role, both at home and abroad, had purpose. Through the sheer force of their optimism and courage, they overcame a national debt, like ours today, amounting to more than 100 percent of GDP. Growth was everything.

There was also a sense of national cohesion that is probably impossible to duplicate short of America adopting a policy of national service for young people, as is the practice in many other countries, including Israel and, until recently, Germany. For one year after either high school or college graduation, students fulfill a national service requirement in the military, the public school system, or some other community support effort before they drift off into our increasingly segmented society. A U.S. national service requirement would almost surely decrease society's fragmentation and would likely begin a process of creating new social cohesion: We're all in this together.

America's task is now clear: to produce the kind of economic and psychological transformation that will achieve average annual growth rates of 3 percent or more. That's the difference between America thriving despite its debt and collapsing under the weight of its debt. The United States can either be the world's anchor of stability, bastion of economic verve, and beacon of hope, or we can reside permanently in the land of the mediocre where the country continues to tear itself apart. The time is now. The notion that decline is inevitable is a myth. Americans are fighters. They are also dreamers and discoverers. But the window for the new president to act is open only very briefly. Change, both good and bad, too often unfolds exponentially, sometimes with brute force. Sometimes our comfortable sense of stability, the view that time is on our side, proves to be a dangerous illusion. That's why the time to act is now.

EIGHT

A Nation of Dreamers and Discoverers

In the nineteenth century, Britain was the world's dominant economic power. Like the United States today, it found itself with a problematic economy, including rapidly declining tax revenues. Britain's leaders responded with policies that sound familiar: (1) infrastructure spending (new schools, hospitals, sewers, and a new police force) combined with (2) encouragement of new innovation (railroads) and (3) an attack against crony capitalism (removal of the protectionist Corn Laws of the 1840s) to create a level playing field.

British journalists John Micklethwait and Adrian Wooldridge write, "Between 1815 and 1870, British Liberals replaced a government based on patronage, sweeping aside the special privileges for the East India Company, West Indian sugar makers and British landowners" that were holding the economy back. Policymakers attacked Corporate Capitalism, simplified and better targeted government, and reinvented the state, introducing competitive exams for civil servants. Most importantly, Britain's leaders "became allies of the new economic forces that were reshaping Britain." To create a level playing field, they enacted legal reforms that included allowing anybody to form a limited liability company. The reforms worked.

Today there is no reason the American people cannot join together behind a similar plan to reboot the U.S. economy. The place to start is to develop a better story. At the heart of any successful economy is a compelling narrative that captures the imagination. As Nobel Prize–winning economist Robert Shiller shrewdly observed: "Popular, emotionally relevant narratives sometimes inspire us to go out and spend, start businesses, build new factories and office buildings, and hire new employees; at other times, they put fear in our hearts and impel us to sit tight, save our resources, curtail spending, and reduce risk. They either stimulate our 'animal spirits' or muffle them."

Narratives are at the center of a successful economy. They offer signposts to guide the economic traveler. They can affect human behavior. Narratives also reflect the zeitgeist. They can be positive, or they can lead to a fearful hunkering down, leaving people afraid of embracing new opportunities. One aspect of the role of narrative may be neurological. We may be hardwired to think the next decade will always be just like the last decade. Particularly in Washington, D.C., innovation is too often thought about only in terms of how it will hurt us economically, as opposed to how innovation could be transformational, leading to greater prosperity and an improvement in the quality of life. So narrative is at the center of a successful economy, but narrative bias can also be a significant factor leading to economic failure.

The great Indian reformer Mahatma Gandhi understood the role of thoughts and language in influencing human behavior. Gandhi warned the Indian people: "Keep thoughts positive. Thoughts make words, words make behaviors, behaviors make habits, habits make values, values make destiny."

America historically has had a series of impressive economic narratives. In 1945, for example, a narrative of optimism prevailed. Victorious veterans returning home from World War II would make the United States into a global economic power backed by a dramatically expanding middle class with rising incomes. People believed in the story. Everybody had skin in the game. Congress enacted the GI Bill to pay for veterans' educational expenses. An American economic juggernaut surged.

In the early 1980s, after Federal Reserve Chairman Paul Volcker broke the back of the 1970s double-digit inflation and interest rates, the next narrative was clear: With the stagflation dragon slain, a new era of rising stock markets and prosperity was inevitable, powered by fiscal reforms that ended tax-bracket creep for middle-class families and indexed the tax code against future inflation.

Then came the 1990s. The world economy benefited from the collapse of the Berlin Wall and the end of the Cold War. The new American economic narrative: A "peace dividend" of reduced defense spending would help balance budgets and allow government to concentrate less on defense and more on domestic economic growth propelled by the globalization of markets. A sense of policy predictability reassured markets.

In the early 2000s, however, the next narrative proved faulty. A real estate boom was supposed to be the economic profession's great achievement. The middle class, the narrative maintained, was dramatically expanding. Home ownership and home prices would continue upward. Booming stock markets and prosperity would never end. What housing bubble?

Slowly, partisan stalemate set in. Little by little serious problems went unresolved. Yet the financial system thrived. Then, in 2008, the party ended in crisis. The secondary mortgage market began to collapse. Many average working families lost their homes. Borrowing went from an easy affair to a tortuous process with a risk-averse banking system ever ready to foreclose. Meanwhile, the children of these fiscally challenged homeowners faced college student loans they often couldn't pay back. And the military disappointments in Iraq and Afghanistan, not to mention the emergence of worldwide terrorism, added to the sense of disillusionment.

What is the narrative today that is influencing economic decision-making? Sadly, the story line each night on the evening news is (1) no one's running a massively debt-ridden world of declining growth rates and rising geopolitical risk; (2) the U.S. economy could be hit by contagion from this global uncertainty; (3) monetary stimulus may have kept us out of depression but has been powerless to raise income across the board in any sustained, dramatic way; (4) in economic policy, macroeconomics has failed; the economy's entrepreneurial dreamers and discoverers are, with some exceptions, in hibernation; (5) in Washington, D.C., Corporate Capitalism reigns supreme; and (6) in the field of economics, even America's best economic minds have joined in a partisan feud of policy stalemate. There is little talk of compromise as the big thinkers, brimming with hubris, engage in the intellectual equivalent of cream-pie throwing during a period of perhaps the greatest economic, financial, and geopolitical uncertainty in history.

And, to make matters worse, the final chapter of America's sad narrative is that three-quarters of the nation's bank-held investment capital has been centralized in the coffers of a small group of giant, relatively risk-averse zombie American banks now highly vulnerable to foreign government–sponsored cyber attacks. It is also difficult not to look at these giant banks and see deep similarities to the quasi-government guaranteed lending institutions Fannie Mae and Freddie Mac before the financial crisis. Our only hope is that the U.S. technology sector eventually promotes the kind of effective technologies in finance that circumvent the zombie banks.

Here's more of the narrative: Since 2000, while the U.S. economy has wallowed increasingly in partisan stalemate, the global monetary system has become a high-risk casino. The value of every global asset (stocks, bonds, and real estate) is in doubt because of serious questions about the underlying strength of the economy to support those asset valuations being propped up by an ocean of central bank liquidity.

For central bankers, identifying the value of assets has become a risky voyage into the land of the unknown. Former New York Federal Reserve official Terry Checki calls this the "leaps and bounds rule." When financial market expansion jumps ahead of real economic activity, the result is always trouble. As former Clinton Treasury official Roger Altman has put it, financial panics are always waiting just outside the door "because the velocity of global money flows increases each year, driven by the pressure for investment returns." In the United States, the difference today versus a decade or so ago is that those stock market investment returns, pumped up by a generously easy monetary policy, have become the economy's primary engine for consumption and prosperity. That is not a healthy long-term economic situation.

Today's narrative is that the world economy is dangerously out of balance. It is the victim of what investment manager and Pulitzer Prize–winning author Liaquat Ahamed calls "a fundamental design flaw that makes it unstable." While 75 percent of the world (including China, Japan, and Europe) has been dangerously dependent on exports for growth at a time of plummeting trade, rising protectionism, and declining consumption because of rapidly aging demographics, the United States has its own problem: It depends too much on the stock market for growth. The more that foreign capital flows into the U.S. economy in a flight to safety from a threatening world, the more U.S. interest rates fall (or fail to rise) even with a pickup in the U.S. economy. What happens then? U.S. financial risk is in danger of becoming underpriced, just as it was in the period before September 2008. Main Street Capitalism of widespread business startups is swept aside as central bank–driven stock market returns become the dominant engine for growth, always dependent on the central bank's liquidity. But is this any way to run an economy?

As the analyst Criton Zoakos observes about this situation, "This may be the most volatile, unpredictable, and potentially explosive period since the end of the Second World War." He's talking about the potential for a new era of financial panics. History shows that prior to World War II, panics were a fact of life. The relatively stable financial system of the postwar era has been an historical anomaly. As far back as the year 1340, England defaulted on its war debt, causing an enormous financial crisis. Then, beginning in the 1770s, financial panics came at least once a decade, sometimes every few years.

Is the world returning to an era of regular financial panics? It is difficult to say. Central bankers have a poor track record evaluating financial asset prices to determine whether they are overvalued, undervalued, or just right.

What does appear certain is that today's policy of central bank bond buying to pump up the stock market within a climate of slow GDP growth risks a rising tide of income inequality and political resentment that could threaten the foundational pillars of capitalism itself. Policy experts think they can anticipate political risk. They never do. Look at how they blew the call on the Brexit vote in June 2016. British Labor Party voters in northern England shocked the elites and proved to be the tipping point for Britain's decision to leave the European Union. Back in the United States, the real incomes of average working families have remained relatively lackluster since the turn of the century. Average folk are quietly angry. Yet our policymakers remain in stalemate. The establishment still seems unsure what this ruckus is all about.

America's new narrative should begin with the fact that the United States has a lot of impressive building blocks to construct a much more powerful and equitable economy. For starters, America is in an economically unique position. Its dependence on exports in a world of currency warfare and declining trade is relatively small, around 12 percent of GDP. By contrast, many countries have economies much more dependent on exports, among the major economies from 26 percent to 44 percent of GDP. When global trade collapsed after the 2008 financial crisis, these economies took the largest hit. America enjoys a more balanced economy, with a historically powerful consumer base, a historically cutting-edge entrepreneurial culture that has served as the global laboratory for technological innovation, and a still-expanding workforce. The rest of the world would love to have America's building blocks with which to construct a successful economic future.

The secular stagnation theory of slow growth baked in the cake, moreover, assumes the U.S. economy is a closed system. The theory ignores the fact that Americans have the ability to invest abroad and, if Washington modernizes its immigration policies, to attract the best of the world's entrepreneurial talent for more business startups in America. The United States has a history of attracting some of the world's most talented innovators. With a reformed global foreign exchange system that ends today's rampant currency manipulation, and a raft of Main Street Capitalism's business startups to maintain domestic employment at the highest levels, America's ability to resume its leadership role as a major global producer of goods and services and technological leader may be unlimited.

The building blocks are still in place for a more vibrant American economy. But policymakers must first produce a compelling game plan that recognizes the role not just of financial capital but of people to an economy's success.

Am I being too optimistic? Consider this: The most surprising development since the 2008 financial crisis has been the unexpected hunger by foreign investors and central banks for, of all things, U.S. assets. Yes, as strange as it sounds, since the financial crisis foreigners have been big buyers of everything American. And it's not just rich Chinese and Russian investors who poured investment capital into safe U.S. government bonds and real estate to escape potential political uncertainty back home. German companies have heavily invested in the United States, buying up mid-sized companies. Foreign investors yearn for safety, but also sense something else—that America may be poised for extraordinary economic achievement.

Here are the numbers: Since 2008, foreigners have accumulated roughly $23 trillion of U.S. financial assets (not counting financial derivatives) in the form of Treasury securities, corporate stocks and bonds, and foreign direct investment, according to the Federal Reserve. By comparison, in the 20 years prior to 2008, foreigners accumulated less than $14 trillion in U.S. financial assets. Incredibly, U.S. asset purchases today by foreigners are happening at more than double the rate that occurred during the pre–financial crisis era.

How could this be? This strange and surprising buy-American infatuation? The story was not supposed to unfold this way. After all, after the 2008 crisis, one thing seemed certain: The United States was the international goat. The U.S. financial system was at the center of the crisis. The so-called Washington Consensus of privatization, deregulation, free trade, and liberalized financial markets was supposedly forever discredited. The United States would be forced to take a backseat in global economic policy. True, the Federal Reserve's quantitative easing policies attracted foreign capital. When the Fed phased out that bond-buying program, the foreigners kept buying all things American anyway.

The reason for these surprising capital inflows may be that as uncertain as things look in the United States, the rest of the world looks worse. In other words, America has been the winner of the Least Ugly Person Beauty Pageant. But global investors also know the following:

> FIRST, the world economy is quickly undergoing a deglobalization process. An ugly re-regionalization of global trade and investment is unfolding. A lot of Asian economic and financial flows are staying in Asia, European flows within Europe, and the same within the Americas—a process with unknown economic consequences. Protectionism is also on the rise, according to the World Trade Organization. The global economic order is breaking down.

> SECOND, it is clear that the United States is different from all the other major global economies. It may be the best equipped to

withstand this decline in global trade and to succeed in this new re-regionalized world economy of rapid technological change. Despite enormous problems, the U.S. economy may be the most flexible, and thus most capable of succeeding, of the world's economies. This will be particularly true if technological break-throughs continue to force a revolution in the financial sector, making it more conducive to funding entrepreneurial risk.

THIRD, Americans for the most part are still committed to defending the integrity of the U.S. Constitution and the rule of law. It is difficult to overestimate the degree to which foreign investors value the fact that when you own something in America, some new political order cannot come along and arbitrarily change the terms of ownership. That's why the U.S. economy has been the world's investment magnet.

The United States has one other advantage. Americans have an extraordinary ability for self-criticism and self-correction. Popular Hollywood movies are often a bottom-up reflection of America's unique penchant for self-criticism. Consider the extraordinarily honest inward look inherent in six popular American films from the last several years. These movies and their popularity reflect a public that has finally figured out the establishment's swindle and is desperate for anyone to tell them the truth. They dramatize the reasons for the American people's anger.

The Big Short lays down a marker about Wall Street greed and corruption. More importantly, the film inadvertently reveals that no one to date has offered any guarantee that another financial crisis won't happen again. It reflects the fact that the American people are still deeply troubled by the corruption of the financial establishment.

Concussion, starring Will Smith, is about big-time corporate corruption, in this case in the National Football League. Players are treated like commodities, their brains smashed and permanently damaged. Instead of mobilizing solutions, the NFL engages in a widespread cover-up. The popularity of the movie demonstrates the fact that the American people are incensed by the corruption of the corporate establishment and yearn for the level playing field of a more Main Street form of capitalism.

Spotlight tells the true story of the widespread molestation of children by the Catholic Church. The movie's popularity is illustrative of the fact that the American people are appalled at the corruption of the religious establishment.

Sicario is about drug trafficking by the Mexican cartels. The movie makes clear that the U.S. federal agencies responsible for policing drug trafficking have been compromised. The film's popularity reflects Americans' horror at the corruption and incompetence of the federal government.

The blockbuster *American Sniper* is a fact-based movie about the life of U.S. Navy SEAL Christopher Kyle. Played by Bradley Cooper, Kyle is a heroic figure engaged in mindless killing, and he bears the brutal psychological cost of that violence.

American Sniper is a profoundly antiwar movie and has been extremely popular. With its overwhelming endorsement of the film, what the public seems to be asking is, how high a price are we willing to pay as Americans to maintain our empire? How many military dollars are we willing to spend with no clear direction and no victories? The popularity of the movie demonstrates the American people's concerns about whether the United States can survive economically while trying to police the world without any clear strategic purpose. To be sure, the public is not anti-defense. In the age of ISIS, Americans want more defense. But they want smarter defense strategies than in the past that reflect a shrewder understanding of the complicated threats in a dangerous world and of the potential and limitations of military power.

Finally, the movie *Joy* celebrates bottom-up entrepreneurial dreaming. The central character, Joy Mangano, played by Academy Award winner Jennifer Lawrence, follows her lifelong ambition to invent her way (through the self-wringing Miracle Mop) to a better life. The movie is an unexpected Hollywood celebration of Main Street Capitalism, the Great Equalizer.

The six movies show that important debates are underway throughout American society about the country's future direction. That is an extraordinarily positive development, a demonstration of the public's anger but also its willingness to consider and accept change. Our new president must tap into this public anger and desperation for new solutions.

By contrast, many other parts of the world lack the ability to engage in such aggressive negative self-reflection. Imagine France publicly cataloguing all its foul-ups the way America does. For decades, for example, French policymakers have known of the political and economic isolation and alienation of its young male Muslim population. During business trips to Paris as far back as the mid-1980s, in my meetings French officials would often privately comment that one out of eight males aged 18 to 28 living in greater Paris were Muslim. But they might as well have been living in Damascus. They had not been assimilated into French society. Yet no one in the French political system did much to correct the situation. The terrorist killings in 2015 in Paris and the 2016 truck massacre in Nice were tragic but, for me, were not surprising.

Perhaps America has a penchant for negative self-reflection because its society has the advantage of not being one "tribe" but a giant melting pot of people from different cultural backgrounds. For example, in New York City, some 800 languages are spoken. Without continual change based on periodic critical self-reflection, the American "experiment" would have failed long ago. The melting pot would have cracked into pieces.

The American economic system can be rebooted. By contrast, Europe may be in a different situation. It faces an uncertain economic future but surprisingly little apparent flexibility for change. The European economy is tied in a knot of governmental and corporate lethargy. Massive sovereign debt and a big bank–dominated financial system that lacks much depth in liquidity are weighing down the economy. There is an ongoing demographic headache. Today Europeans 65 or older who are not working account for 42 of every 100 workers. By 2026, that number will be 65 per 100, according to Eurostat, the statistical office of the European Union. A shrinking labor force will make it extraordinarily difficult to support such massive debt. If demographics is destiny, then Europe's economic future is dismal. Yet when you mention the issue of this demographic challenge to European policymakers, they change the subject. Or at least most do. (The same is true for Japan's policy leaders, whose country is in a similar situation.) And large portions of both Europe's and Japan's populations are fundamentally opposed to immigration.

As strange as it sounds, in the decades after World War II, the European economies were nothing like that. They were vibrant. They had developed a can-do attitude about rebuilding their war-torn economy. Europe's economies actually grew much faster than the U.S. economy. Europe's Main Street capitalist economy was firing on all cylinders. As economists Jesús Fernández-Villaverde and Lee Ohanian point out: "European firms rapidly adopted and developed new technologies and became vigorous competitors. Its people worked longer hours than in the United States." In 1950, France's per-capita GDP was 50 percent of the U.S. level. By 1980, that figure had jumped to an impressive 80 percent, according to the Penn World Table.

But then look at what happened. France's common-sense political center went into hiding. In 1981, French Socialist Party leader François Mitterrand became president. The climate changed as government intruded into large segments of the economy. Even several years later, when the government tried to back off some from socialist policies because of the highly negative reaction of the financial markets, the impression was nevertheless set in stone. The incentives to begin new enterprises and invest in new plant and equipment were never the same. "The result was a large drop in the number of hours employees worked, in business investment, and in the creation of new economic activity and the adoption and development of new technologies," note Ohanian and Fernández-Villaverde.

Between 1976 and 2007, Europe's entrepreneurial sector—its timid attempt at a more innovative capitalism—proved to be a complete flop. Defined by market capitalization, only one European startup, the Norwegian firm Renewable Energy Corporation, has been able to match the dozens of dazzlingly successful U.S. startups from that same period, including Apple, Microsoft, and Oracle. Since 1990, Europe's venture capital industry has had returns of about 2 percent. The returns of similar American firms have averaged more than 13 percent. Total manufacturing productivity growth, a key measure of an economy's health, has since the early 1980s been flat for most of Europe. Bernie Sanders, call your office!

In the past several years, slow economic growth combined with an influx of Middle Eastern refugees has given the green light to Europe's populist parties, led in France by Marine Le Pen's National Front. In the event of a steep European recession in the next several years, a populist uprising and Le Pen takeover in France seem inevitable. Such a development would create the real possibility of the breakup of the European Union, the end of the euro, and overall financial chaos.

There is one other reason for the huge disparity in performance between Europe and the United States: America's common-sense political center understood that the U.S. system of liberalized capital markets, although not perfect as the 2008 financial crisis demonstrated, has a much greater capacity to fund entrepreneurial risk. Despite its flaws, the empowering nature of Main Street Capitalism is a force for positive advancement for folks on the middle and lower rungs of the economic ladder. Main Street Capitalism is the Great Equalizer. Of course, such innovative, free-market capitalism is not perfectly efficient. But as economist John Cochrane noted, paraphrasing Winston Churchill on democracy: "Free markets are the worst system ever devised—except for all the others."

Since the early 1980s and for the next several decades, America's capital markets grew to be much deeper, much freer, and more nimble than Europe's markets. In Europe, incredibly 40 percent of venture capital funding still comes from one large financial dinosaur—a bureaucratic behemoth called the European Investment Fund where insider political favoritism runs rampant. (The relevant situations in China and Japan are arguably worse. They have Corporate Capitalism run amok.)

It is no surprise that the European financial sector, dominated by big universal banks, is shrinking. Italy's banks haven't changed much from their state just before the 2008 financial crisis—that is, they are still deeply undercapitalized. Europe's corporate bond market as a percentage of GDP has dramatically shrunk. Its venture capital market is relatively small.

As a result, the European economy has lost out on a whopping $5 trillion in additional funding had the Continent had more of an American-style financial system, warts and all, according to the London-based think tank New Financial. As English billionaire businessman Simon Nixon wrote in the New York Times, "The challenge for European policymakers is to find ways to deepen capital markets." If that fails to happen, no amount of the European Central Bank's quantitative easing or any other exotic monetary stimulus will make much of a difference.

In today's ugly global environment, the only hope of protecting American working families is with more robust rates of economic growth. But to achieve more vibrant growth, America needs more than the normal fiscal and monetary adjustments, as important as those goals are. The United States again needs a new politics and a revolution in spirit and attitude based on a better understanding of how humans make decisions. Average folk need to sense more than ever that the common-sense center is alive and well and that the Gordian Knot of Washington policy stalemate is in the process of being cut. Policymakers need to show they have a more realistic assessment of the limitations, and unintended consequences, of their policy tools and, that they recognize that risk and failure are both essential components of private-sector success.

Average working families also need to sense that a paradigm shift is underway. Washington, D.C., has to become engaged in bipartisan problem solving. And when new technologies appear, the policy community should make sure that these breakthroughs are admired, not obstructed, for their ability to challenge the status quo in the marketplace. Economic success begins with a new mindset.

And here's the ultimate issue: Our policy experts mistakenly argue the simplistic notion that "money" is the driver of human behavior. Not true. What we have learned since the 2008 crisis is just the opposite. The central bankers opened the taps, flooding the world with liquidity by amounts never before seen in history. Those efforts produced an important lesson. In the aftermath of the crisis, what's clear is that money alone isn't the solution to creating prosperity. Money is little more than a measuring tool—and, in a sense, is a reflection of our values as a society.

After the 2008 crisis, a massive flood of stimulus "money" failed to drive human behavior, at least to a level as high as expected by the standards of past recoveries. The role of money in an economy's success is a lot more complicated. As economics writer Adam Davidson described the process in *The New York Times*, "What actually matters is what we make and do and feel and want." In short, at the heart of economics are people. When all is said and done, the people's collective Main Street attitude and mood matter enormously. True, central bank liquidity may pump up the stock market. But whether a person breaks away from an existing job to start a new business entails a far more complicated set of calculations and emotions. I'm talking here less about affairs of the head than about affairs of the heart—the drive to dream, to create, to desperately want to change the world.

Today's challenge is to make ordinary folk believe in the future not only as confident consumers but as innovative entrepreneurial producers. That confidence to take risks, to engage in economic reinvention, has slowed. Main Street Capitalism has been jettisoned as a legitimate way to view the workings of the economy. As a result, the rate of business startups, while picking up a bit in 2016, has seen a remarkable decline since 2010. In the game of economic reinvention, attitude is everything. And today our fearful attitude is killing our economy. Americans for all practical purposes "got chicken." In some cases, they have lost belief in the American idea.

The American people desperately need to have a national discussion about the true source of prosperity. The essential questions: Does that prosperity require more than policies that maintain and protect the existing wealth base, preserving the financial status quo at asset price levels that may be inflated? Is the secret more than central bank–supplied "money"? Is the answer the unleashing of people's dynamism and confidence in the future, not just as consumers but also as creative, entrepreneurially minded producers? What's the role of leadership in igniting that dynamism? And how do we jump-start the process?

A new politics that champions Main Street Capitalism's innovation and daring requires leadership. The American people are so desperate for effective leadership, so angry at what is happening to their country, that in a 2015 national poll they chose Darth Vader, the evil villain from the movie series *Star Wars*, when asked to identify from a list whom they would prefer to lead the country. Darth Vader may be a bad guy, the public seemed to be saying, but at least for once we'd have a compelling leader.

Earlier in this book, I discussed the limitations of economic knowledge, which begs the question: Why should the analyses, prescriptions, and compromises outlined in this book be considered gospel? Answer: They shouldn't. There is no magic formula to achieve overnight economic success. No ideological road map of divine inspiration. Economic reform is a process of trial and error. Regulatory overreach (i.e., the death of innovation by a thousand small cuts) is not a process economists can easily model. Many members of Congress, moreover, no doubt feel that if a large corporation with plants, factories, and offices in their district is facing pressure from the competitive process of creative destruction, they have a responsibility to intervene to protect the existing jobs base. But rest assured, the thousand cuts of intervention will come at a cost. They will slow the process of innovation and reduce the U.S. economy's overall potential to create a wellspring of broad-based prosperity.

So, to summarize, here's a new economic narrative of reform for the new president of the United States. The goal: to create a climate more welcoming of greater business startups in all sectors of the economy, propelled by greater innovative daring.

Main Street Capitalism's 14-Point Plan

1. **GRAND BARGAINS WITH CONGRESS.** Establish a new paradigm with bold policy compromises. Strike a bipartisan grand bargain—entitlement reform in exchange for infrastructure spending (designated not by Congress or the administration but by a distinguished independent panel, as with the earlier military base closing commission). A second grand bargain: Tort reform in exchange for a change in Medicare's policies with drug companies. Put a check on medical and legal corporate welfare. Challenge the medical-industrial complex.

2. **BRING OUR CAPITAL HOME.** In exchange for enticing U.S. corporations via a one-time tax holiday to repatriate capital back to the United States, insist those firms purchase specific amounts of special infrastructure bonds paying 1 percent.

3. **AVERT DEBT CRISES.** With the world more than $180 trillion in debt, call for a global debt summit for the purpose of setting down contingency plans (potential rescheduling and write-downs) in the event of a debt crisis and a time when the world's central banks have run out of monetary ammunition. Engage in contingency planning.

4. **TAX REFORM (REAGAN 2.0).** Reform the tax system, shifting it away from the stock "coupon clippers" in favor of jobs-producing enterprises. Tax corporate profits at the same rate as individual income. Reform the estate tax, raising the amount allowed to be exempted as an incentive for more startups.

5. **INVEST IN YOUTH.** Make every American child at birth a stock-holding capitalist with an investment account and modest low-interest loan. Set up a new system that facilitates investment in America's future innovators. Pursue Gallup's proposed "strengths-based organization" to identify and find the next generation's superstars. Facilitate the shift of the trillions of dollars of private investment capital sitting idle on the sidelines to finance the investment ideas of the millennial generation.

6. **RECREATE A GLOBAL FINANCIAL ARCHITECTURE.** Call for a global summit on the world's financial architecture, the role of the dollar, the global macroeconomic significance of emerging market excess supply capacity, and debt. Organize a Plaza II Accord to begin discussions on greater currency coordination. But also "think globally, but act locally." Become a champion of local community banks, the workhorses of the U.S. financial system. With the globalization and dramatic expansion of cross-border bandwidth, America needs a massive, new coordinated effort to prevent a simultaneous cyber attack on the codependent sectors involving the electric grid, financial transactions, and telecommunications.

7. **ENCOURAGE NEW ENTERPRISES.** Urge the Federal Reserve to reevaluate its policy of "financial repression" and to reexamine its definition of "money" in the twenty-first-century economy. Make part of the central bank's mandate the encouraging of large financial institutions to specify an increment of new credit to young enterprises. Have the government's statisticians redefine inflation (which it underestimates) and employment (which it overestimates). Adopt the Kauffman Foundation's proposal to allow shareholders in firms going public to vote to opt out of the onerously expensive Sarbanes-Oxley rules and regulations. Pay special attention to encouraging women, who are starting firms at up to twice the rate as men.

8. **THE 3.5 SOLUTION.** Improve the management of the U.S. government's non-financial assets, increasing the annual return by 3.5 percent for a bonanza of billions, or even trillions, of dollars in new revenue.

9. **MODESTLY RAISE THE MINIMUM WAGE.** Careful, incremental raising of the minimum wage will help compensate for flat wages while not threatening small business solvency.

10. **INCREASE WORKER MOBILITY.** Provide vouchers for disadvantaged families to move from states with modest employment opportunities to states with economies in need of new employees.

11. **WELCOME FOREIGN GENIUSES.** Achieve comprehensive immigration reform with the primary goal of enticing the Einsteins, Picassos, Curies, and Neels of the world to set up shop in the United States.

12. **THE PAUSE THAT REFRESHES.** Declare a two-year holiday on new regulations that are not specifically tied to an immediate, pending health or safety issue. Call this "the pause that refreshes." Establish a bipartisan panel that targets "The Ugly 50"—the 50 most egregious cases from the 2010s in which corporations have used lobbying pressure to influence the regulation process to the disadvantage of their competitors or potential competitors. Roll back those lobbied changes. Make a powerful statement to the Corporate Capitalist system. The Chinese have a phrase, "To scare the monkey, kill the chicken." Kill The Ugly 50. Increase antitrust scrutiny of the corporate sector.

13. **FUND ADULT TECH EDUCATION.** Fix the U.S. community college system, which has forgotten its mission. Provide federal grants for community college adult education on evenings and weekends to update information technology and Internet-related skills.

14. **REINVENT GOVERNMENT.** Pass legislation to reform the patent system as well as legislation to modernize the Civil Service Reform Act of 1978.

To enact such an agenda, America's new president needs to lead a national economic growth crusade. What is required is uncommon courage and character to jolt Washington policymakers into an aggressive attitude of problem-solving. We are living in extraordinary times with major tectonic shifts in global economics, finance, and geopolitics. Why shouldn't Americans demand extraordinary leadership at such a critical time? The stakes could not be higher. Our new president must reject the forces of the status quo. This is the time for a leader for all Americans.

Chinese history offers a sobering reminder. Six hundred years ago, China was the world's great empire. The West was an uncivilized backwater. As economic historian Niall Ferguson has observed:

> Just look at the star lineup of Chinese inventions. Gun powder, ink, matches, paper, the suspension bridge and the printing press—which the Chinese discovered in the 11th century but Gutenberg in Germany didn't get around to discovering until four centuries later. Time seemed to be on China's side.
>
> Yet by the mid-17th century, the wheels went flying off. Power had become centralized. Collapse happened in a decade. Everything turned inward which created a fragility to the system.

For centuries, the great Chinese empire basked in the sweet spot of prosperity. Then, in a flash, it all vanished. The most advanced society in the world centralized, turned inward, and collapsed. Could the same thing happen to America? It is impossible to say for sure.

But one thing is certain: Leadership is essential if we are to avoid both the socialist illusion and the stifling effects of the corporate stranglehold. There are just as compelling examples on the upside, where inspiring leadership made all the difference, as there are on the downside. In 1942, for example, from a tiny radio transmitting office in the basement of Britain's War Department, Winston Churchill rallied a disillusioned population into not giving up despite the near certainty of a Nazi victory. The British people found a sudden inner grassroots dynamism. They endured. They innovated. They were victorious in combating an enemy intent on annihilating them.

Several decades ago, Deng Xiaoping, the great Chinese economic reformer, embraced a vision that moved his country out of a disappointing collectivist system into a hybrid market-based system. Since his death in 1997, China's economy unfortunately has been compromised by less imaginative and inspiring leadership that caters to an elite Communist Party membership amid a climate of mass high-level corruption. Today Deng must be rolling over in his grave to see what is happening to his country's political and economic systems.

At the beginning of the twentieth century, Theodore Roosevelt saw an America rapidly industrializing and successfully shaped that industrialization. During a time of lightning-quick industrialization and its excesses, he brought America into the modern age by the sheer force of his personality.

Societies can change, for better or worse, and change quickly. Economies are ruled by psychology. There is as much reason to be hopeful as there is to be pessimistic if our new president steps forward boldly and America wakes up.

The process of renewal starts by realizing that what we do, day in and day out, is bigger than ourselves. We are part of a collective effort to expand the economic pie—not just for some but for all. We are all part of a noble economic experiment of purpose that is inconsistent with the partisan economic policy food fight taking place in Washington, D.C. We are a country of dreamers and discoverers traditionally supported by a majority open to common-sense compromise. We want programs and policies to make ever-larger segments of society capital owners of the country's productive wealth.

Now our challenge is to begin the tough, gnarly, sweaty process of change. Saying "we're economically mediocre, but thankfully not as mediocre as the rest of the world" simply doesn't cut it as a game plan for our children's economic future. We can do much better. There are no facts about the future. The great investor Warren Buffett summed up the situation this way: "Though we invest abroad as well, the mother lode of opportunity resides in America." His deeply held belief is that "America's best days lie ahead." That's something we can all believe in—and work toward. But the clock is ticking. The time for audacious reform, for a paradigm shift toward a high-growth Main Street Capitalist attitude, is now.

Acknowledgments

It would be difficult not to first acknowledge the tremendous effort of my agent Jim Levine. When the publishing world said readers are no longer interested in serious books on economics (unless written by Kim Kardashian), he said, "Nonsense!" The same is true of Clive Priddle of PublicAffairs Books and its founder Peter Osnos. These individuals recognized the growing frustration and anger of working- and middle-class families at the loss of economic opportunity. Additional thanks go to Norman MacAfee for his superb editorial suggestions and insistence that the book's message be one of hope. Thanks also to Beth Partin for her editorial insights.

This is a book written with the help of many friends. So many gave advice, direction, and encouragement, it is difficult to know where to begin in expressing my gratitude.

But let me start with Jeffrey Garten of the Yale School of Management. Early on he provided the essential encouragement to take on the task of writing this book. Rob Johnson of the Institute for New Economic Thinking was also an early advocate whose advice influenced almost every chapter. He particularly stressed that I explore the issue of the medical cartel in the context of entitlement reform. Another essential early promoter was former Bill Clinton adviser Rob Shapiro of Sonecon. He provided key insights on the role of bipartisanship in laying the groundwork for economic prosperity. Bob Merry, an important author of presidential biographies, early on encouraged me to begin with a description of my background growing up in working-class Baltimore. Shelby Coffey read the manuscript several times, providing important guidance and creative direction.

High-tech investor Christopher Schroeder served as a kind of guru on the changing nature of technological innovation. His advice was unvarnished and invaluable. Ned Phelps, the Nobel Prize winner, encouraged me to simplify certain chapters with the goal of broadening the book's audience. Dino Kos, the former New York Federal Reserve official, provided important help in describing the limitations of monetary policy. Adam Walinsky, the former Robert Kennedy aide, read the manuscript with a wickedly brutal eye. The notion that current Hollywood movies reflect national sentiment was his idea. Energy executive Robin West offered several points that dramatically bolstered my arguments. Criton Zoakos, a brilliant analyst, urged me to write a preface that stated from the beginning the urgency of dealing with the frustration and anger of today's working- and middle-class families. John and Gina Despres, as always, were unstinting in their support. Gina's advice on tax policy was very helpful.

Investor Scott Bessent stressed that I concentrate on the dangers of ballooning corporate debt, as did investor Stan Druckenmiller, who also provided important insights on the need for entitlement reform. Former *National Geographic* media executive Mike Cascio read the draft several times and gave important advice. Joe Sprung offered the useful point that policymakers need to figure out how to move capital sitting on the sidelines to future young innovators. Joe Kennedy provided important tech advice. Larry Silberman generously made time to read the manuscript several times, noting points of strength and weakness. Nancy Cardwell and Jeffrey Krames offered important early editorial guidance. Richard Clarida, the economist and PIMCO advisor, urged me to concentrate more on the great globalization conundrum. Former Bundesbank official Stefan Schoenberg provided guidance on European banking issues, as did the former European central banker Gerd Häusler. Journalist John Berry read several drafts and provided important suggestions on the reform of America's community colleges. Jeff Bell's encouragement was beyond the call.

Others who generously offered their time by reading the manuscript and offering helpful suggestions include Bruce Bartlett, Michael Anderson, Mike Bates, Bill Brock, Mac Carey, Jürgen Stark, Lance Choos, Lew Eisenberg, Mel Krauss, Marc Leland, Fred Barnes, Harald Malmgren, Adam Posen, Jim Sims, Bill Sweetser, and Mort Kondracke. If I have inadvertently omitted anyone who provided help, I offer my sincere apologies.

As every business executive knows, a back office can make or break an enterprise. Angela Wilkes, managing editor of *The International Economy*, offered both editorial and fact-checking help beyond the call. Josef Neusser, who has come into his own as a policy strategist and business manager, was instrumental in picking up the slack with my consulting business during times I was preoccupied. And last but not least, Jean Wells, my executive assistant, worked tirelessly in preparing a blizzard of manuscript drafts. Her editorial suggestions were superb. The book would not have happened without her help.

My now extended family—Peter and Amanda, Sarah and Ian, and David, Jr.—provided useful advice as, of course, did my wife Vickie, who became the "author's widow" yet still offered encouragement, support, and several vital suggestions. Her warning early on: "Only write a second book if there is something you desperately need to say."

A Word on Sources

In writing *The Great Equalizer*, I have drawn on a broad array of sources. To begin, in my almost 30 years of providing editorial direction to *The International Economy* magazine, hundreds of scholars, policymakers, and journalists, in presenting their views, have influenced my thinking. Articles written since 2002 are available on the magazine's website at www.international-economy.com.

In addition, I have quoted from, been influenced by, or reflected on a number of books, articles, speeches, and databases on the subjects of macroeconomics, income inequality, the financial markets, high-tech innovators, and monetary policy. Although I have used a variety of publicly available sources, some of the book's discussions reflect my personal experiences and conversations on the trading floors of a number of financial institutions, and with politicians and policymakers worldwide.

It is virtually certain that some sources that have broadly influenced my thinking over the years have slipped through the cracks. For this likely omission, I extend my apologies.

Bibliography

Books

Akerlof, George A., and Robert J. Shiller. *Animal Spirits: How Human Psychology Drives the Economy, and Why It Matters for Global Capitalism.* Princeton, NJ: Princeton University Press, 2009.

Bartley, Robert L. *The Seven Fat Years: And How to Do It Again.* New York: Free Press, 1992.

Brenner, Reuven. *History: The Human Gamble.* Chicago: University of Chicago Press, 1983.

Buchholz, Todd G. *The Price of Prosperity: How Rich Nations Fail and How to Renew Them.* New York: HarperCollins, 2016.

Bush, Jonathan. *Where Does It Hurt? An Entrepreneur's Guide to Fixing Health Care.* New York: Portfolio, 2014.

Christensen, Clayton. *The Innovator's Dilemma: When New Technologies Cause Great Firms to Fail.* New York: Harvard Business Review Press, 2016.

Clinton, Bill. *Between Hope and History: Meeting America's Challenges for the 21st Century.* New York: Random House, 1996.

Cowen, Tyler. *The Great Stagnation: How America Ate All the Low-Hanging Fruit of Modern History, Got Sick, and Will (Eventually) Feel Better.* New York: Penguin, 2012.

Detter, Dag, and Stefan Fölster. *The Public Wealth of Nations: How Management of Public Assets Can Boost or Bust Economic Growth, 2015 Edition.* New York: Palgrave Macmillan, 2016.

Dobbs, Richard, James Manyika, and Jonathan Woetzel. *No Ordinary Disruption: The Four Global Forces Breaking All the Trends.* New York: PublicAffairs, 2015.

Drucker, Peter. *The End of Economic Man: The Origins of Totalitarianism.* Piscataway, NJ: Transaction, 1995.

Evans, Harold. *They Made America: From Steam Engine to the Search Engine: Two Centuries of Innovators.* New York: Little, Brown, 2004.

Ferguson, Niall. *Empire: The Rise and Demise of the British World Order and the Lessons for Global Power.* New York: Basic Books, 2003.

Ford, Martin. *The Rise of the Robots: Technology and the Threat of a Jobless Future.* New York: Basic Books, 2015.

Galinsky, Adam, and Maurice Schweitzer. *Friend and Foe: When to Cooperate, When to Compete, and How to Succeed at Both.* New York: Crown Business, 2015.

Gilder, George. *The Scandal of Money: Why Wall Street Recovers but the Economy Never Does*. Washington, DC: Regnery Publishing, 2016.

Gordon, Robert J. *The Rise and Fall of American Growth*. Princeton, NJ: Princeton University Press, 2016.

Hoffman, Reid, Ben Casnocha, and Chris Yeh. *The Alliance: Managing Talent in the Networked Age*. Boston: Harvard Business Review Press, 2014.

Hufbauer, Gary C., and Wendy Dobson. *World Capital Markets: Challenge to the G-10*. Washington, DC: Institute for International Economics, 2001.

Huntington, Samuel P. *The Clash of Civilizations and the Remaking of World Order*. New York: Simon and Schuster, 1996.

Johnson, Paul. *Modern Times: The World from the Twenties to the Nineties*. New York: Harper Perennial Modern Classics, 2001.

Keynes, John Maynard. *The General Theory of Employment, Interest, and Money*. New York: Harcourt Brace and World, 1965.

Kurtzman, Joel. *Unleashing the Second American Century: Four Forces for Economic Dominance*. New York: PublicAffairs, 2014.

Lawrence, Robert Z. *Blue-Collar Blues: Is Trade to Blame for Rising U.S. Income Inequality?* Washington, DC: Peterson Institute for International Economics, 2008.

Mann, Thomas E., and Norman J. Ornstein. *It's Worse Than It Looks*. New York: Basic Books, 2012.

Mayer-Schönberger, Viktor, and Kenneth Cukier. *Big Data: A Revolution That Will Transform How We Live, Work, and Think*. Boston: Houghton Mifflin Harcourt, 2013.

Micklethwait, John, and Adrian Wooldridge. *The Fourth Revolution: The Global Race to Reinvent the State*. New York: Penguin Press, 2014.

Miller, John H. *A Crude Look at the Whole: The Science of Complex Systems in Business, Life, and Society*. New York: Basic Books, 2016.

Ophuls, William. *Immoderate Greatness: Why Civilizations Fail*. Create Space, 2012.

Parker, Richard. *John Kenneth Galbraith: His Life, His Politics, His Economics*. Chicago: University of Chicago Press, 2005.

Phelps, Edmund S. *Mass Flourishing: How Grassroots Innovation Created Jobs, Challenge and Change*. Princeton, NJ: Princeton University Press, 2013.

Piketty, Thomas. *Capital in the Twenty-First Century*. Cambridge, MA: Belknap Press, 2014.

Rajan, Raghuram G., and Luigi Zingales. *Saving Capitalism from the Capitalists: Unleashing the Power of Financial Markets to Create Wealth and Spread Opportunity*. New York: Crown Business, 2003.

Reagan, Ronald. *An American Life: The Autobiography*. New York: Simon and Schuster, 1990.

Reich, Robert B. *Saving Capitalism: For the Many, Not the Few*. New York: Alfred A. Knopf, 2015.

Ridley, Matt. *The Evolution of Everything: How New Ideas Emerge*. New York: Harper Collins, 2015.

Rifkin, Jeremy R. *The Zero Marginal Cost Society: The Internet of Things, the Collaborative Commons, and the Eclipse of Capitalism*. New York: St. Martin's Press, 2014.

Schumacher, E. F. *Small Is Beautiful: Economics As If People Mattered.* London: Blond and Briggs, 1973.

Sims, Peter. *Little Bets: How Breakthrough Ideas Emerge from Small Discoveries.* New York: Free Press, 2011.

Soros, George. *George Soros on Globalization.* New York: PublicAffairs, 2002.

Stiglitz, Joseph E. *Globalization and Its Discontents.* New York: W. W. Norton, 2002.

———. *Rewriting the Rules of the American Economy: An Agenda for Growth and Shared Prosperity.* New York: W. W. Norton, 2015.

Tapscott, Don, and Anthony D. Williams. *Wikinomics: How Mass Collaboration Changes Everything.* New York: Portfolio, 2006.

Thiel, Peter. *Zero to One: Notes on Startups, or How to Build the Future.* New York: Crown Publishing, 2014.

Thomas, Evan. *Robert Kennedy: His Life.* New York: Simon and Schuster, 2000.

Articles, Speeches, and Databases

Aarons-Mele, Morra. "More Women Starting Businesses Isn't Necessarily Good News." *Harvard Business Review,* June 25, 2014.

Ahmed, Murad. "Davos: Smart Machines Set to Transform Society." *Financial Times,* January 20, 2016.

Altman, Roger. "Why the Fed Needs Summers' Firefighting Skills." *Financial Times,* August 13, 2013.

Apple. "Record-Breaking Holiday Season for the App Store." Press release, January 6, 2016.

Armenta, Maria. "Google CEO Received $100.5 Million in 2015 Total Compensation." *Wall Street Journal,* April 19, 2016.

Bank for International Settlements. "Debt Service Ratio for the Private Non-financial Sector." May 26, 2016.

Belfiore, Michael. "The Robots Are Coming." *Aeon,* March 12, 2014.

Belvedere, Matthew. "Making the Rich Poorer Isn't the American Dream." CNBC.com, January 23, 2014.

Bernanke, Ben. "Why Are Interest Rates So Low?" Ben Bernanke's Blog. Brookings Institution, March 31, 2015.

Bernstein, Jared. "Dethrone 'King Dollar.'" *New York Times,* August 27, 2014.

Bhalla, Surjit S. "Today's Golden Age of Poverty Reduction." *The International Economy* (Spring 2006).

Blinder, Alan. "'Pikettymania' and Inequality in the U.S." *Wall Street Journal,* June 23, 2014.

Bono, interview with Charlie Rose, May 17, 2013.

Bounds, Andrew. "The Need for Policy Rethink to Favour Scale-Ups Rather Than Startups." *Financial Times,* June 7, 2016.

Bratton, Ethan, and JahanZaib Mehmood Chaudhary. "Largest 100 Banks in the World." SNL Interactive, S&P Global Market Intelligence, April 12, 2016.

Brittan, Samuel. "Look Behind the Myth of Global Imbalances." *Financial Times,* January 6, 2011.

———. "Why the World Economy Is Still Spluttering Away." *Financial Times*, February 9, 2012.

Brooks, David. "Midlife Crisis Economics." *New York Times*, December 26, 2011.

———. "The Zero-Sum Moment." *New York Times*, March 20, 2015.

Buffett, Warren. "Why Stocks Beat Gold and Bonds." CNN Money, February 9, 2012.

Bunting, Madeleine. "Small Is Beautiful—an Economic Idea That Has Sadly Been Forgotten." *The Guardian*, November 10, 2011.

Buttonwood. "Muddled Models." *The Economist*, July 20, 2012.

Carter, Graydon. "The Pariah Shortage." *Vanity Fair*, July 30, 2013.

Case, Anne, and Angus Deaton. "Rising Morbidity and Mortality in Midlife Among White Non-Hispanic Americans in the 21st Century." *Proceedings of the National Academy of Sciences*, September 17, 2015.

Cassidy, Bill, and Louis Woodhill. "Dismal Growth Needs the 3.5% Solution." *Wall Street Journal*, April 30, 2015.

Cendrowski, Scott. "Here's What You May Not Know About the Chinese Stock Market." *Fortune*, September 2, 2015.

Center on Budget and Policy Priorities. "Policy Basics: Where Do Our Federal Tax Dollars Go?" March 4, 2016.

"Central Banks Alone Cannot Conjure Growth." Editorial. *Financial Times*, February 20, 2016.

Citizens for Tax Justice. "Fortune 500 Companies Hold a Record $2.4 Trillion Offshore." March 4, 2016.

Cochrane, John H. "Growth Is Central." *The Grumpy Economist* blog, October 26, 2015.

Codevilla, Angelo M. "America's Ruling Class—and the Perils of Revolution." *American Spectator* (July–August 2010).

Cohn, D'vera, and Paul Taylor. "Baby Boomers Approach 65—Glumly." Pew Research Center, December 20, 2010.

Congressional Budget Office. "The Budget and Economic Outlook: 2016–2026." Table 2-1, January 2016.

Cooper, Helene. "Air Force Fires Nine Officers in Scandal over Cheating on Proficiency Tests." *New York Times*, March 27, 2014.

"The Corruption of America." *Stansberry's Investment Advisory*, December 2011.

Cowen, Tyler. "Is Innovation Over? The Case Against Pessimism." *Foreign Affairs* (March–April 2016).

Coy, Peter. "The Mystery of America's Missing Capital Investment." *Bloomberg Businessweek*, March 17, 2016.

Curtin, S. C., S. J. Ventura, and G. M. Martinez. "Recent Declines in Nonmarital Childbearing in the United States." National Center for Health Statistics data brief no. 162, Centers for Disease Control and Prevention, August 2014.

Davenport, David. "America's Drift Toward 'Socialism' Is Generational, But Also Educational." *Forbes*, February 26, 2016.

Davidson, Adam. "The Money Issue." *New York Times*, May 3, 2015.

Davison, Remy. "The Five Worst Decisions Ever Made by the European Union." TheConversation.com, September 6, 2012.

"Demographics a Ticking Time Bomb." *China Economic Quarterly* (June 2012).

DeMuth, Christopher. "Capital for the Masses." *Wall Street Journal*, April 8, 2014.

Dhume, Sadanand. "India's Half-Done Reforms: Compared with Its Past, India Has Prospered over the Past 25 Years. But in Many Ways It Still Lags Its Peers in Asia." Blog. *The Times of India*, July 27, 2016.

Dobbs, Richard, Susan Lund, Jonathan Woetzel, and Mina Mutafchieva. "Debt and (Not Much) Deleveraging." McKinsey Global Institute, February 2015.

Domenici, Pete, and Alice Rivlin. "Restore America's Future." Bipartisan Policy Center, November 2010.

Drell, Lauren. "Female Founders Series." Mashable.com, August 16, 2012.

Durden, Tyler. "Stanley Druckenmiller: 'We Have an Entitlement Problem.'" ZeroHedge.com, February 21, 2013.

Easterbrook, Gregg. "Death of the Middle Class? Think Again." *Reuters*, September 23, 2010.

"Economics Needs to Reflect a Post-Crisis World: The Dismal Science Should Be Grounded in Reality to Stay Relevant." Editorial. *Financial Times*, September 25, 2014.

Edwards, Jim. "How China Accumulated $28 Trillion in Debt in Such a Short Time." *Business Insider*, January 6, 2016.

Ekins, Emily. "57 Percent of Americans Say Only Kids Who Win Should Get Trophies." Reason.com, August 19, 2014.

———. "Millennials Don't Know What 'Socialism' Means." Reason.com, July 16, 2014.

Ekins, Emily, and Joy Pullmann. "Why So Many Millennials Are Socialists." Reason-Rupe Surveys, Reason.com, February 17, 2016.

Evans-Pritchard, Ambrose. "China Has Now Become the Biggest Risk to the World Economy." *The Telegraph*, November 15, 2009.

———. "Is the Whole Theory of Secular Stagnation a Hoax?" *The Telegraph*, January 6, 2016.

Feldstein, Martin. "The Tax Reform Evidence from 1986." *Wall Street Journal*, October 24, 2011.

Fenby, Jonathan. "Cracks in China." *The Spectator*, March 24, 2012.

Fernández-Villaverde, Jesús, and Lee E. Ohanian. "European Economic Errors for the U.S. to Avoid." *Wall Street Journal*, December 29, 2014.

Florida, Richard. "Is Life Better in America's Red States?" *New York Times*, January 3, 2015.

Garten, Jeffrey. "The Future of Globalization." *The International Economy* (Winter 2016).

Gates, Bill. "GatesNotes." Blog. July 26, 2016.

Gayathri, Amrutha. "China's Military Paper Warns U.S. of Armed Conflict over Sea Dispute." *International Business Times*, April 21, 2012.

Gillespie, Patrick. "Junk Territory: U.S. Corporate Debt Ratings Near 15-Year Low." *CNN Money*, March 24, 2016.

"The Global Debt Clock." *The Economist*, March 7, 2012.

"Global Markets Catch the Chinese Flu." *Wall Street Journal*, October 17, 2014.

Gramm, Phil. "What's Wrong with the Golden Goose." *Wall Street Journal*, April 21, 2015.

Gramm, Phil, and Steve McMillin. "The Real Causes of Income Inequality." *Wall Street Journal*, April 6, 2012.

Grant, David. "Entitlement Reform: Why Obama Faces Tough Sell to Supporters." *M Newsletter*, November 21, 2012.

"The Great Innovation Debate." *The Economist*, January 12, 2016.

Greenspan, Alan. "The Reagan Legacy." Remarks at the Ronald Reagan Library, Simi Valley, California, April 9, 2003.

Greider, William. "Why Was Paul Krugman So Wrong?" *The Nation*, April 1, 2013.

Hathaway, Ian, and Robert E. Litan. "Declining Business Dynamism in the United States: A Look at States and Metros." Brookings Institution, May 2014.

Hilsenrath, Jon, and Brian Blackstone. "Central Banks Diversify Their Arsenals." *Wall Street Journal*, January 27, 2012.

"How Much Do Corporations Pay in Taxes?" Tax Foundation, February 2015.

Huddleston, Tom, Jr. "Tim Cook Is Not Apple's Highest-Paid Executive." *Fortune*, January 7, 2016.

InsideGov.com. "2015 United States Budget." Analysis using data from the White House Office of Management and Budget and the Council of Economic Advisers. www.omb.gov.

International Monetary Fund. "Household Debt to GDP for United States [HDTG-PDUSQ163N]." Retrieved from FRED, Federal Reserve Bank of St. Louis. fred.stlouisfed.org/series/HDTGPDUSQ163N, July 18, 2016.

———. "United States: Gross Domestic Product, Current Prices (National Currency)." World Economic Outlook Database, April 2016. https://www.imf.org/external/pubs/ft/weo/2016/01/weodata/index.aspx.

International Telecommunication Union. "ICT Facts & Figures: The World in 2015." Geneva, May 2015.

Ipsos MORI. "People in Western Countries Pessimistic About Future for Young People." April 14, 2014.

"Is the European Central Bank Losing Credibility? A Symposium of Views." *The International Economy* (Spring 2012).

Japan Exchange Group. "Market Cap of Japanese Stock Markets." Website, July 29, 2016.

Josten, R. Bruce. "Ten Truths About America's Entitlement Programs." U.S. Chamber of Commerce, June 18, 2013.

Kaka, Noshir, and Anu Madgavkar. "India's Ascent: Five Opportunities for Growth and Transformation." McKinsey and Company, August 2016.

Kennedy, Robert F. Speech in Detroit, Michigan, May 5, 1967.

Kessler, Andy. "China's Economic Hinge Point." *Wall Street Journal*, February 1, 2016.

———. "What's the Matter with Wall Street?" *Wall Street Journal*, September 28, 2010.

Kinsley, Michael. "About Rising Inflation, Please Remain Worried." *Bloomberg*, January 19, 2012.

Kleinfield, N. R. "The People Who Were PATCO." *New York Times*, September 28, 1986.

Kohut, Andrew. "What Will Become of America's Kids?" Pew Research Center, May 12, 2014.

Kosar, Kevin R. "The Common Perception Is True." *The Weekly Standard*, May 25, 2015.

Krugman, Paul. "Earth to Ben Bernanke." *New York Times*, April 24, 2012.

———. "How Did Economists Get It So Wrong?" *New York Times*, September 2, 2009.

Kynge, James, and Jonathan Wheatley. "Emerging Asia: The Ill Wind of Deflation." *Financial Times*, October 4, 2015.

Lachman, Desmond. "No Recovery for the American Worker." *The American*, January 29, 2011.

Lazear, Edward P. "How Not to Prevent the Next Financial Meltdown." *Wall Street Journal*, October 2, 2015.

Leonard, Andrew. "Krugman's Critics Go on the Warpath." *Salon*, September 15, 2009.

"Let the Job-Creators In." *The Economist*, June 9, 2012.

Lowenstein, Roger. "The Villain." *The Atlantic*, April 2012.

Luce, Edward. "America's Three Takes on the Crisis." *Financial Times*, March 18, 2012.

Maddison Project. http://www.ggdc.net/maddison/maddison-project/home.htm, 2013.

Mallaby, Sebastian. "The 'Buffett Rule' Is a Sorry Excuse for Tax Reform." *Financial Times*, April 13, 2012.

Malmgren, Harald B. "Why the Fed Can Tell When a Recession Starts." *Advisor Perspectives*, February 15, 2016.

Manyika, James, Jonathan Woetzel, Richard Dobbs, Jaana Remes, Eric Labaye, and Andrew Jordan. "Can Long-Term Global Growth Be Saved?" McKinsey Global Institute, January 2015.

Marr, Bernard. "What Impact Will Artificial Intelligence Have on Our Jobs?" World Economic Forum, July 27, 2015.

Marsh, David. "Why Beijing Is Promoting the SDR." *OMFIF Analysis*, April 11, 2016.

Martin, Paul. "How Canada Cut Its Deficits and Debt." *The International Economy* (Spring 2012).

McGinnis, John O. "Innovation and Inequality." *National Affairs* (Winter 2013).

McGurn, William. "Grow, Baby, Grow!" *Wall Street Journal*, February 15, 2016.

McMahon, Dinny, and Bob Davis. "Stalled Project Shows Why China's Economy Is Wobbling." *Wall Street Journal*, July 24, 2013.

Mead, Walter Russell. "The Myth of America's Decline." *Wall Street Journal*, April 9, 2012.

Mellman, Mark. "Relationship of Parties and Policies." *The Hill*, March 13, 2013.

Melloan, George. "Inattention-to-the-Deficit Disorder." *Wall Street Journal*, May 27, 2016.

Meyerson, Harold. "The Coming Job Apocalypse." *Washington Post*, March 27, 2014.

Micklethwait, John, and Adrian Wooldridge. "In Search of Gladstonian Republicans." *Wall Street Journal*, May 30, 2014.

Mills, Karen. "Why Small-Business Lending Is Not Recovering." *HBS Working Knowledge*. Editorial, August 4, 2014.

Mills, Karen Gordon, and Brayden McCarthy. "State of Small Business Lending: Credit Access During the Recovery and How Technology May Change the Game." Harvard Business School working paper, July 22, 2014.

Mishel, Lawrence, Josh Bivens, Elise Gould, and Heidi Shierholz. "Wealth Groups' Shares of Assets, by Asset Type, 2010." Table 6.6 in *The State of Working America*. Economic Policy Institute series. Ithaca: Cornell University Press, 2012, 2015.

Moore, Stephen. "We've Become a Nation of Takers, Not Makers." *Wall Street Journal*, April 1, 2011.

Münchau, Wolfgang. "There Is No Spanish Siesta for the Euro Zone." *Financial Times*, March 18, 2012.

Murray, Charles. "Why Economics Can't Explain Our Cultural Divide." *Wall Street Journal*, March 16, 2012.

Nager, Adams. "Calling Out China's Mercantilism." *The International Economy* (Spring 2016).

Nakamura, Yuji, and Toshiro Hasegawa. "Hong Kong Poised to Top Japan as World's No. 3 Stock Market." *Bloomberg*, April 10, 2015.

New York City Department of City Planning. "New York City Population: Population Facts." July 19, 2016. www1.nyc.gov/site/planning/data-maps/nyc-population/population-facts.page.

Nixon, Simon. "Are the Euro-Zone's Pockets Deep Enough?" *Wall Street Journal*, January 18, 2015.

Norton, Leslie P. "Still Banking on Treasuries." *Barron's*, December 19, 2011.

Organisation for Economic Co-operation and Development Better Life Index. "Income." www.oecdbetterlifeindex.org/topics/income/.

———. "Employed Population." stats.oecd.org.

Packer, George. "No Death, No Taxes." *The New Yorker*, November 28, 2011.

Perry, Mark J. "Charts of the Day: Another Look at How America's Middle Class Is Disappearing into Higher Income Households." *AEIdeas*, December 30, 2015.

———. "Some Demographic Trends That Might Explain the Stagnation and Decline in U.S. Household Income." *AEIdeas*, December 19, 2015.

Perry, Mark S., and Thomas A. Hemphill. "Regulations Are a Really Big Drag on U.S. Growth." *Investor's Business Daily*, May 13, 2016.

Phelps, Edmund S. "Less Innovation, More Inequality." *New York Times*, April 8, 2014.

Piketty, Thomas, and Emmanuel Saez. "How Progressive Is the U.S. Federal Tax System? A Historical and International Perspective." *Journal of Economic Perspectives* 21, no. 1 (Winter 2007); and supporting data from Excel file containing stand-alone results at http://elsa.berkeley.edu/~saez/jep-results-standalone.xls.

Pollock, Alex. "Elastic Currency with a Vengeance." *The American*, November 29, 2011.

———. "There's Usually a Banking Crisis Somewhere." *The American*, September 21, 2011.

Quiggin, John. "Doing More with Less: The Economic Lessons of Peak Paper." *Aeon*, February 12, 2016.

Racanelli, Vito J. "Is America Becoming an Anti-Risk Welfare State." *Barron's*, April 30, 2012.

Rapoport, Michael. "Toxic Assets Still Lurking at Banks." *Wall Street Journal*, February 7, 2011.

Ratcliffe, Caroline, and Signe-Mary McKernan. "Who Is Most Worried About Student-Loan Debt." *Communities and Banking*, Federal Reserve Bank of Boston (Winter 2015).

Reich, Robert B. "Big Tech Has Become Way Too Powerful." *New York Times*, September 20, 2015.

———. "China and the American Jobs Machine." *Wall Street Journal*, November 17, 2009.

"The Retreat from Everywhere." *The Economist*, April 21, 2012.

Richards, Parker. "Sixty-Four Students Charged With Honor Code Violations." *The Dartmouth*, January 7, 2015.

Rifkin, Jeremy. "The Rise of Anti-Capitalism." *New York Times*, March 15, 2014.

Rohde, Robert A., and Richard A. Muller. "Air Pollution in China: Mapping of Concentrations and Sources." *PLOS ONE*, August 20, 2015.

Rose, Stephen. "The Growing Size and Incomes of the Upper Middle Class." Urban Institute, June 21, 2016.

Roser, Max. "World Poverty." OurWorldInData.org, 2016.

Rubin, Richard. "GE Deploys Army of Lobbyists to Preserve Low Effective Tax Rate." *Bloomberg*, February 16, 2011.

Saez, Emmanuel. "Striking It Richer: The Evolution of Top Incomes in the United States (updated with 2014 preliminary estimates)." University of California at Berkeley, June 25, 2015.

Samuelson, Robert. "A Country in Denial About Its Fiscal Future." *Washington Post*, December 26, 2011.

———. "The New Era of Muddle-nomics." *Washington Post*, October 6, 2014.

———. "Why There's a Debt Stalemate." *Washington Post*, November 18, 2011.

Saphir, Ann. "U.S. Small Business Borrowing Sank in 2015: PayNet." *Reuters*, February 1, 2016.

Schramm, Carl, Robert Litan, and Dane Stangler. "New Business, Not Small Business, Is What Creates Jobs." *Wall Street Journal*, November 6, 2009.

Schwab, Charles. "The Fed Votes No Confidence." *Wall Street Journal*, February 6, 2012.

Shapiro, Robert J. "Income Growth and Decline Under Recent U.S. Presidents and the New Challenge to Restore Broad Economic Prosperity." Center for Effective Public Management, Brookings Institution, March 5, 2015.

Sharma, Ruchir. "The Global Slowdown Hits the U.S." *Wall Street Journal*, January 12, 2016.

———. "How Spending Sapped the Global Recovery." *Wall Street Journal*, January 15, 2015.

Sherman, Gabriel. "The End of Wall Street as They Knew It." *New York Magazine*, February 5, 2012.

Shermer, Michael. "Wrong Again: Why Experts' Predictions Fail, Especially About the Future." *Huffington Post*, March 5, 2012.

Shiller, Robert J. "Why Innovation Is Still Capitalism's Star." *New York Times*, August 18, 2013.

Simon, Ruth. "Big Banks Cut Back on Loans to Small Business." *Wall Street Journal*, November 26, 2015.

Slaughter, Matthew J. "The Myths of China's Currency 'Manipulation.'" *Wall Street Journal*, January 8, 2016.

"Small Business Economic Trends: Small Business Optimism Sees Third Month of Modest Gains." National Federation of Independent Business website. July 2016 Report.

Social Security Administration. "Ratio of Social Security Covered Workers to Beneficiaries, Calendar Years 1940–2013." Website. https://www.ssa.gov/history/ratios.html.

———. "Update 2016." SSA Publication No. 05-10003.

Sola, Katie, and Emily Canal. "Here Are the States with the Most Billionaires." *Forbes*, March 5, 2016.

Steiner, Sheyna. "Survey: How Americans Contend With Unexpected Expenses." Bankrate.com, January 6, 2016.

Stock, James H., and Mark W. Watson. "Disentangling the Channels of the 2007–2009 Recession." Brookings Institution, March 13, 2012.

Surowiecki, James. "The Pay Is Too Damn Low." *The New Yorker*, August 12 and 19, 2013.

Swanson, Ana. "How China Used More Cement in 3 Years Than the U.S. Did in the Entire 20th Century." *Washington Post*, March 24, 2015.

Tawny, John. "Stop Fretting About Income Inequality." *Forbes*, October 2, 2009.

Thaler, Richard H., and Sendhil Mullainathan. "Behavioral Economics." Library of Economics and Liberty, 2015.

Thomas, Evan. "Attack from the Left: Paul Krugman's Poison Pen." *Newsweek*, March 27, 2009.

Thompson, Derek. "The Mysterious Death of Entrepreneurship in America." *The Atlantic*, May 2014.

———. "Would Doubling Taxes on the Rich Create More Jobs?" *The Atlantic*, November 2011.

Timiraos, Nick, and Kris Hudson. "How a Two-Tier Economy Is Reshaping the U.S. Marketplace." *Wall Street Journal*, January 28, 2015.

Ullmann, Owen. "Crony Capitalism: American Style." *The International Economy* (July–August 1999).

U.S. Census Bureau. "Income and Poverty in the United States: 2014, Table A-1. Households' Total Money Income, Race, and Hispanic Origin of Householder: 1967 to 2014." September 2015. www.census.gov/library/publications/2015/demo/p60-252.html.

U.S. Department of Commerce, Bureau of Economic Analysis. "Table 1.1.1. Percent Change from Preceding Period in Real Gross Domestic Product." National Income and Product Accounts. www.bea.gov.

U.S. Department of Labor. "History of Federal Minimum Wage Rates Under the Fair Labor Standards Act, 1938–2009." www.dol.gov/whd/minwage/chart.htm.

U.S. Department of Labor, Bureau of Labor Statistics. "Employment, Hours, and

Earnings from the Current Employment Statistics Survey (National), January 2013 to April 2016." 2016, https://www.dol.gov.

——. "Employment by Major Industry Sector, Agriculture, Forestry, Fishing, and Hunting, 2014."

——. "Employment Projections." www.bls.gov/emp/ep_chart_001.htm, March 15, 2016.

——. "Occupational Outlook Handbook, Computer and Information Technology Occupations, December 17, 2015."

U.S. Department of Labor, Bureau of Labor Statistics, and the Census Bureau. *Current Population Survey.* Annual Social and Economic Supplement, 2014.

Warshawsky, Mark J., and Andrew G. Biggs. "Income Inequality and Rising Health-Care Costs." *Wall Street Journal,* October 6, 2014.

Watts, Anthony. "Great Moments in Failed Prediction." WattsUpWithThat.com, January 19, 2013.

Wei, Lingling, and Bob Davis. "Debt That Once Boosted Its Cities Now Burdens China." *Wall Street Journal,* January 28, 2015.

Wessel, David. "Big Issues the Budget May Miss." *Wall Street Journal,* February 10, 2011.

Wildau, Gabriel, and Don Weinland. "China Debt Load Reaches Record High as Risk to Economy Mounts." *Financial Times,* April 24, 2016.

Winship, Scott. "Hillary and Bernie, Tax Fantasists." *Wall Street Journal,* March 28, 2016.

Wolf, Charles, Jr. "Chinese Fire Drill." *The International Economy,* Summer 2010.

Wolf, Martin. "China's Great Economic Shift Needs to Begin." *Financial Times,* January 19, 2016.

——. "Europe's Banks Are Too Feeble to Spur Growth." *Financial Times,* October 29, 2014.

——. "This Time Will Never Be Different." *Financial Times,* September 28, 2009.

——. "What We Can Learn from Japan's Decades of Trouble." *Financial Times,* January 13, 2010.

World Bank. "2.17 World Development Indicators: Reproductive Health, Total Fertility Rate." 2014.

——. GDP growth (annual percentage), from national accounts data. www.worldbank.org.

"WSJ Dollar Index—BUXX." *Wall Street Journal.* quotes.wsj.com/index/XX/BUXX.

Yongding, Yu. "A Different Road Forward." *China Daily,* December 23, 2010.

Zacks, Mitch. "Are We Headed for a Currency War?" *Zacks Investment Management,* March 22, 2016.

Zakaria, Fareed. "Is America Losing Its Mojo?" *Newsweek,* November 23, 2009.

Zuckerman, Mortimer. "Fight Inequality with Better Jobs." *Wall Street Journal,* March 3, 2014.

Index

Abe, Shinzo, 148
Affirm (company), 61
Afghanistan, 94
African Americans, 20
Ahamed, Liaquat, 182
AI. *See* artificial intelligence
air traffic controller incident, 25–27
Alibaba Group, 93
Altman, Roger, 182
Amazon, 93, 108
An American Life (Reagan), 24
The American President (film), 81–82
American Sniper (film), 187
Andreessen, Marc, 8, 40, 71, 80, 176
AngelList, 73
anger, public's, 4–6, 7, 90, 144, 171–172
Apple, 56, 61, 62, 69, 72, 85, 93, 189
Apple operating system, 70–71
Apple Pay, 90–91
Arab Spring, 34, 92
The Art of the Start (Kawasaki), 107
artificial intelligence (AI), 62, 65, 101,
    116–117
Asia, 14, 31
assets: U.S., foreign investors in, 184–185
Atlanta, Georgia, 162
The Atlantic, 17
ATM, 107
AT&T, 73
attitude, 8, 9, 67, 68–69, 75, 197; bottom-
    up, 94–95, 156, 188; economic growth
    and, 18–19, 79, 81, 158, 166, 191, 192; vs.
    money, 191–192; toward risk-taking, 55
Australia, 141–142
Austria, 150
automobile industry, 72–73, 113–115
Axelrod, David, 92
Ayres, Whit, 19

baby boomers: entitlements and, 119,
    120–121
Baker, Dean, 78
Baker, James, 59, 163
Bank for International Settlements, 50
bank messaging system, global, 141
Bank of America, 87–88
Bank of Japan, 35, 131, 148
banking: hackers and, 141; politicized,
    87–88. *See also* banks
Bankrate.com, 11
banks: collateralized debt and, 44;
    community and regional, vs. big, 85,
    90; estimated prices of securitized
    assets and, 44; European and
    Eurozone, 142; smaller and medium-
    sized, 107. *See also* banking; big banks;
    central bankers; central banks; Federal
    Reserve; *other specific banks*
Base Realignment and Closure (BRAC)
    Act, 106
Basel Accords: big banks and, 105
Bear Stearns, 42
Becker, Gary, 38
Bedford-Stuyvesant Restoration
    Corporation, 14
Bentham, Jeremy, 38
Bernanke, Ben, 33
Bessent, Scott, 5, 87
Betamax, 70–71
Bhalla, Surjit, 12
Biden, Joe, 14, 147
big banks: Basel Accords and, 105;
    consolidation of, 85, 87–90; control of
    financial risk and, 103–105; domination
    of, post-financial crisis and, 85–90;
    financial crisis (2008) and, 1–2, 3; illegal
    banking practices of, 88; largest four, big

social improvement, as career goal, 101–102
social media, 160
social mobility, 162
Social Security, 21, 50, 116–122, 129–130, 132; billionaires and, 127
socialism, 12–13; vs. capitalism, 15; economic system under, 15
Society for Worldwide Interbank Financial Telecommunication (SWIFT) system, 141
SoFi, 90
Solow, Robert, 61
Sony, 70–71
Soros, George, 127
Soros Fund Management, 84
South Carolina Public Service Commission, 102
South Korea, 141–142, 168
Southeast Asia, 141–142
Soviet Union, 32, 89, 142
SpaceX, 61
Spiegel, Evan, 64
Spotlight (film), 187
Sprung, Joseph, 174, 175
Stagflation, 26
Standard and Poor's, 44
Star Wars (film), 192
steam power, 63–64
Stiglitz, Joseph, 30, 176
stock market, 42; in Japan, 131–132
Stockton, Paul, 152
Striking It Richer (Saez), 5
Summers, Larry, 53, 63, 65, 92, 153, 171
Sutton, Willie, 40
Sweden, 108
SWIFT system. *See* Society for Worldwide Interbank Financial Telecommunication system
Systrom, Kevin, 64

tax reform, 109–111, 162–165, 194; business income and capital gains and, 164; corporate tax rate and, 163–164; estate taxation and, 164–165. *See also* taxation

Tax Reform Act of 1986, 109–110, 170
taxation, 46–47, 78, 89, 98, 107, 120, 173; income tax rate, 170–171. *See also* tax reform
taxpayer-funded bailouts, 89, 115
teachers' unions, 166
tech sector: centralization, 93; Corporate Capitalism in, 92–93; interrelated disciplines of, 60; rule of law and, 99–100
technology: need for summit on, 52–53; nineteenth century, 63–64; shared, 143
telecommunications industry, 152
television, 94
terrorism, 155, 188
Tesla, 61
Tetlock, Philip, 33
Texas Tech, 166
texting: vs. conversation, 160
Thaler, Richard, 38–39
The Theory of Moral Sentiments (Smith), 38
Thiel, Peter, 66, 85–86, 95, 98–99, 158
Third Way, 119
Thomas, Evan, 14
Thompson, Derek, 17
Thorne, David, 76
3D printing, 57, 167
3.5 solution (management of non-financial assets), 195
Tim Hortons (Canadian company), 163
Tobin, James, 39
trade, 5; trade obstructionism and, 5, 15. *See also* free trade; free trade agreements; global trade; trade deficits
trade deficits, 143–144, 148. *See also* trade
trade obstructionism, 5, 15. *See also* trade
Trump, Donald, 5, 52, 60, 74–75, 120, 137–138, 143–144, 165, 172
Turkle, Sherry, 160
Twitter/blogging phenomenon, 94–95

Uber, 102–103
Udacity, 75, 161
"The Ugly 50," 106, 195
Ullmann, Owen, 96–97

DAVID M. SMICK advises some of the world's most successful investors. His bestselling book *The World Is Curved* predicted the great financial crisis. He is the chairman and CEO of the financial-market advisory firm Johnson Smick International and the founder, publisher, and editor of *The International Economy* magazine. He has published widely, including in the *New York Times, Wall Street Journal*, and *Washington Post*.

PublicAffairs is a publishing house founded in 1997. It is a tribute to the standards, values, and flair of three persons who have served as mentors to countless reporters, writers, editors, and book people of all kinds, including me.

I. F. STONE, proprietor of *I. F. Stone's Weekly*, combined a commitment to the First Amendment with entrepreneurial zeal and reporting skill and became one of the great independent journalists in American history. At the age of eighty, Izzy published *The Trial of Socrates*, which was a national bestseller. He wrote the book after he taught himself ancient Greek.

BENJAMIN C. BRADLEE was for nearly thirty years the charismatic editorial leader of *The Washington Post*. It was Ben who gave the *Post* the range and courage to pursue such historic issues as Watergate. He supported his reporters with a tenacity that made them fearless and it is no accident that so many became authors of influential, best-selling books.

ROBERT L. BERNSTEIN, the chief executive of Random House for more than a quarter century, guided one of the nation's premier publishing houses. Bob was personally responsible for many books of political dissent and argument that challenged tyranny around the globe. He is also the founder and longtime chair of Human Rights Watch, one of the most respected human rights organizations in the world.

•   •   •

For fifty years, the banner of Public Affairs Press was carried by its owner Morris B. Schnapper, who published Gandhi, Nasser, Toynbee, Truman, and about 1,500 other authors. In 1983, Schnapper was described by *The Washington Post* as "a redoubtable gadfly." His legacy will endure in the books to come.

Peter Osnos, *Founder and Editor-at-Large*